AF386883

THE LAST
SECRETS OF
THE NAZIS

THE LAST SECRETS OF THE NAZIS

KRZYSZTOF DROZDOWSKI

Pen & Sword

MILITARY

AN IMPRINT OF PEN & SWORD BOOKS LTD.
YORKSHIRE – PHILADELPHIA

First published in the Polish language in 2023 by
Wydawnictwo Replika as Ostatnie tajemnice nazistów

First published in Great Britain in 2026 by
PEN AND SWORD MILITARY
An imprint of
Pen & Sword Books Limited
Yorkshire – Philadelphia

Copyright © Krzysztof Drozdowski, 2026

Print ISBN 978 1 03618 238 0
ePUB ISBN 978 1 03618 240 3
ePDF ISBN 978 1 03618 241 0

Typeset in Times New Roman 11/14 by
SJmagic DESIGN SERVICES, India.
Printed and bound in the UK by CPI Group (UK) Ltd.

The Publisher's authorised representative in the EU for product safety is
Authorised Rep Compliance Ltd., Ground Floor, 71 Lower Baggot Street,
Dublin D02 P593, Ireland.
www.arccompliance.com

For a complete list of Pen & Sword titles please contact
PEN & SWORD BOOKS LIMITED
George House, Units 12 & 13, Beevor Street, Off Pontefract Road,
Barnsley, South Yorkshire, S71 1HN, England
E-mail: enquiries@pen-and-sword.co.uk
Website: www.pen-and-sword.co.uk

or

PEN AND SWORD BOOKS
1950 Lawrence Rd, Havertown, PA 19083, USA
E-mail: uspen-and-sword@casematepublishers.com
Website: www.penandswordbooks.com

Contents

Introduction

Nearly eighty years have passed since the end of the Second World War. Despite the war between Russia and Ukraine (still ongoing as of 2026…), we tend to believe we live in a relatively safe world, economically stable, ideologically adrift, with new technologies advancing at an almost alarming pace.

The author of this book has witnessed the birth of the internet, mobile telephones, and many other inventions that have permanently transformed our lives. And yet, we remain fascinated by the mysteries and enigmas of the past. Still-classified documents and sealed archives, particularly those held in Russia, continue to fuel conspiracy theories and keep long-unresolved histories alive.

Just when we think these are matters of distant history, others treat them as tools of active historical policy, invoking the threat of declassifying files that, in the view of certain authorities, should never see the light of day. This fuels our anticipation of future discoveries and chance finds.

At the same time, it opens the door for those who attempt to falsify documents or entire diaries, either to provoke a new sensation or to profit from deceit. Was that not, after all, the aim of Konrad Kujau, the German illustrator who spent considerable time forging what he claimed were Hitler's diaries in the 1980s? Another case of a forged diary, a story that came to light in recent months, is also covered in this volume.

I have tried to present the most compelling unresolved episodes from the Third Reich era. I have approached many of these topics with what might be called a 'cool head', aware that some may never be fully explained. Even so, we must continue to probe, to search for new documents, and to pursue the truth as far as possible.

At the same time, I have endeavoured to write in a manner that is accessible and engaging for readers. I leave it to you to judge whether I have succeeded. This kind of project required careful consideration of which subjects deserved further investigation. I hope I have managed to select the most intriguing and mysterious among them.

It is customary, at the end of such a work, to thank those who have offered support during the writing process. While many people deserve gratitude, three individuals merit special acknowledgment, including my wife, Karolina. I am acutely aware of how much effort she must invest so that I can concentrate on my work in peace. Frequent travel, research trips, and long hours spent writing often separate me from most domestic responsibilities. Fortunately, my wife bears it all with stoic calm. Though sometimes... but that's another story.

Dear Readers, I present to you the fruit of my labour. I take full responsibility for any errors, speculations, or assumptions. As always, I encourage you to get in touch after reading and share your thoughts and reflections. This time is no different.

Krzysztof Drozdowski

Chapter 1

Rudolf Hess's Secret Mission

'Oh God, oh my God! He's flown to England!' These were Hitler's first words upon opening the thin envelope handed to him by one of Rudolf Hess's adjutants.

He was standing in the grand hall of the Reich Chancellery, a vast and opulent space that, even before 1939, had impressed every visitor who passed through its doors. Guests were made to walk a long way before they could even catch a glimpse of the Führer's face, a psychological tactic that ensured they felt small in the presence of the so-called 'little corporal', as Hitler was mockingly referred to among some Wehrmacht generals.

Hitler's first order upon hearing the news was to summon Martin Bormann, his private secretary, followed shortly by Hermann Göring. The bloated and morphine-addicted commander-in-chief of the Luftwaffe was a shadow of the First World War flying ace he had once been. Desperately, the Nazi leadership searched for a way to contain the embarrassment.

On 10 May 1941, at precisely 5:45 pm German summertime, Rudolf Hess (Hitler's deputy) climbed into a Messerschmitt Bf 110 fitted with auxiliary fuel tanks and took off alone from Augsburg. Officially, it was yet another training flight. In truth, it was a cover. His real destination was Britain. His aim was to meet with members of the British aristocracy in an attempt to broker peace between Britain and the Third Reich.

'In the event of failure, mein Führer, please declare that I have gone mad,' he wrote in a letter to Hitler shortly before departure.

Rudolf Hess was born on 26 April 1894 in Alexandria, Egypt, the son of a merchant father, Fritz Hess, and his wife Klara. Raised in luxurious surroundings, he was groomed to take over the family business, with his father placing great emphasis on his son's education.

Between 1900 and 1906, Hess attended a German Protestant school in Alexandria. He and his younger brother Alfred later received private

The wreckage of the Messerschmitt Bf 110D bomber in which Rudolf Hess, Adolf Hitler's deputy, flew to Scotland hoping to negotiate peace with Great Britain. (*Public domain*)

tutoring from an Egyptian governess. Every summer, the family returned to their estate in Germany to spend the holidays.

When Rudolf was 14, the family returned permanently to their homeland. Hess enrolled at an Evangelical school in Bad Godesberg, where particular emphasis was placed on mathematics and the natural sciences. After completing what was known as the '*kleine Matura*' (lower school-leaving certificate), he continued his education for a year at the École Supérieure de Commerce in Neuchâtel, Switzerland. He then began a merchant apprenticeship in Hamburg.

In 1914, following the outbreak of the First World War, he volunteered for military service. During the Battle of Ypres, he displayed notable bravery and was awarded the Iron Cross, 2nd Class. At the Battle of Verdun in 1916, he sustained injuries to his arm and hand, although these would not be the only wounds he suffered during the war. On 23 July 1917, he was struck by shrapnel from an artillery shell, and later that year, on 8 August, he received a serious gunshot wound during an assault on a hill in the Romanian Carpathians.

In March 1918, having passed his flight qualification tests, he began training as a pilot. By October, he had officially joined the Jagdstaffel 35B fighter squadron, stationed in Givry. However, he did not have the opportunity to shoot down a single enemy aircraft. The war ended in defeat for Germany in November 1918. The squadron was disbanded, and Hess was demobilised.

Returning to civilian life, he settled in Munich, where in 1920 he began studying political science. To support himself financially, he worked as a sales representative for a furniture company. Still searching for direction in life, he joined the Thule Society, as well as the Freikorps. At the same time, he attended lectures in history and economics, during which he became acquainted with Karl Haushofer.

Deputy Führer Rudolf Hess (third from right) at the official opening of the IV Winter Olympic Games in Garmisch-Partenkirchen, 6 February 1936. To his right are the IOC President Count de Baillet-Latour and Adolf Hitler. (*Bundesarchiv, R 8076 Bild-0019 / CC-BY-SA 3.0*)

In June 1920, having recently met Adolf Hitler and been thoroughly captivated by him, Hess became a member of the NSDAP. Two years later, in 1922, he joined the SA. He also took part in the Munich Putsch on 8 November 1923. Armed, he entered the *Bürgerbräukeller* beer hall alongside Hitler. Hess's task was to detain the Bavarian Prime Minister and several of his ministers who were present and transport them by car to a pre-selected location.

Later, in the mountains near Tegernsee, he held two ministers of the Bavarian government, both opponents of the Nazis, as hostages under guard. When news reached him on 9 November that the coup had been crushed, he released the ministers and managed to cross the Austrian border, avoiding arrest.

However, in May 1924, he voluntarily surrendered to the authorities and was sentenced to eighteen months in prison. He served his sentence alongside Hitler at Landsberg Fortress, where he typed up the manuscript of *Mein Kampf*, dictated to him by Hitler.

On 1 January 1925, Hess was released from prison. When the NSDAP was reactivated in February, he was issued membership card number 16, and gradually gained increasing importance both in Hitler's activities and within the party structure.

On 21 April 1933, Hess was appointed Deputy Führer of the NSDAP. In December of that year, following the Nazi's seizure of power in the elections, he joined the government as a Minister without Portfolio and was actively involved in introducing restrictive measures targeting the Jewish population.

After the outbreak of war in 1939, Hess's influence within Hitler's inner circle waned, eclipsed by that of the Führer's secretary, Martin Bormann. Hess was an advocate of reaching a peace agreement with the Western Allies and turning the full force of Germany's might against Bolshevism. This was one of the reasons behind his decision to undertake his solo flight to Scotland in 1941.

After parachuting from his aircraft, he was captured by a local farmer, who alerted the police. An interrogation was needed, but no one present spoke German. This is where a Polish connection appears, which we shall return to later.

Hess's pre-war contacts proved useless and he remained imprisoned throughout the war. That is the official version. But there are two others, long spoken of only in hushed tones.

On 17 August 1987, a guard at Berlin's Spandau Prison discovered Hess's lifeless body in a garden summerhouse. He had been strangled. He was 93 years old at the time. Would a man of such age truly commit suicide?

Research into the matter is hampered by the British authorities, who placed a long-term classification order on numerous documents related to Hitler's former deputy. Historians continue to ask: what truly drove him to make that fateful flight? And did Hitler really know nothing about it?

Hess was likely aware of the impending attack on the East, known as Operation *Barbarossa*. Had he succeeded in bringing about an end to the war between the Third Reich and Great Britain, he would have been hailed as a hero.

Unfortunately, a BBC radio broadcast in the evening of 10 May announced that Rudolf Hess, Hitler's deputy, had parachuted into Scotland and that his aim had been to meet with the Duke of Hamilton, whom he had first met in 1936 during the Berlin Olympics. This news meant Hitler could no longer cling to the hope that Hess had failed to reach his destination, or that the British might keep the incident secret out of fear that Stalin would accuse them of negotiating behind the Soviet Union's back.

The trial of the Nazi war criminals before the Nuremberg Tribunal began on 20 November 1945. Each of the four victorious powers sought to present its most prominent captured prisoners. Rudolf Hess was among those indicted for war crimes.

His conduct in the dock was highly controversial. For much of the proceedings, he remained silent or pretended not to understand what was happening. He refused to wear the headphones through which the trial was being translated into German, and appeared utterly uninterested in his own fate.

Hess surprised everyone during his final statement. While most of the accused sought to downplay their guilt or portray themselves in a more favourable light, Hess declared that he had done his duty as a National Socialist and that he continued to believe in and trust Hitler until the end.

He was sentenced to life imprisonment and indeed spent the remainder of his life in Spandau Prison.

He remained there for forty years, twenty-one of which he spent as the sole prisoner number 7. It was not until 1969 that he agreed to see his family. The meeting with his wife, Ilse Hess, and their son, Wolf Rüdiger, took place on 24 December at a British military hospital, where he had been transferred due to declining health.

This detail gave rise to a theory that he had avoided his family out of fear of being recognised. According to this line of thought, the man imprisoned in Spandau was not Rudolf Hess at all, but an impostor planted by the British, while the 'real' Deputy Führer had been secretly murdered.

The case was further complicated by the fact that Hess's alleged suicide also occurred while under British watch. Did someone perhaps assist the 'Hess double' in ending his life, fearing that, in his final days, he might reveal the truth?

According to the official report, on 17 August 1987 Hess hanged himself using an electrical cable. In the days that followed, all traces of his presence in the prison were removed. It was only many years later that a photograph of the alleged cable was made public. It turned out to be so long that, had it actually been used for hanging, the victim would have had to be lying down.

Hess's death occurred shortly after the Soviets ceased raising objections to his potential release from prison. Was Hess murdered by the British, fearful that once freed he might reveal what had happened to him between 1941 and 1945 while in custody? Might he have disclosed details about negotiations between the Germans and the British? After all, Hitler had great admiration for the proud sons of Albion.

Or perhaps it would have emerged that Hess was not really Hess at all, but a double?

Perhaps it is time for a touch of conspiracy theory.

> My Führer, by the time you receive this letter, I will be in England. You can imagine that the decision to take this step was not an easy one for me, as a 40-year-old is bound to life by very different ties than a 20-year-old…

This was the opening sentence of the letter Hess had entrusted to his adjutant, Karl Heinz Pinsch, who then delivered it to Hitler. The Führer was furious, although, as history tells us, he was also an excellent actor. It is entirely possible that Hitler's display of shock and outrage was nothing more than a performance.

While Hess was still flying over German territory, Göring attempted to stop him, issuing orders for the aircraft to be shot down at all costs. The interception was meant to take place over occupied Holland, but it is here where we arrive at the heart of a certain conspiracy theory, which claims that after the fighter aircraft with Hess on board was indeed shot down, a double was substituted in his place.

Two key arguments are often cited in support of this idea. The first concerns the flight path. Over the North Sea, Hess is said to have made several inexplicable manoeuvres. He later claimed these were meant to burn off excess fuel before landing. But if so much fuel needed to be jettisoned, why had he taken two extra fuel tanks in the first place?

The second argument involves discrepancies in the aircraft's serial numbers. The number seen in a photograph taken before departure does not match the one on the wreckage that crashed in Scotland. However, proponents of this theory assume that the first photograph was taken on the day of the flight itself and not earlier, for instance, during a previous, unsuccessful attempt, on 10 January 1940.

Before Hess took off from Augsburg airfield in this first attempt, he handed his adjutant, Pintsch, two envelopes with strict instructions not to open them for at least four hours. One contained instructions for the adjutant; the other, a letter addressed to Hitler. However, due to deteriorating weather conditions, Hess was forced to turn back after two hours. Naturally, Pintsch did not wait the instructed amount of time and opened the envelope addressed to him. In it, his superior explained that he had flown to Great Britain.[1]

Another theory suggests that Hess was murdered by the British upon his arrival in Scotland, where he had hoped to receive support from members of the upper class who were said to be fascinated by Hitler. This remains a sensitive and uncomfortable subject to this day.

Rudolf Hess with Joachim von Ribbentrop in the defendants' dock at Nuremberg. (*Author's archive*)

However, the idea that Hitler's deputy was killed during the war and replaced with a double is implausible. Such an act would have been pointless, and this theory can be reasonably dismissed.

The matter appears quite different when it comes to Hess's death at the age of 93. It is technically possible to hang oneself with an electrical cable while lying down, but what raises doubt, however, is the location of the ligature mark on the neck. In a typical hanging, the mark should be positioned much higher across the middle of the neck. A lower position suggests the person may simply have been strangled. And if that was the case, why?

After the Soviet authorities ceased objecting to Hess's early release, there remained a lingering fear that he might reveal various pieces of information to the world both concerning himself and the mission he had undertaken.

In 2019, DNA testing was carried out using a blood sample that had been miraculously preserved from one of Hess's earlier medical examinations. The sample was compared with one from the Hess family. An attempt to conduct such a test had been made earlier, but following the death of Hess's son, Wolf Rüdiger, the family withdrew from the public eye and avoided any contact with the media.

The test results confirmed a match. This means that the Rudolf Hess who died in Spandau Prison was indeed the real Hess, not a double. Unless, of course, the sample was switched, but that is something we will likely never know.

We must now return to the moment when Hess, having landed in a Scottish farmer's field, was arrested by the Home Guard. Its members decided to take him to a holding cell in Giffnock, where they awaited the arrival of government officials to begin formal questioning.

Rudolf Hess in the garden of Spandau Prison, July 1983. (*Author's archive*)

After midnight, however, it was not a British officer who arrived but a man in civilian clothing, a Pole. Some of those present were no doubt puzzled by the fact that no one asked to see his identification, nor even questioned his identity.

This Pole was Roman Roger Adam Maria Guido Battaglia, born on 5 April 1903. He was the son of Roger and Kazimiera, née Kirchmayer. In 1927, he had completed a law degree at the Faculty of Law and Administration of the Jagiellonian University, and later graduated from the Kraków School of Commerce and the Solvay Institute in Brussels, earning a doctorate in law. From 26 October 1927 to 10 October 1929, he worked as a trainee at the Ministry of Foreign Affairs in Warsaw. Then, from 10 October 1929 to 31 January 1931, he served as a secretary and legal adviser to the Polish-German Mixed Arbitral Tribunal in Paris. From 1 March 1935, he served as a counsellor at the General Commissariat of the Republic of Poland in the Free City of Danzig, and during the Second World War, worked at the Polish Consulate in Glasgow.

Recalling the events of May 1941, Battaglia described the room where Hess had been taken by the Home Guard: 'In the large room, there were around a dozen people mostly Home Guard officers, along with a few civilians clearly excited by the event. In the centre of the room, seated comfortably in an armchair, was a massive dark-haired man dressed in a German Luftwaffe captain's uniform.'

When he asked Hess the reason for his visit, Hess enigmatically replied that he had a message for the Duke of Hamilton, with whom he shared a mutual acquaintance, and that the message concerned matters of utmost importance to the British Air Force.

Battaglia sat down opposite the prisoner and spoke with him in German for two hours – a language none of the British present understood. When the interrogation ended, the guest stood up and calmly left the station. He got into the car of one of the British officers, who then drove him off in an unknown direction.

'Don't you think we're being a bit too gentle with this German?' asked the driver, Colonel Hardie.

'If you want my opinion,' the Pole replied, 'that airman has been treated far too leniently.'

Battaglia's arrival at the Home Guard station later caused irritation. It was a mystery to members of the British security services why he was there, and remains so to this day.

Chapter 2

Himmler's Secret Game

The head and architect of the SS's power, Heinrich Himmler, was long considered a model of loyalty. A faithful paladin to Hitler, he carried out the most brutal and difficult orders without question. The Führer knew that even if Himmler lacked the skills required for a given task such as commanding an army group in 1945, he would make up for it with his zeal and unwavering devotion.

Yet Himmler had another side. Behind the scenes, he was playing his own private game, aiming to one day replace Hitler as the next Führer. One key element of this secret plan involved negotiating peace with the Western Allies while preparing for a decisive confrontation with the Soviets.

On 14 January 1943, in the Antifa Hotel in Casablanca, the British Prime Minister Winston Churchill, US President Franklin Delano Roosevelt, and the embattled leader of the Free French, Charles de Gaulle, came together for a crucial meeting. De Gaulle had initially refused to attend the conference, and only changed his mind after being pressured by Churchill, who had threatened to recognise Henri Giraud, then also in Casablanca, as the legitimate leader of the Free French. The great absentee from this meeting was the leader of the USSR, Joseph Stalin, who refused to leave the country due to the ongoing Battle of Stalingrad.

During the conference, it was jointly agreed that the primary objective of the Allies would be the unconditional surrender of the Axis powers and the opening of a second front. The decision that Germany must surrender simultaneously to all three major Allied powers ultimately served as little more than a diplomatic smokescreen. In reality, both Stalin and Churchill continued to conduct secret negotiations with German representatives almost until the very end of the war, exploring the possibility of a separate peace. Talks were held with virtually anyone who came forward.

From 1943 onwards, Reichsführer-SS Heinrich Himmler also began playing his own game with the Allies. These efforts, however, were kept under the strictest secrecy, although each side had entirely different reasons for maintaining that silence.

At the time, Himmler stood at the peak of his power, and the risks he took could easily have cost him his life. That is why he never negotiated directly. Instead, he acted through his trusted associate, Walter Schellenberg. But who exactly was this man?

Walter Friedrich Schellenberg was born on 16 January 1910 in Saarbrücken, then part of the German Empire. In 1929, he began studying law at the University of Bonn. Upon completing his degree four years later, he joined the NSDAP and subsequently the SS. Two years after that, he was assigned to the SD (*Sicherheitsdienst*, the Nazi Security Service), where he worked in counterintelligence, eventually becoming head of counterintelligence division 'Amt FIVE' within Department IV of the Gestapo, part of the Reich Main Security Office (RSHA).

In November 1939, he gained notoriety for the abduction of two MI6 agents, Major Richard Stevens and Captain Sigismund Payne Best, from the Dutch town of Venlo, an operation that earned him the Iron Cross. In 1940, he led operations in Portugal with the aim of kidnapping the former king, now Duke of Windsor, Edward VIII. The attempt failed and resulted

Adolf Hitler and Heinrich Himmler. Two loyal allies, for now … (*NAC*)

in Schellenberg developing a kidney ailment caused by a drug administered as part of the mission. Despite this failure, his career continued to advance.

On 21 June 1941, Schellenberg was appointed head of Department VI of the RSHA, responsible for foreign intelligence, and successfully tracked and dismantled the Soviet espionage network known as the Red Orchestra (Rote Kapelle). Working closely with Himmler, he plotted the dissolution of the Abwehr (military intelligence) and its incorporation into the SD as Amt Mil.

As head of the SS intelligence apparatus, he made Himmler increasingly dependent on him. According to his own memoirs, Schellenberg claimed that as early as 1942, he knew the Third Reich was destined to lose the war, though this assertion seems rather unlikely.

Returning to Himmler and his pursuit of a peace settlement: in October 1943, the head of the Political Warfare Executive (PWE), an organisation established in Britain two years earlier, received a letter from Himmler outlining a six-point peace proposal.

In the letter, Himmler stated that peace would include the withdrawal of German forces from occupied Western Europe and the re-establishment of an independent and free Poland. In return, he sought assurances that there would be no Allied invasion of Western Europe and that the bombing of Germany would cease.

The head of the PWE, Brendan Bracken, commented on the Reichsführer's proposal as follows: 'Of course, HH's [Heinrich Himmler's] proposal is unrealistic, but it also shows just how desperate the top figures of the Nazi regime have become in their assessment of the military situation.'

As Himmler's previous efforts had yielded no results, in 1944 Schellenberg began urging his superior to commit open treason and initiate peace negotiations with the Western Allies. He proposed

SS-Brigadeführer Walter Friedrich Schellenberg (1910-1952) was head of the *Sicherheitsdienst* (SD) intelligence service. (*Bundesarchiv, Bild 101III-Alber-178-04A/ Alber, Kurt / CC-BY-SA 3.0*)

doing so through a representative of the Red Cross, the Swedish Count Folke Bernadotte.[1]

The Allies ultimately rejected all attempts to reach a separate peace. The British, in particular, were keen to erase any traces of potential collaboration. After the war, the Nuremberg Tribunal found Schellenberg guilty of membership in the SS and the SD security service, both of which had been declared criminal organisations. In 1949 he was sentenced to six years in prison, but was released in June 1951 and died a year later in Turin.

During the night of 20/21 April 1945, Himmler, keen to present himself favourably to the Western leaders and increase his chances of being recognised by the West as the new leader of the Third Reich, met with Norbert Masur, a representative of the Swedish branch of the World Jewish Congress.

From the report submitted by Masur upon his return to Stockholm, we learn how the rather complex preparations for the trip unfolded:

> Due to the unusual and uncertain nature of the meeting with Himmler, the section did not want to make a decision especially as it was not possible to consult New York on the matter. It was therefore decided to leave the final decision to the volunteer undertaking the mission: whether to proceed or not.
>
> We discussed the matter with the Swedish Ministry for Foreign Affairs, which was firmly of the view that direct contact with Himmler would be valuable and yield meaningful results, fully in line with Sweden's desire to support humanitarian rescue efforts. The three local Allied embassies we informed had no objections; in fact, the representative of the War Refugee Board based in Stockholm actively encouraged us to proceed.
>
> We therefore asked Dr Kersten to inform Himmler that a member of our section, acting as a private citizen, would travel for this purpose. Himmler accepted this arrangement. Several of our members volunteered for the journey. In the end, I was chosen to go.

Masur travelled to Germany, accompanied by the aforementioned Felix Kersten, Himmler's personal masseur. They stayed at Kersten's estate in

Folke Bernadotte (1895-1948), Count of Wisborg, was a Swedish diplomat who was assassinated in Jerusalem by Jewish assassins from the Lehi paramilitary terrorist organisation. (*Wikimedia Commons/USHMM*)

Hartzwalde. From there, equipped with documents from the Swedish Ministry for Foreign Affairs, they proceeded to the meeting the following day.

Also present during the discussions were Dr Brandt and Walter Schellenberg. Masur recounted that Himmler greeted him dressed in full ceremonial uniform, adorned with all his medals and decorations with a simple 'Guten Tag'. Masur had expected the more typical Third Reich salutation: 'Heil Hitler!'

The meeting was originally scheduled to take place several hours earlier. However, 20 April was Hitler's birthday, and the Reichsführer could not fail to appear in the Führer's bunker on such an occasion.

The two-and-a-half-hour conversation proved successful for Masur, who later characterised his interlocutor as follows:

> There is no doubt that Himmler was intelligent and well-educated, but he was no master of concealing the truth. His cynicism came through particularly clearly when he spoke of the impending catastrophe. One especially telling remark was made as he took leave of Kersten: 'The worthy part of the German nation will go down with us – what happens to the rest is of no importance.'
>
> Unlike Hitler, he behaved rationally in his dealings with Jews. Hitler, of course, expressed open hatred. Himmler's actions were devoid of emotion. He murdered with cold calculation as long as it served his purposes, and he was capable of taking a different course if it better suited his political agenda. What could have motivated him, towards the end of the war, to make minor concessions to us? He never asked for anything in return. He certainly did not believe that

such gestures would be enough to save his own skin. He was too intelligent for that; he knew all too well that the list of his crimes was long.

Perhaps he wished to be remembered in the annals of history in a better light than those who bore the principal responsibility for Germany's crimes.[2]

Thanks to this intervention, Himmler ordered the release of 1,000 Jewish women from the Ravensbrück concentration camp. They were transported in white buses bearing the Red Cross emblem to Denmark, and from there by train to Sweden.

The White Buses expedition of 1945 was the largest and most significant humanitarian operation carried out by Sweden in the past century. It was also, in all likelihood, the boldest and most successful undertaking by the Swedish government in the twentieth century.[3]

Masur, together with Dr Kersten, departed immediately after the meeting, flying to Copenhagen. From there, they travelled by ferry and then by train to the Swedish capital.

Himmler made no demands in exchange for the release of the female prisoners. He only requested that the ongoing negotiations be kept strictly confidential.[4] It was not so much that he had begun to care about the Jews, who were of no concern to him, but rather that he hoped to open a channel of communication that could be used for further talks on reaching a separate peace.[5]

The efforts of Swedish Count Bernadotte were not limited to the rescue of Jews from German concentration camps, however. On the night of 23/24 April, another meeting took place between him and Himmler. This was arranged by Schellenberg, who encouraged Bernadotte to initiate negotiations between his superior and Dwight Eisenhower.

Himmler was said to be offering the surrender of German forces fighting on the Western Front, as well as in Denmark and Norway. Bernadotte suggested that for Germany to capitulate, a personal meeting with the American supreme commander was not necessary; it would suffice simply to issue the appropriate order.

The situation in Norway, however, was different. No fighting was taking place there, and the German garrisons had no one to whom they could surrender. The prospect of opening surrender talks in Norway created an opportunity for a face-to-face meeting, or so Himmler hoped.

His meeting with Bernadotte took place at the Swedish Legation in Lübeck. It is worth letting the diplomat speak for himself:

> That night, with its extraordinary atmosphere of defeat, I shall never forget – Himmler arrived (...) at around half past eleven. Moments later, the air raid sirens began to wail. I asked the head of the Gestapo whether he wished to go down to the shelter, but I also pointed out that I could not guarantee we would be alone there – clearly, we could not prevent others living in the building, or passers-by, from seeking refuge in the cellar.
>
> Himmler hesitated for a moment, then decided to go down. Several Swedes and Germans were already in the shelter. Himmler spoke with his compatriots, asked how they were feeling – he was clearly trying to gauge the mood of the people. It was evident that no one recognised him. I observed him closely during the hour we spent in the shelter. He was very tired and agitated; it was clear he was struggling to maintain his composure.[6]

After the air raid warning ended, the three men resumed their discussions. The course of the conversation is known to us from the accounts of both Bernadotte and Schellenberg, which are broadly consistent.

Himmler reportedly claimed that, until then, he had been unable to make binding decisions regarding a surrender on the Western

SS-Obersturmbannführer Heinz Linge (1913-1980) was Adolf Hitler's valet from 1939. (*Bundesarchiv, Bild 146-1982-044-11/CC-BY-SA 3.0*)

Front. Now, however, given that Hitler had declared he would remain in the Berlin bunker, and even, as Himmler put it, with uncertainty as to whether the Führer was still alive at all, he felt he could be more open to negotiations.

He even made a formal declaration:

> In the present situation, I have a free hand. In order to save as much of Germany as possible from Russian invasion, I am prepared to surrender on the Western Front so that the forces of the Western powers can move eastward as quickly as possible. By contrast, I do not wish to surrender on the Eastern Front. I have always been a sworn enemy of Bolshevism and shall remain so until the end. At the beginning of the war, I fought fiercely against the German-Russian pact. Would you be willing to pass such a declaration to the Swedish Foreign Minister, so that the Western powers might understand the nature of my proposal?

Himmler also reportedly stated that, if his plans could not be realised, he would take command of a battalion fighting on the Eastern Front and fall in battle.

As Bernadotte had anticipated, the proposal was completely rejected. However, this did not prompt Himmler to carry out his dramatic promise of seeking death at the front.

At the conclusion of the talks, Himmler drafted a letter intended for the Swedish Foreign Minister, Christian Günther. After the war, Bernadotte would recall that:

> Towards the evening [28 April], I was sitting by the radio, listening to the Atlantic Service. Suddenly, my name was mentioned. Then came the announcement that, according to reports from London and New York, I was conducting negotiations with the head of the SS, Minister Himmler, concerning Germany's surrender. 'Well, now the entire matter is lost,' was my first reaction. 'Now I can no longer conduct any negotiations at all.'[7]

The news of Himmler's plot, broadcast over the radio, was received at the Kriegsmarine headquarters. According to Heinz Macher, Himmler's adjutant, Großadmiral Karl Dönitz likely telephoned Himmler to request clarification. On the issue of surrendering forces on the Western Front, while continuing the fight in the East, the two reportedly held similar views.

If such a call did indeed take place, Himmler would have known that the information would almost certainly reach the ears of the Führer. As Dönitz later recalled, when asked whether the radio reports were true, Himmler firmly denied them. He also stated that he would not be issuing any public statement on the matter. He may have hoped that the message would be dismissed as an Allied bluff, aimed at sowing discord between himself and Hitler.

In reality, Himmler was furious. He raged at Schellenberg, accusing him of drawing him into the negotiations. But there was nothing more he could do. The threats directed at Schellenberg likely stemmed more from a need to vent his frustration, or even from a sense of fear for his own life.

As Himmler had feared, at 9:00 pm that same day, the sensational news also reached the Führer's bunker beneath the Reich Chancellery. The handwritten note informing of the betrayal was carried to Hitler by Werner Lorenz, who handed it to Hitler's personal valet, Heinz Linge, whom he encountered en route. Without reading its contents, Linge passed the note directly to the Führer.

The reaction was not long in coming. As Lorenz had predicted, Hitler flew into a rage. Immediately after finishing his tirade about the betrayal by the always-loyal 'Heini', he made his way to the room where, just hours earlier, a wounded Field Marshal Robert Ritter von Greim had arrived, accompanied by Hitler's favourite test pilot, Hanna Reitsch.

'A traitor cannot be my successor! He must never be allowed to replace me! Von Greim, you are to depart immediately and arrest Heinrich Himmler then decide what is to be done with him!' Hitler ordered the field marshal.[8]

Himmler, meanwhile, was still in the Baltic port city of Lübeck, some 300 kilometres (186 miles) from Berlin. It was most likely this distance that saved him from immediate execution. He had chosen a police barracks as his temporary headquarters, where he indulged in one of his great passions: astrology. Walter Schellenberg, aware of this weakness, used it to his advantage as he travelled to meet his superior.

> I realised that my position in relation to Himmler had become so precarious that I might face the threat of physical elimination. That is why I brought an astrologer from Hamburg with me.

Himmler knew this man and held him in high regard. He could never resist hearing his horoscope, and I was certain that the astrologer's presence would help soften the Reichsführer's reaction to the bad news.

I would prefer not to recount the first part of my conversation with Himmler here. It was not easy, and looking back on it now, I still cannot understand how everything turned out so favourably for me.

For some time, we discussed the reasons why the Allies had refused to negotiate with us. Himmler was bitterly disappointed, and what troubled him most was the fact that all the details had been published in the international press. He was also concerned that his letter to the Swedish Foreign Minister might be made public.

We then turned to the issue of Denmark and Norway. The fact that Himmler saw me, who had inspired his peace overtures, as responsible for a failure that could have disastrous consequences for his relationship with Hitler did not seem to provide the best foundation for a plan to save the Scandinavian countries.

Nevertheless, with the help of the astrologer, I managed to persuade him. After reflecting on the matter, he finally granted me permission to discuss with Count Bernadotte the possibility of ending the German occupation of Norway and interning the German occupying forces in Sweden for the remaining duration of the war.[9]

With this clever move, Schellenberg secured his own safety. That very same day, he left for Flensburg and then continued with Count Bernadotte to neutral Sweden.[10] There, he held talks regarding the surrender of German forces stationed in Denmark and Norway; an area of primary concern for the Swedish ruling elite.

Despite his demotion, Himmler was still guarded by a detachment of loyal SS men. However, he feared that a larger Wehrmacht unit might attempt to capture him and deliver him to Hitler or simply shoot him on the spot.

In a state of nervous tension, he relocated his headquarters to Kalkhorst, near Travemünde, where he intended to wait and see how events would unfold.

Chapter 3

'Wunderwaffe' Counterfeit – Paper Money

If one were to count all the *'Wunderwaffe'*, the so-called miracle weapons developed between 1939 and 1945 that were intended to secure Germany's victory, there would be over 150 projects. Yet there is one that is rarely included in such lists, despite having had the potential to eliminate Britain from the war altogether. Unlike many of the other schemes, this project did not involve plans to kill as many enemy soldiers as possible.

In 1959, divers recovered crates containing counterfeit British pounds from Austria's Lake Toplitz. At the time, it was believed that these were all the forged banknotes produced under what became known as Operation *Bernhard*. However, for many years afterwards, forged currency remained in circulation. This continued until all banknotes with a denomination greater than £5 were withdrawn. It is worth revisiting this story.

Following Germany's victory over Poland in 1939, and with the security of the pact with the USSR, in 1940 Hitler began redeploying his divisions to the West. The objective was to defeat France and, at least for a time, to persuade Britain to cooperate or at the very least, to remain neutral. Along the way, however, it was deemed necessary to deal with Denmark and Norway, so that these natural 'aircraft carriers' looming over the Third Reich would pose no threat to its army.

While the defeat of France turned out to be a surprisingly easy task for the Wehrmacht, fighting the British proved to be far more difficult. Victory could have been achieved in 1940, but two obstacles stood in the way: first, the boastful and attention-seeking Hermann Göring and his Luftwaffe; and second, the weather, an age-old force that has changed the course of battles and even entire wars throughout history. Since defeating the enemy on the battlefield was no longer feasible, more unconventional and even surprising methods had to be considered.

In May 1942, SS-Hauptsturmführer Bernhard Krüger, five years older and five ranks below, stood before SS-Brigadeführer Walther Schellenberg. We know the course of the conversation thanks to the memoir Krüger would write in 1957. He declared that Schellenberg announced:

> I've asked you to report to me, in order to inform you of an important order I received late yesterday evening from the Reichsführer-SS. I proposed to the Reichsführer that the execution of a certain undertaking be entrusted to you, and that, accordingly, it be carried out under your name as Operation *Bernhard*. Given your achievements to date, I am convinced I have chosen the right man for the task.

To Krüger, it was clear why he had been chosen to command individuals of Jewish origin. In the event of failure, or indeed in the event of success, they were all to be eliminated. Witnesses were not needed.

Bernhard Krüger's reaction to the proposal was later described by his granddaughter:

> If, at the time, he had any scruples while sitting in Schellenberg's office, he could presumably always console himself with the thought [of eliminating the witnesses]. Beyond that, he was ambitious. 'What was I supposed to do? Tell me what you would have done,' he later asked Professor Hans Fricke during a television interview, without expecting an answer. After all, until then, he had only been forging passports, carrying out routine tasks in the intelligence services. 'And then suddenly something like this lands in your lap!' he exclaimed. 'Saying no would have been regarded as disobeying an order.' He was too dutiful for that. 'And to say I wasn't up to the task… well, one does have ambitions!' he admitted.[1]

According to his surviving memoirs, Krüger was aware of two major challenges presented by the new task he had been given in the service of the Third Reich. The first, and quite significant, was that the British pound had until then been considered impossible to counterfeit. How, then, could one achieve the impossible? The second challenge was of an entirely different nature and concerned human behaviour, or rather, how to compel prisoners to work efficiently and effectively. Krüger described it as follows:

> Gaining control over prisoners who had become rightless, degraded human beings did not require any special character traits. Winning them over, encouraging them and inspiring them to exert themselves in a way that stood in direct opposition to their beliefs, their sense of justice and their understanding of dignity, this required me to gain their trust. To achieve the intended goal, I couldn't simply stand up and shout: 'I trust you, so you should trust me!' That was impossible, unthinkable. The prisoners would not have believed a single word I said. Me with the eagle on my sleeve and the death's head on my cap. At best, they would have taken me for a complete idiot.[2]

Of course, the road from concept to execution is long and fraught with obstacles. The Germans, however, had a distinct advantage: in their concentration camps, they held hundreds of thousands of people from a wide range of professions and with a vast array of skills.

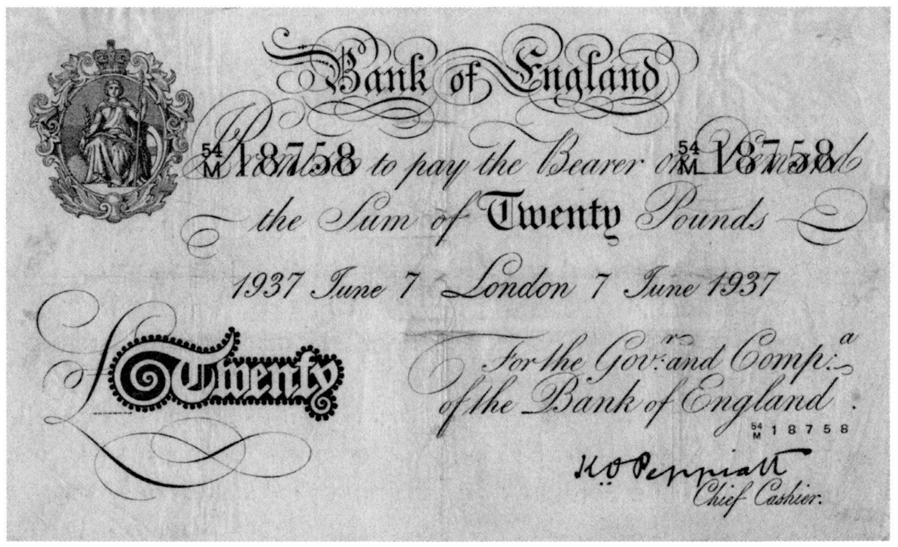

A counterfeit £10 banknote, produced as part of the German Operation *Bernhard*. (*Author's archive*)

This potential had to be exploited. In most camps, special roll calls were conducted during which prisoners were ordered to step forward if they were printers, engravers, painters, graphic artists, paper specialists, bankers, electroplaters, or experts in photographic reproduction. Those selected were transferred to Sachsenhausen concentration camp, which became their new place of imprisonment, albeit under slightly different conditions. Initially, the camp authorities designated Block 19 for the secret operation. Later, Block 18 was added to the project as well.

After his first visit to the camp, Krüger jotted down a few reflections about the prisoners: 'In their traditional blue-and-white striped uniforms, these are people stripped of all rights nothing more, nothing less. Those with decent work fare better. But who has such work? Very few. Jews, homosexuals, and the like certainly not.'[3]

He also described his first impression of the camp itself:

A high wall, massive guard towers equipped with machine guns give it the feel of a world apart. What stands out is the order and cleanliness that prevail here. Just as striking is the efficient and precise operation of the SS guard unit. Discipline has penetrated to the bone. If that discipline is also imposed on the prisoners... then the camp is a harsh school. A school that must feel even more oppressive than Prussian drill, because the word 'freedom' holds no meaning here.[4]

The prisoners who arrived at the camp were first directed to the shower room, where they were required to wash themselves. When someone shouted that the Germans intended to gas them, a few prisoners jumped out of the windows. Outside, however, SS men stood ready with their weapons. After bathing, now dressed in ragged camp uniforms, the prisoners were ordered to attend roll call. Eighty Jewish men stood before a well-fed, clean-shaven man in an immaculate uniform; the man on whom their fate now depended.

On 20 August 1942, Krüger selected thirty-nine individuals from the group. As he made his way among the prisoners, he questioned each about their profession, skills, and city of origin. He had to choose only the most capable. He deemed that just thirty-nine of them were suitable for the task. As the project expanded, additional specialists were brought in. The final list of prisoners involved in Operation *Bernhard*, dated 14 April

1945, contained 141 names. By that time, however, five of the prisoners had already died. Entry number 113 on the list, Viennese illustrator Karl Sussmann, died at the end of April under unexplained circumstances.[5] Thus, the project ultimately involved a total of 146 individuals, of whom 140 survived.

Krüger, in plain and direct language, explained to 'his Jews', as he called the group of counterfeiters under his command, the simple rules he expected them to follow:

> From today onwards, you are under my authority. I place great importance on smooth cooperation without disruption and exemplary behaviour. Ensure both within your community and beyond it. In many respects, your daily life in the camp will now differ from what you have previously experienced. The SS-Untersturmführers standing beside me, Marocka and Weber, are in charge of official supervision. You may always turn to them. Both are required to treat you properly and are responsible for order in Block 19. Work begins daily at 7:00 and finishes at 16:00. There is a lunch break from 12:00 to 13:00. No work on Sundays. If you have complaints, I want to be informed of them, whatever their nature. I am equally available for personal matters. As of today, you are exempt from attending the general camp roll call. Do you understand me?[6]

The prisoners themselves had varying opinions about their superior after the war, though favourable views tended to prevail. Avraham Krakowski described him as follows: 'Krüger himself was a mystery to me. I understood that, to him, we were like hens laying golden eggs, and so we had to be guarded and well fed. We were producing British pounds for them. When we were weak or overworked, the quality of our product suffered too. All the same, he was our guardian angel in an SS uniform.'

Another counterfeiter, Georg Kohn, testified after the war: 'Sturmbannführer Krüger behaved calmly towards us, never used violence, and was always cordial. In my opinion, this was likely nothing more than a clever tactic on his part, intended to ensure that the production of counterfeit money… for which he was responsible, continued without disruption.'[7]

Interestingly, Krüger was by no means the first to be tasked with producing counterfeit banknotes, and was well aware of this fact. His first steps after receiving the assignment led him to a small workshop: 'The key turned silently as I opened the door to those mysterious rooms which, since October 1939, had held something elusive, although the tension surrounding Operation *Andreas* had long since faded.'[8]

The aforementioned Operation *Andreas* was overseen by Alfred Naujocks, who had also been responsible for carrying out the Gleiwitz operation in 1939. Naujocks was born on 20 September 1911 in Kiel. Until the age of 8, he suffered from tuberculosis, which caused him to miss school. When he eventually returned, he often skipped classes. At the age of 16, he dropped out of education and began training as an orthopaedic technician. In 1930, he started working as a car mechanic. However, due to the economic crisis in Germany, he lost his job and was unable to find another. He eventually found employment with his father, although he did not receive regular wages. On 1 August 1931, he joined the NSDAP and the SS. Within the organisation, he became known for his adventurous and combative nature. At the end of July that same year, he and two companions were involved in a shoot-out with members of the Communist Party of Germany (KPD). In 1932, he joined the *Sicherheitsdienst* (SD).

In January 1935, he was promoted to the rank of SS-Untersturmführer (equivalent to second lieutenant) and was transferred to the Eastern section, to an Abwehr post stationed there. At the same time, he was entrusted for the first time with managerial responsibilities. His work included counterintelligence operations, safeguarding information relating to the German armaments industry, and combating foreign espionage.

In the autumn of 1937, Naujocks was transferred to the foreign intelligence service. His name appears on the list of candidates to be awarded the Commemorative Medal of 13 March 1938. In 1974, former SD commander Wilhelm Höttl testified that Naujocks

Salomon Smolianoff (1899-1976) was a Jewish counterfeiter who was involved in Operation *Bernhard*. (*National Archives of Sweden*)

was among the forty to sixty individuals who made up the SD operational group *Einsatzkommando Österreich*.

In 1939, Naujocks was given a new assignment: the production of counterfeit money. Work began in 1940 and a facility used for forging banknotes was set up in the Spechthausen paper mill near Berlin, where prisoners were tasked with forging the currency. The head of production was an expert in the field, a Jewish counterfeiter from the capital, Salomon Smolianoff, who was serving a prison sentence at the time and was a wanted criminal in several European countries. Interestingly, it was Bernhard Krüger, who would later head Operation *Bernhard*, who had put Smolianoff behind bars in 1936.

Released from his cell, Smolianoff began working in a role where he could fully utilise his skills. However, by 1942, only 3 million counterfeit banknotes of various denominations had been produced, and these were far from perfect replicas. The flaws were easily noticeable to experts.[9] Ultimately, Naujocks was removed from the project following a dispute with Heydrich, and the entire operation was shut down. Shut down but not forgotten.

On the path to success, Krüger's counterfeiters encountered a wide range of difficulties. British banknotes had as many as 150 different security features. However, the main problem lay in identifying the correct type of paper used to print the pound notes. After a year of trials and experiments, they discovered that the British were using old linen mailbags, and that the production technique dated back to the eighteenth century. The German counterfeiters achieved a similar result by producing paper from old linen rags: the resulting material had the right crispness, durability, and weight, and it fluoresced correctly under UV light.

By 1943, production had reached a level of 650,000 banknotes per month. Notes ranging in denomination from £5 to £1,000 were printed, though only the lower denominations were released into circulation. Fearing exposure of the operation, the decision was made not to use the £500 and £1,000 notes. But what to do with the already printed high-value currency?

Originally, the plan had been to use aircraft to drop the counterfeit money over English cities. By 1943, however, this was practically impossible. The banknotes were therefore introduced into circulation via neutral countries such as Spain and Portugal, and later in Denmark, Norway, Switzerland, Turkey, and even Egypt. From these locations, the counterfeit currency quickly found its way to Britain, causing massive economic damage. The forgeries were so widespread that the pound lost 75% of its value, and banks in Western countries ceased accepting British currency for exchange, as they were unable to distinguish the originals from the forgeries, especially since every banknote produced in Sachsenhausen bore a serial number corresponding to one that was genuinely in circulation. The counterfeit notes were even used to pay certain spies. The most famous example is Elias Bazna, better known by his codename 'Cicero', who operated within the British Embassy in Ankara. From 1943 onwards, he passed highly classified documents to the Germans stolen from the British ambassador, which concerned, among other things, the Allied landings in France and the opening of the Second Front in the West.

As the months passed, Germany's production capabilities steadily diminished. Turkey, which had previously supplied the necessary paper, began to sense the shifting balance of power and increasingly aligned its sympathies with the Allies.

Two years earlier, Hitler had explicitly forbidden the counterfeiting of US dollars, unwilling to provoke the giant across the Atlantic. By now, however, the geopolitical situation looked markedly different. In December 1944, the production of counterfeit pounds was brought to an end, and efforts were redirected towards the US dollar.

The first series of banknotes rolled off the printing presses in May 1945. By then, the Red Army was advancing at an alarming pace towards the gates of Sachsenhausen camp. The secret of what had taken place over the past few years in blocks 18 and 19 could not be allowed to fall into Soviet hands. The counterfeit currency, along with all related materials and equipment, was carefully packed into wooden crates and transported to the Ebensee camp in Austria.

However, the Soviet threat continued to grow there, as well. Everything was repacked, with each crate containing £200,000 and dumped into Lake Toplitz and the River Enns. In August 1945, Edward Reid, a former banker employed in section B1B of MI5, the British intelligence division responsible for gathering information on the enemy, compiled a report in which, quoting the testimony of one of the SS men, he revealed the German plans related to the counterfeit banknotes: 'The forgeries were so expertly executed that, for anyone without specialist knowledge, distinguishing them from the genuine article was virtually impossible,' wrote Reid. 'Overall, it can be said that the German objective to destroy foreign confidence in Bank of England notes was achieved. The counterfeiting of British banknotes became so widespread that no one in neutral countries would accept sterling unless it was at a significant discount,' he concluded.

And the German success was by no means insignificant. As part of Operation *Bernhard*, a total of 8,965,080 banknotes were printed, with a combined value of £134,610,945 an amount equivalent to nearly the entire gold reserve of the Bank of England.

Bernhard Krüger was arrested by the British after the war and spent three years in prison. Upon his release in 1948, he took up employment at a factory that, during the war, had supplied paper for the operation he had overseen. In 1955, he was accused of the deaths of four prisoners whom he had allegedly removed from his team of counterfeiters after they contracted tuberculosis. However, the German prosecution concluded that the accusations were insufficiently substantiated, and the case was closed. Krüger went on to live a quiet life with his family, enjoying time with his grandchildren, collecting stamps, and writing his memoirs. He died in 1989.

Chapter 4

The Lost Treasures of the 'War Diary'

The subject of missing treasures or works of art from the Third Reich still fires the imagination of thousands of treasure hunters. And this is not without reason. We know the stories of many treasures discovered in various hiding places, tunnels, and mine shafts, yet many smaller caches may still remain undiscovered. Of course, the search also continues for those great treasures that make headlines in newspapers and news portals. In recent years, we witnessed another chapter in the search for the Amber Room,[1] this time in Hitler's former headquarters, the Wolf's Lair, and earlier, the search for the 'golden train' at the 65th kilometre of the railway line to Wałbrzych, a case so sensational that it even echoed as far away as Japan.[2]

Despite rational arguments suggesting that such immense riches will never be found, almost every year a new batch of stories emerges about gold and valuables, supposedly hidden almost within arm's reach. Paradoxically, more books are written about the history of treasures *not* being found than about searches that actually end in success.

From time to time, however, the media reports on the discovery of precious items that are not necessarily gold bars from the Reichsbank. These objects, though of much lesser monetary value, are priceless for deepening our understanding of certain historical facts, and sometimes for the finders themselves. Recently, the treasure-hunting community was electrified by reports of the so-called War Diary, said to indicate the location of forty-eight chests containing 10 tons of gold. It is worth taking a closer look at this story.

Among all kinds of seekers of Nazi gold, the figure of Günther Grundmann looms almost as a cult icon and at the same time as a key to future discoveries. Grundmann was a German historian and art conservator, who from 1942 onwards, was tasked with selecting, securing, and hiding the most important works of art located within the Reich, as well as those looted during the war. Refusing such work was, of course, out of the question, or perhaps he simply had no desire to refuse.

The prospect of gathering thousands of works of art from almost all of Europe under his own supervision was a tempting vision. And so, from the very start, he threw himself into the task with zeal, dispatching letters to fellow collectors, museums, and art galleries. Yet he was not the sort to remain chained to a desk, waiting for replies. He set out into the field, determined to see with his own eyes what was worth preserving and what could be discarded. After all, there was never enough time for everything.

The scale of his operations is evident from the sheer numbers: from private collectors alone he received 552 paintings, 90 sculptures, 373 pieces of furniture, 11 portfolios of graphics, and thousands of objects of decorative art. And all this had been gathered by 21 June 1944, the date of the last entry on Grundmann's list. This, of course, did not mean that the mysterious conservator ceased his work. On the contrary, he continued to appear in the field almost daily, accompanied by armed SS men assigned to protect him.

By the end of 1944, as the front drew closer, the authorities of Breslau (now Wrocław) called on residents to deposit their valuables and precious objects in bank vaults. These were ultimately transferred to the cellars of the Police Presidium. Since Breslau was designated to defend itself as a fortress until the last soldier, the city was not expected to be left standing. That meant the accumulated treasures had to be evacuated.

Günther Grundmann (1892-1976) was a German art historian and conservator of monuments. An author of books and articles on Silesian art, he created the so-called Grundmann List – an encoded register of locations where the authorities of the Third Reich hid works of art to protect them from wartime destruction. (*Schondorf.pl*)

It was at this moment that SS-Sturmbannführer Egon Ollenhauser entered the scene. As Grundmann's assistant, he was entrusted with the task of transporting and securing the collected deposits. He was accompanied by SS-Hauptsturmführer Herbert Klose and SS-Hauptsturmführer Gustav Seifert, both serving in the *Ordnungspolizei* (OrPo).

Ollenhauser is said to have compiled a diary of some 500 pages, in which he recorded information about the hiding places of the deposits. It points to twelve potential locations, including the palace at Minkowskie in Upper Silesia. Hidden in these caches, alongside gold and jewellery, were allegedly wartime-lost paintings by Botticelli, Rubens, Cézanne, Caravaggio, Monet, Dürer, Raphael, and Rembrandt.

Yet despite intensive searches and much-publicised announcements, the current owners of the palace have not revealed a single discovery. Doubts, therefore, continue to multiply, both about the information provided by the diary's custodians and about the document itself. And there are many more question marks. Two individuals supposedly confirming the diary's authenticity later stated that they had never taken part in the research and had never endorsed its validity. That fact alone was enough to arouse suspicion.

According to Krzysztof 'Czarny' Krzyżanowski, who reported on the conference at which the diary was presented, he was allowed to view only a few pages. It was possible, however, to examine it closely from the outside

Gold looted and hidden by the Germans in the Merkers-Kieselbach salt mine, 15 April 1945. (*Public domain*)

and learn that only some pages contained writing, while the greater part remained blank. At the same time, the diary was said to be accompanied by other documents not disclosed by the foundation, such as a 'location map'.

The open question remains whether Egon Ollenhauser ever existed at all, or whether he was merely a creation of Herbert Klose, the only person to provide information about him. Klose, however, was hardly a reliable witness. During interrogations he evaded questions, contradicted himself, and repeatedly changed his testimony. Was this deliberate?

Soon afterwards, however, the riddle of the 'war diary' was solved: it turned out to be yet another historical forgery. The passages included in the diary had, in fact, been copied after the war from accounts given by German refugees fleeing Lower Silesia in 1945. Decades later, someone transcribed these reports word for word onto the pages of the diary. This revealed that the supposed diary could not have been created before the 1970s. In many ways, the story, albeit on a smaller scale, echoes the case of the forged Hitler Diaries, produced by Konrad Kujau.

<h1 style="text-align:center">Chapter 5</h1>

The Golden Treasure of Bydgoszcz

The most popular land of mystery and legend about hidden Nazi treasures is, of course, Lower Silesia in Poland. Yet, as we can increasingly see, other regions of the country are also rich in such stories. One example is Bydgoszcz, the city on the River Brda, and its surroundings. During the Second World War, the Bydgoszcz airfield hosted, among others, the 4th Reserve Close Reconnaissance Squadron (4. *Ergänzung Nahaüfklarung Gruppe Bromberg*), which was stationed in the city from 1941 onwards. In 1944, one of its soldiers was a 22-year-old unteroffizier named Karl Tränkle.

One December day, the unit received an unusual order. Tränkle, along with three comrades, was assigned to carry it out. They were instructed to

A document confirming service in a Wehrmacht unit stationed in Bydgoszcz. (*Institute of National Remembrance*)

select a site and bury roughly 700 kilograms of gold. The chosen location was near the barracks at the Bydgoszcz airfield. The soldiers carried out the order diligently, although after the war they could never explain how an additional 80 kilograms of gold bars had come into their possession.

A few days after completing their task, Tränkle undertook a solo flight north. Reaching the Tuchola Forest near Czersk, he dropped the cargo he was carrying, carefully marked the spot on his map, and then returned 100 kilometres (60 miles) south to the airfield at Szwederowo.

By now, the war was drawing to a close. On 22 January 1945, the last aircrew departed from Bydgoszcz. Five days later, it was free of the German occupier. Tränkle was taken prisoner, and in the years that followed he lived with the memories of a war fading into the past and with the secret of the golden deposit he had once guarded.

Such an account can be found in the documents preserved in the archives of the Institute of National Remembrance. In this entire story, at least three puzzling questions arise:

- How did those 700 kilograms of gold end up in Bydgoszcz?
- Was the additional 80 kilograms dropped near Czersk part of the treasure the soldiers were supposed to bury, which they decided to keep aside for themselves?
- Did someone on the ground collect the drop and hide it? After all, it is hard to believe that postwar treasure hunters – of whom there was no shortage – would fail to have stumbled upon gold bars weighing a total of 80 kilograms simply lying in the grass or moss.

And so the key question remains: does the German gold buried near the Bydgoszcz airfield still lie there?

After the war, Germans possessing knowledge of looted valuables, gold, or paintings hidden in the territories incorporated into Poland turned up in droves at Polish consulates and other institutions. On 30 September 1986, Consul Stanisław Kantorski opened and read a letter addressed to him by a German merchant named Kurt Tränkle. What caused great surprise was that, at least initially, the sender did not demand the customary finder's fee and even declared his willingness to come to Poland almost immediately to point out the location of the hidden treasure. This visit, however, was complicated by a significant reduction in the income of Tränkle's business, which he explained in his letter: 'I run a catering business together with my wife, and it is impossible for us to take a long leave since we manage the business on our own. Our monthly expenses car, telephone, insurance, etc. amount to 5,000 to 6,000 DM, which must be paid at the end of each month. My absence would reduce both turnover and income.'

Of course, covering Tränkle's potential losses was out of the question for formal and legal reasons, so his proposal was rejected. Yet he did not give up and suggested two solutions that, from his point of view, seemed reasonable:

> First proposal – You will take from my warehouse goods worth around 50,000 DM (the goods will be purchased at current gross prices + VAT).

> Second proposal – You will buy from me tableware worth 50,000 DM of your choice at the current prices, that is, the gross price + VAT.

By this stage, the matter began to look anything but serious. It even suggested an attempt by the enterprising German to prop up his failing business – as if the story of the gold were meant merely to lend credibility to the entire scheme.

The ambassador, however, chose to place his trust in his interlocutor and allowed the matter to proceed further. He referred the case to the Legal and Treaty Department of the Ministry of Foreign Affairs, which in turn passed it on to the Foreign Department of the Ministry of Finance. From there, a request for an opinion was forwarded to the Social and Administrative Department of the Ministry of the Interior. Ultimately, the issue of the German gold landed in the Economic Section of Department V of the Ministry of the Interior.

In addition to analysing the materials, it was decided, on the basis of the data already obtained, to carry out an onsite inspection. The task was entrusted to a team from the Provincial Office of Internal Affairs for Security Service matters in Bydgoszcz. The investigation lasted several days, and on 17 December, Colonel Stefan Stefanowski, Deputy Head of the WUSW for Security Service in Bydgoszcz, sent a report to headquarters. It read:

> Since the end of the Second World War, the small airfield in Bydgoszcz has been completely modernised and expanded. Numerous new facilities necessary for modern aviation

technology have been built, while the old ones were demolished. Near the barracks by the airfield, new residential districts have been constructed: Błonie, Wzgórze Wolności, Szwederowo, and Wyżyny with outbound roads leading towards Poznań and Inowrocław, including bypass routes. In the vicinity of the airfield, single-family housing estates have also arisen: Trzciniec and Białe Błota.

In view of such development, both of the airfield itself and the surrounding areas, I consider it impossible to determine precisely the site of the hidden gold. Regarding the alleged gold drop near Czersk (the Tuchola Forest), it should be noted that identifying the location of the drop is highly unlikely – the forests have been felled, replanted, and have grown naturally. These woods are heavily frequented by mushroom pickers, and such a 'treasure' could well have been discovered long ago.

After analysing the report, which took such a negative stance on the possibility of finding gold in Bydgoszcz, a decision was made to close the investigation and end cooperation with the German. His assistance onsite was not used. We do not know why, at least not officially.

So, does Nazi gold still lie buried somewhere near the airfield? To this day, no one has announced the discovery of such a treasure.

Chapter 6

The Guard or the Doctor?

On 1 October 1946, just before 3:00 pm, a guard unlocked the heavy steel door leading to the cell of the most important prisoner in Nuremberg: Hermann Göring. The prisoner rose to his feet and followed the guard to the elevator that carried them up to the floor where the courtroom was located. It was there, over the previous months, that German crimes committed during the war years had been laid bare. It was there that the former Reichsmarschall, having regained his strength thanks to the forced withdrawal from morphine, tried to argue that the Allies judging the Germans had themselves committed war crimes. Precisely at 3:00 pm, Göring and his guard stepped out of the elevator and walked towards the place where he would hear his sentence.

Judge Lawrence read the verdict: 'The accused, Hermann Wilhelm Göring. The International Military Tribunal sentences you to death by hanging.'

The death penalty could hardly have been – and indeed was not – a surprise for Göring. He had hoped, however, that as a soldier he would be granted the dignity of facing a firing squad. Death by hanging was a disgrace to a man of arms. Fifteen days of life remained to him.

In the final days of the Third Reich, when Germans lived in misery and despair and their cities lay in ruins, Göring remained safely distant from Berlin and from Adolf Hitler, who awaited the inevitable end in the bunker beneath the Reich Chancellery. Göring had last met his Führer on 20 April, when celebrating his birthday. But it was, in truth, little more than a macabre dance around the coffin.

From Berlin Göring travelled south to Obersalzberg, which many regarded as the heart of the mythical Alpine Redoubt. A considerable number of Germans believed that from there, a new offensive would be launched, one that would change the course of the war and drive the Bolshevik armies from their land.

Left: Hermann Wilhelm Göring (1893-1946), a fighter ace from the First World War, was one of the founders and leading figures of the Third Reich. He served as Reich Minister of Aviation from 1933 to 1945, and commander of the German Air Force, the Luftwaffe, from 1935 to 1945. (*Bundesarchiv, Bild 146-1979-089-22/CC-BY-SA 3.0*)

Below: Göring during the Nuremberg Trial, March 1946. (*Public domain*)

At 10:00 pm on 23 April, knowing that Hitler had no intention of leaving Berlin and still seeing himself as his nominal deputy and successor, Göring sent a telegram stating that if he did not receive a reply, he would feel obliged to assume power.

Most publications repeat the version that Hitler was shown by his secretary, Martin Bormann. But what is the truth?

To answer this question, it is worth examining the text of Göring's own telegram:

> Mein Führer!
> General Koller informed me today of reports passed on to him by Colonel General Jodl and General Christian, according to which you had delegated certain decisions to me. (…). These statements were so surprising and serious to me that I felt obliged to assume that if I received no reply by 22:00, it would mean that you had lost your freedom of action, that in this case the conditions of your decree were fulfilled, and I would act in the best understanding of the interests of our homeland and our people (…).

As can be seen from the contents of the message, Göring – who considered himself Hitler's successor – was not attempting to seize power by force, nor did he issue any conditions. On the contrary, he was asking Hitler whether he had correctly interpreted the current situation. The wording of the telegram is cautious and entirely rational. Why, then, was its sender accused of treason? The answer lies with Martin Bormann, who jealously guarded access to the Führer.

Practically since Rudolf Hess's flight to England in May 1941, anyone seeking to reach Hitler had to do so through Bormann. Hitler always valued him for being able to distil even highly complex issues into a few simple sentences. This time as well, the message addressed directly to the Führer passed into the secretary's hands. In the upper echelons of power, it was no secret that Bormann harboured no affection for Himmler, and even less for Göring. He awaited the chance to eliminate them both, and in each case that chance came only in the final days of the Third Reich.

Bormann convinced Hitler that his deputy was attempting a coup. As Albert Speer later recalled, Bormann exclaimed with excitement: 'Göring is betraying you (…) tonight, at midnight, he is taking over your office, mein Führer!'

By this time Hitler was already a wreck of a man. Nothing remained of the magnetic force that once drew people to him and captivated them in fiery speeches. Now he was subject to constant mood swings, propped up by the narcotic injections of Dr Theo Morell. It was therefore easy for Bormann to manipulate the Führer, eliminating potential and often imaginary opponents. This is precisely what he did with the Minister of Aviation. He had little difficulty persuading Hitler that the Reichsmarschall was a schemer, a degenerate, a morphine addict, and so forth.

Göring was blamed for all the misfortunes that had befallen the Third Reich. The final charge was, to a large extent, justified. Had it not been for his boast that the Luftwaffe would finish off the British Expeditionary Corps at Dunkirk, England might long ago have been brought to its knees as a vassal of the Reich. In that case, the situation on the Eastern Front would have looked entirely different. Perhaps there would have been no defeat at Stalingrad, where the Luftwaffe once again faltered. But such speculation is futile, although it became fuel for Hitler's frustration as the war was slipping away. That frustration could now be poured out on a single, tangible target.

Bormann did not even wait for the Führer's instructions. He set to work to destroy his rival and to savour the satisfaction, even in the final days of the war. His first telegram went to SS-Obersturmbannführer Bernhard Frank, who commanded the SS unit stationed at the foot of the Obersalzberg, ordering him to surround the villa of the supposed traitor and arrest the now-former Reichsmarschall.

Naturally, Göring received no reply to his telegram, so he calmly began preparing to assume succession, together with his wife Emmy and daughter Edda. He ordered the guard posts around the villa to be reinforced, including the anti-aircraft defences. He summoned Hans Lammers, head of the Reich Chancellery. Lammers hardly ever parted with the briefcase in which, since 29 June 1941, he had carried the document that was now to be put into effect. It contained the following declaration: 'In the event that illness or other circumstances prevent me from fulfilling my duties, even temporarily [...] I appoint as my deputy, in all functions I perform, the Reichsmarschall of Greater Germany, Hermann Göring.'

Meanwhile, Bormann was sending out further telegrams to all key figures who were to learn of the official version of Göring's 'treason'. By evening, when a detachment of SS men surrounded the Reichsmarschall's villa, a telegram finally arrived from Berlin. It was a message from Hitler himself. The demoted Reichsmarschall read its contents in disbelief: 'The decree of 29 June 1941, shall take effect only when I issue the relevant order. There can be no question of freedom of action. Therefore, I forbid you from taking any steps in the direction you propose.'

Göring was terrified. He realised that all the telegrams he had sent to Ribbentrop, Himmler, and the OKW would now be used against him. At 8:00 pm the telephone line was cut. Two hours later, the commander of the SS unit that had closed the ring around the villa stepped inside.

SS-Obersturmbannführer Frank declared that Göring was under arrest, raising his right hand in the Nazi salute as he did so. Within twenty-four hours, Göring's situation had become dire. An air raid by British bombers virtually wiped his villa off the face of the earth. He himself, along with his wife, daughter, and closest staff, driven on by SS men, took shelter in the underground tunnels built during the villa's construction. No one had ever imagined they might prove useful. And yet, they did.

Frank's unit was relieved on Himmler's orders, and another detachment was sent to guard the Reichsmarschall. The new SS men were considerably friendlier, even offering to transport Göring wherever he wished. Such an offer did not need to be repeated. The Reichsmarschall climbed into his

Nr.	Marinenachrichtendienst					Ltg.-Nr.
Aufgen., den 23.4. 19 45	Wieder an	Tag	Uhrzeit	Ltg.	durch	Uhrzeitgruppen
um 0056 Uhr						1811/11 frr
von Ltg.						2352/14 frr
durch Schl.						
Verzögerungsverm.						Geheim!

Fernspruch	Funkspruch	von:	Obersalzberg
Fernschreiben	Posttelegramm		

Mein Führer:

General Koller hat mir heute auf Grund von Mitteilungen, die ihm Generaloberst Jodl und General Christian gemacht hatten, eine Darstellung gegeben, wonach Sie in gewissen Entscheidungen auf mich verwiesen hätten und dabei betonten, dass ich, falls Verhandlungen notwendig würden, dazu leichter in der Lage wäre als Sie in Berlin. Die Äusserungen waren für mich derart überraschend und ernst, dass ich mich verpflichtet fühlte, falls bis 2200 Uhr keine Antwort erfolgt, nehme ich an, dass Sie Ihrer Handlungsfreiheit beraubt sind. Ich werde dann die Voraussetzungen Ihres Erlasses als gegeben ansehen und zum Wohle von Volk und Vaterland handeln. Was ich in diesen schwersten Stunden meines Lebens für Sie empfinde, das wissen Sie und kann ich durch Worte nicht ausdrücken. Gott schütze Sie und lasse Sie trotz alledem baldmöglichst hierher kommen.

Ihr getreuer Hermann Göring

The telegram Göring sent to Hitler, inquiring about the possible assumption of power in Germany, a move for which he was declared a traitor. (*Public domain*)

armoured Maybach with his family and ordered to be driven to Mauterndorf Castle, located about 64 kilometres (40 miles) from Salzburg.

On 1 May, a message arrived from Berlin announcing Hitler's death. This made the situation even more complicated. Göring had every reason to believe that Bormann would now use his power to have him executed. Yet no one was willing to make a decision either to carry out a death sentence or to release the prisoner. It was no longer clear where the centre of power in the collapsing Reich truly lay.

Finally, on 6 May, Field Marshal Albert Kesselring ordered the prisoner's release. At the same time, a unit from the 12th Luftwaffe Signal Regiment happened to be passing near the castle. Seeing their superior walking in the company of SS men, the soldiers decided to greet him. Noticing that his own men vastly outnumbered Himmler's guards, Göring ordered the castle to be seized. Thus, a clash broke out between the Luftwaffe and the Waffen-SS.

Immediately after his release, the former Reichsmarschall sent a letter to Grand Admiral Dönitz, offering himself as a negotiator with the Americans. He also dispatched a message to General Eisenhower's staff, inviting them to peace talks at nearby Fischhorn Castle (Austria). To his surprise, the proposal was accepted. Göring reluctantly set out to meet Brigadier General Robert Stack, a Texan, who approached from the opposite direction. The two men met roughly halfway, exchanged greetings, and Stack invited his guest into the sedan in which he had arrived. At that moment, Göring's twelve years of life in luxury came to an irreversible end. Indeed, the courtesy shown to a Nazi dignitary also marked the end of the American's career.

Hearing in Nuremberg the sentence condemning him to death by hanging, Göring resolved that his life could not end in such a way. Although he had forbidden his defence counsel to submit an appeal for clemency, when he learned that it had been filed regardless, he allowed himself a flicker of hope that somehow it might succeed, or at least that the method of execution might be changed.

On his last night before death, Göring sat at a small table and wrote his final letter. In it he stated:

> I have considered it an affront to decency and good taste to turn
> our execution into a spectacle for sensation-hungry reporters,
> photographers, and the curious crowd. The form of this 'grand

finale' is a visible testimony to the degeneration of the tribunal and the prosecutors. Pure theatre from beginning to end pure theatre! All of this is a miserable comedy!

I understand perfectly well that our enemies wish to dispose of us, driven either by fear or by hatred. But it would be to their credit if they carried out the whole matter as soldiers would.

I myself intend to die without all this sensation and circus.

I want to emphasize once again that I do not feel in the slightest degree obliged, morally or in any other way, to submit to the death sentence and subsequent execution imposed by the enemies of myself and of Germany.

I intend to depart into the hereafter joyfully, and I shall regard death as liberation.

I rely on Divine mercy! I deeply regret that I cannot help my companions in misfortune (especially Field Marshal Keitel and Colonel General Jodl) to avoid the public spectacle that is intended to be made of our deaths.

All the precautions applied to us prisoners to prevent us from harming ourselves were not for our good, but solely to preserve us for that great spectacle.

But it shall be without me.[1]

The following day, at around 7:30 pm, Pastor Gerecke entered Göring's cell. He noticed that the former Reichsmarschall seemed more subdued than in previous days, and they spoke about reconciliation with the Savior. At 8:30, the guards were changed. Private Gordon Bingham looked through the peephole into the cell. He saw the prisoner lying on his bed, wearing shoes, trousers, and a jacket, reading a book. About twenty minutes later, Göring went to the toilet, disappearing briefly from the guard's view. Afterwards he busied himself tidying his desk and preparing to sleep. But he would not yet rest in Morpheus's embrace.

At 9:30 pm, urologist Dr Pflücker entered the cell. He had been distributing luminal tablets to prisoners suffering from insomnia. He spoke with Göring for about three minutes. The guard later testified that he saw Göring swallow a capsule handed to him by the doctor, who later claimed it was filled with baking soda, so that the Reichsmarschall would not fall asleep that night; he was to be fully prepared for his final walk to the gallows. The doctor then measured his pulse, exchanged a few words, and, in farewell, shook Göring's hand. This was strictly forbidden, yet as Dr Pflücker explained: 'Since we were seeing each other for the last time, it would have been difficult for me, as a doctor, not to make such a gesture.'[2]

Was it then that the doctor handed Göring the cyanide capsule?

At 11:00 pm, Harold F. Johnson looked into the cell through the peephole. The prisoner was lying on his back without moving, seemingly asleep. The guard, as the later investigation showed, did not see his left arm, which rested alongside his body. He lay motionless until about 11:40, when he folded his hands on his chest and turned his head towards the wall. He remained in this position for two or three minutes, then once again laid his arms alongside his body. 'It was exactly 11:44; I remember it well because I looked at my watch', Johnson later testified.

Sixteen minutes later, Göring was supposed to plunge through the open trapdoor with a noose tightening around his neck. Yet precisely at that time, the entire prison was thrown into alarm and all the lights were switched on. The corridors echoed with the clatter of hobnailed boots. The characteristic smell of bitter almonds could also be detected. Sergeant Daniel E. Hauberger shouted at the top of his voice: 'Göring is dead!'

Several letters were found on Göring's body. When had he written them? They were dated five days earlier. Yet it is obvious that they were not actually composed then or, if written on that date, they had not been kept in the cell, and someone must have placed them there during the commotion surrounding the prisoner's death.

One of the letters was addressed to the warden:

> To the prison warden.
> From the moment of my imprisonment, I always carried a poison capsule with me. When I was transferred to the prison in Mondorf, I had three capsules. The first I kept hidden in my clothing, so that it could easily be found during a search. The second I would place beneath the coat rack while undressing, and when dressing again I would take it with me. I hid it so skilfully, both in Mondorf and here, that despite frequent and meticulous searches of the cell, it was never discovered. During the trial sessions I kept it inside my shoes.
>
> The third capsule is still in the container with my toiletry items, specifically in a round box of skin-care cream. Had I wished, I could have used it twice while in Mondorf.

None of those who carried out the searches can be blamed for anything, since finding the capsule bordered on the impossible. It could only have been a matter of sheer chance.[3]

The remaining letters were addressed to the Allied Control Council in Germany, the military authority based in Berlin that exercised power over occupied Germany on behalf of the United States, Great Britain, France, and the Soviet Union, as well as letters to his wife Emmy, and to Pastor Gerecke.

The open question remains: how did Göring come into possession of the capsule containing 35 millimetres of the poison hydrogen cyanide? One suspect was an American prison guard, who was said to have smuggled a cyanide ampoule from the storage of personal belongings. However, it seems far more likely that the capsule was slipped to him by Dr Pflücker while measuring his pulse. The doctor was also the last person to visit Göring in his cell. Yet is this lead correct? That will likely remain a mystery forever.

The body of Hermann Göring, First World War flying ace, Reichsmarschall and Minister of Aviation, Reich Master of the Hunt was cremated, and his ashes thrown into the River Isar, so that his grave would not become a site of pilgrimage for potential Nazi sympathizers.

Chapter 7

The Last Knight of the Wehrmacht?

On 1 September 1939, the German armies set out to conquer Poland. In launching the war, the German Reich deployed 1.85 million soldiers, 11,000 artillery pieces, 2,800 tanks, and 2,000 aircraft. As Hitler declared, however, this was not to be an ordinary war. It was not about seizing a defined territory. Its purpose was the physical annihilation of the enemy.

When speaking at a commanders' conference on the eve of signing the Ribbentrop-Molotov Pact, Hitler announced that:

> The destruction of Poland is our first task. The objective must not be to reach a designated line, but to destroy a living force. Even if war were to break out in the West, the destruction of Poland must be our first task. The decision must be immediate because of the season. I shall provide some reason for the outbreak of war for propaganda purposes. It matters little whether it is credible or not. The victor will not be asked whether he spoke the truth or not. In matters concerning the initiation and conduct of war, it is not law that counts, but victory. Be merciless, be brutal.[1]

Thus, following the Wehrmacht troops came the *Einsatzgruppen* (EG), composed of policemen as well as members of the SD and the Gestapo, tasked with securing the rear. This 'security' consisted of selecting and murdering as many people as possible belonging to the so-called leadership strata of the nation, as well as all Jews. These units had already received their baptism of fire during the occupation of what remained of the Czechoslovak state.

There were eight *Einsatzgruppen* operating in Polish territories, including six designated with Roman numerals:

To carry out – in Hitler's words – the 'settling of accounts' with the Poles in Bydgoszcz, a detachment separated from *Einsatzkommando* 16, under the command of Jakob Lölgen, was sent from Gdańsk, among other places. (*Author's archive*)

- I – SS-Standartenführer Bruno Streckenbach – operating with the 14th Army of Colonel General Wilhelm List
- II – SS-Obersturmbannführer Emanuel Schäfer – with the 10th Army of General of Artillery Walter von Reichenau
- III – SS-Obersturmbannführer und Regierungsrat Dr Ludwig Fischer – with the 8th Army of General of Infantry Johannes Blaskowitz
- IV – SS-Brigadeführer Lothar Beutel – with the 4th Army of General of Artillery Günther von Kluge
- V – SS-Standartenführer Ernst Damzog – with the 3rd Army of General of Artillery Georg von Küchler
- VI – SS-Oberführer Erich Naumann – operating in Greater Poland
- z.b.v. (*zur besonderen Verwendung* – for special tasks) – SS-Obergruppenführer Udo von Woyrsch and SS-Oberführer Otto Rasch – operating in Upper Silesia and Cieszyn Silesia
- *Einsatzkommando* 16 (EK16) – SS-Sturmbannführer Dr Rudolf Tröger – an independent group operating in Pomerania.

What concerns us most here is the 8th Army, commanded from 1 August 1939 by General Johannes Albrecht Blaskowitz, who was tasked with advancing towards Łódź and then Warsaw. Following it was EG III, which committed numerous brutal murders of Poles and Jews. Not all Wehrmacht commanders accepted such actions.

General Blaskowitz, in a protest sent to Hitler's Chancellery, described an incident that took place on 30 October 1939, in the town of Turek:

> A group of Jews was herded into the synagogue and ordered to crawl between the benches and sing, while the SS men beat them with whips. They were then told to take off their trousers so that they could be beaten on their bare buttocks. One of the Jews, who soiled his trousers out of fear, was forced to smear his excrement on the faces of the other Jews.

The general concluded in his report:

> The attitude of the soldiers towards the SS and the police oscillates between disgust and hatred. Every soldier feels revulsion and loathing for these crimes committed in Poland by members of the Reich and representatives of state authority. He cannot understand how such things, especially when they occur under his protection, so to speak, can go unpunished.

The protest did not stop the German crimes. Hitler completely dismissed Blaskowitz's objections. He considered the general's accusations 'childish' and the methods he wished to employ as akin to those of the 'Salvation Army'.

Combined with the fact that his army had virtually ceased to exist during the Battle of Bzura, it can be said that Blaskowitz's position in Hitler's hierarchy of favoured officers was not very high. Nevertheless, the Führer was sufficiently pleased with his overall success that on 20 October 1939, he promoted Blaskowitz to Commander-in-Chief of *Oberkommando Ost* (Supreme Command East), exercising temporary military authority over occupied Poland. The general was also awarded the Knight's Cross of the Iron Cross. From that point, however, his career became a rollercoaster, and he alternated between receiving command appointments and being sent into the reserve shortly thereafter.

In May 1940 Blaskowitz was given command of the 9th Army, only to be transferred to the reserve in June 1940 on Hitler's orders. At the end

Johannes Blaskowitz as a defendant at the High Command Trial (*Oberkommando der Wehrmacht*) in Nuremberg. (*Public domain*)

of Operation *Fall Gelb*, he served as military commander in northern France, but after its conclusion he was once again sent into the reserve, and from October 1940 he again commanded the 1st Army occupying France. On 12 May 1944, he became commander of Army Group G, tasked with defending southern France. After the assassination attempt on Hitler at the Wolf's Lair on 20 July, Blaskowitz declared his loyalty to the Führer. Following the Allied invasion, he coordinated the evacuation of his army group. On 29 October, he was awarded the Oak Leaves. The citation read:

> Colonel General Blaskowitz commanded the German forces in southwestern France when the Allies landed on the southern coast of France with overwhelming forces and at the same time broke through the German front in Normandy. Yet his determination and excellent leadership proved sufficient for the formations under his command to escape all enemy attempts at encirclement. While continuously fighting heavy battles against a far superior enemy, he led his Army Group back to a state fully fit for battle. In this way he could successfully be incorporated into the new German Western Front.

Soon afterwards, the general was once again placed in the reserve, and from January 1945 he commanded Army Group H in the Netherlands. On 10 April, as commander of 'Fortress Holland', he refused to surrender to the Allies, awaiting orders from the high command. After his subordinate units laid down their arms on 5 May, he capitulated to Canadian General Foulkes at the De Wereld Hotel in Wageningen. He was taken prisoner and interned in a POW camp at Dachau, and later in Allendorf.

After the war, Blaskowitz was held in investigative custody in Nuremberg, where he was interrogated during the High Command Trial of the Wehrmacht. Afterwards, together with 240 generals and admirals, he was required to work at the internment camp in Neustadt for the history department of the American Army. At the beginning of 1948 Blaskowitz was formally charged with war crimes.[2] He was accused of participation in the preparation and conduct of an 'illegal', aggressive war against Poland, which subsequently led to war with Great Britain and France. He then issued a special statement in which he presented his own view of those events:

> After the annexation of Czechoslovakia, we hoped that the Polish question would be resolved peacefully by diplomatic means, since we believed that this time France and England would come to the aid of their ally. In fact, we felt that if political negotiations failed, the Polish question would inevitably lead to war, and thus not only with Poland itself, but also with the Western powers.
>
> When, in mid-June, I received the order from the OKH to prepare for an attack on Poland, I knew that this war had moved even closer to the realm of possibility. This conclusion was only reinforced by the Führer's speech of 22 August 1939, at Obersalzberg, when it apparently seemed to be a fact. From mid-June 1939 to 1 September 1939, the members of my staff engaged in preparations took part in various discussions that took place between the OKH and the army group. During these discussions, issues of a tactical, strategic, and general nature were considered, which were relevant to my future position as Commander-in-Chief of the 8th Army during the planned Polish campaign.
>
> During the Polish campaign, especially during the Kutno operations, I was repeatedly in contact with the Commander-in-Chief of the Army, and he, like the Führer, visited my headquarters. Commanders-in-chief of army groups and armies were from time to time asked to assess the land situation in order to provide recommendations – by telephone, teletype, or wireless, as well as in personal conversations. They actually became advisers to the OKH in their field, so that the positions presented in the attached table included this group, which was the actual advisory council of the Supreme Command of the Armed Forces of Germany.[3]

In addition, Blaskowitz was accused of participating in the execution of Führer Order No. 003830/42 of 18 October 1942, better known as the *Kommandobefehl.* In it, Hitler commanded that all opponents carrying out so-called commando missions in Europe and Africa, even uniformed soldiers who were captured either in combat or while fleeing, were to be wiped out to the last man. It made no difference whether they had landed from a ship, parachuted in, or come down from an aircraft.

On the same day Hitler issued a special annex in which he explained the reasons for his decision. It was the only time in history that the Führer explained one of his orders in writing:

> I have found myself in a situation where I had to issue a severe order for the destruction of sabotage groups, and I shall punish heavily any failure to carry it out. (…) Never in any war have such methods been used as now. (…). The results of such actions are very serious for us. I do not know whether every commander realizes that the destruction of a single power plant results in the loss of many tons of aluminium, which is essential for the construction of aircraft. (…). For the enemy, such operations involve no risk. They drop sabotage groups in uniform while also equiping them with civilian clothes, so that at one moment they can pose as civilians and at another as soldiers. (…) There is no doubt, however, that such actions are contrary to the provisions of the Geneva Convention. (…). I therefore expect that all commanders will understand the necessity of this measure and will with all their energy ensure the execution of this order.

Blaskowitz was also accused that around 7 July 1944, near Poitiers in France, soldiers of the LXXX Corps of the 18th Army under the command of Army Group G, commanded by Blaskowitz himself, carried out the execution of one American and thirty British prisoners of war. He was further accused of participating in the illegal use of prisoners of war for forced labour in violation of the Geneva Conventions. In particular, he was charged with having ordered, in February 1945, that prisoners of war be used in the construction of fortifications.

Despite so many charges, Blaskowitz could hope that he would be treated more favourably than his fellow generals accused in the same trial.

Blaskowitz considered that through his conduct during the war, he had not stained either his honour or his uniform. Since he had opposed the crimes committed by the SS in Poland, this ought to have ensured that he was not placed on the same level as officers who had directly ordered murders.

It remains a mystery to this day why Blaskowitz took his own life. On 5 February 1946, at 7:20 am, after breakfast, as the prisoners returned to their cells, the 64-year-old Blaskowitz suddenly leapt from the line, seized a ladder left in the corridor by painters, placed it against a 2.5-meter-high protective fence, and climbed over it, jumping down into the prison courtyard. He did not die immediately but lived until 10:20 am. The following day, the correspondent of *Dziennik Zachodni* conveyed the news of the former general's death to Polish readers.[4]

Chapter 8

The First Worker of the Third Reich

In the Third Reich every activity had to be formalised. It is therefore no surprise that the economy was also brought under strict control. In place of the trade unions abolished throughout the country, the German Labor Front (*Deutsche Arbeitsfront*, DAF) was created. Like the earlier unions, it was an organisation intended to 'unite all workers'.

The DAF functioned as an appendage of the NSDAP and was divided into eighteen groups, each of which encompassed workers from a different branch of industry. From the very beginning of its activity on 10 May 1933, it was headed by the chronic alcoholic Robert Ley.

Ley was born on 15 February 1890, in Niederbreidenbach, a small village in the Rhineland. He was the seventh of eleven children of Friedrich and Emilie. The family lived very modestly, but despite this Robert studied chemistry at the universities of Jena, Bonn, and Münster. When the First World War broke out, he volunteered for the Imperial Army and spent the first years of service as an artilleryman, before beginning a course as an aerial artillery observer in 1917. At that time, service connected with aviation attracted more and more young men who wanted to test their courage in this entirely new arm of warfare. Ley was shot down during one of his reconnaissance flights and was taken prisoner by the French. Did he suffer head injuries during the crash that caused brain damage, and later

Robert Ley (1890-1945) was a politician and the leader of the German Labour Front (DAF) from 1933 to 1945. (*Public domain*)

on, speech difficulties? There is no absolute certainty, but it cannot be ruled out. What is certain is that his condition worsened as a result of alcoholism.

After the end of the First World War, Ley returned to university and obtained a doctorate. Having completed his studies, he worked as a food chemist in one of the branches of the IG Farben conglomerate. After the occupation of the Ruhr by the French, he became interested in Hitler and the NSDAP. He was looking for a nationalist organisation through which he could channel his hostility towards the occupiers. By 1925 he was already serving as Gauleiter of the South Rhineland district as well as editor of the strongly antisemitic Nazi newspaper *Westdeutscher Beobachter*.

In 1932 he came to Munich, working in the party's main headquarters, the so-called Brown House (*Braunes Haus*). After the resignation of Gregor Strasser, he became head of party organisation (*Reichsorganisationsleiter*); it was a sign that Hitler had rewarded his loyalty. When the trade unions were replaced by the DAF in 1933, Ley was placed at its head.

After the outbreak of the Second World War, Ley's influence and importance within the structures of the Third Reich diminished significantly. He was gradually pushed aside, yet to the very end he remained a loyal companion of Hitler. He saw his Führer for the last time on his birthday, 20 April 1945. The following day he departed for Bavaria, believing he would find safe refuge in the Alpine Fortress (*Alpenfestung*). He was convinced that Hitler would soon join him there as well.

On 16 May Ley was captured by American paratroopers of the 101st Airborne Division in the home of a shoemaker in the village of Schleching. He introduced himself to the soldiers as Dr Ernst Distelmeyer but was unmasked by the town's mayor. Together with other criminals, he was placed in the Palace Hotel in Mondorf-les-Bains, Luxembourg. During this time, he is said to have made as many as three suicide attempts.[1]

When the first Nuremberg Trial began, Ley was included among the most important defendants. He was charged with incitement and preparation for an aggressive war in violation of international law and treaties; with the commission of war crimes, including 'mistreatment of prisoners of war and civilians'; and with crimes against humanity, including murder, extermination, enslavement of civilians, and persecution on racial, religious, and political grounds.

Ley was, of course, outraged by such accusations. He believed that if the Allies wished to execute him, they should shoot him but not call him a criminal and place him before some tribunal. He expressed this view during a conversation with American prison psychiatrist Gustav Gilbert.

On 25 October 1945, at 8:15 am, four days after the charges were formally presented to him, Robert Ley hanged himself in his cell. He accomplished this by sitting on the toilet and using a noose fashioned from strips of torn underwear. He stuffed scraps of torn long johns into his mouth so as not to alert the guard with his death rattle. Ley's brain was subjected to detailed examination in a medical laboratory. His body was thrown, unclothed, into an anonymous grave.

Robert Ley left behind a farewell letter, which was found in his cell:

Farewell, I can no longer endure the shame. Physically, I lack nothing. The food is good, my cell is warm. The Americans behave properly, even in a friendly way. Spiritually, I am in the mood for writing and I can write whatever I wish. I have been given paper and pencil. My health is cared for more than necessary. I smoke and receive tobacco and coffee. I can walk at least 20 minutes a day. So far everything is all right, except for the fact that I will be a criminal, and this I cannot endure (…).

I have always belonged among responsible men. I was with Hitler in the good times, when our plans and hopes were fulfilled. And I would like to be with him also in the worst of times. In everything I did, I was guided by God. He exalted me, and now He has allowed me to fall. I torment myself trying to understand the reasons for my downfall, and here is the result of my reflections:

We denied God, and therefore God denied us. Antisemitism distorted our perspective, and we committed great mistakes. It is hard to admit errors, but the very existence of our nation has been called into question. We, National Socialists, must have the courage to free ourselves from antisemitism. We must tell the youth that it was a mistake. The youth will not believe our enemies. We must see this through to the end. We must accept the Jews with open hearts.

German nation, reconcile with the Jews. Invite him into your home (along with you). We cannot calm the raging sea at once, but we must soothe it gradually, otherwise the consequences will be terrible. Complete reconciliation with the Jews takes precedence over economic and cultural reconstruction. We, the fierce antisemites, must become the first fighters for new ideas. We must show our nation the way.[2]

It is not known what motivated the words written in the letter. Did Ley, sitting in his prison cell, experience a conversion? Such things often occur in prisons, especially among those facing the highest penalty.

Robert Ley's suicide immediately led to the tightening of security measures for the other prisoners. The victors could not allow another case in which one of the accused might escape justice.

At a rally in Bydgoszcz, Robert Ley threatened the Poles, saying they faced annihilation or a life of slavery. (*Author's archive*)

Chapter 9

Josef Mengele

When a 67-year-old man, sunbathing on one of Brazil's beaches, decided to cool himself in the waters of the Atlantic, he did not suspect that it might be the last act of his life. It was 7 February 1979. The air temperature was 29⁰C, ideal conditions for sunbathing and swimming. One could, if only for a moment, forget about failing health. An enlarged prostate, back pain, high blood pressure, rheumatism, and bouts of depression all temporarily receded. What mattered now was only the heat from the sky and the slightly cooler water.

What was meant to bring relief turned out to be a deadly trap. The man swam a few metres from the shore, when he realised that something strange was happening to his body. His limbs stopped cooperating and responding to commands, the result of a sudden cerebral haemorrhage. Andreas Bossert, who had accompanied him since the morning, swam over and attempted to save his companion.

> With one hand I had to hold him back, and with the other make swimming strokes. I fought to keep his head above the surface, but with no ground under my feet it meant we were not moving closer to shore. At last I was so exhausted that I could no longer resist the force of the waves. Then I had the idea of using the strength of the surf: I dived, dug my feet into the sand, and held his body above my head he was still alive at that moment.

Bossert reached the shore, dragging the older man's body behind him. On the beach, a doctor attempted resuscitation, but without success. The deceased was buried as Wolfgang Gerhard in the town of Embu das Artes.

In 1992, DNA tests were conducted which confirmed beyond any doubt that the buried remains in fact belonged to Josef Mengele, the infamous

Three SS officers from KL Auschwitz resting at the nearby Solahütte resort, 1944. (Left to right) Commandant Richard Baer, Dr Josef Mengele, and former commandant Rudolf Höss. (*Public domain*)

'Angel of Death'. He was best remembered by those who encountered him in the concentration camps during the Second World War: 'He was a man who looked like a film star, with a smooth, pleasant face and extremely regular features. He always wore his uniform, appeared clean and elegant, and wherever he went he radiated an atmosphere of fear and uncertainty, for it was known that he carried out selections and sent people to the gas.'

It is worth taking a closer look at his figure.

Josef Mengele was born on 16 March 1911, in Günzburg, the son of Karl and Walburga. His father ran the firm *Mengele & Söhne*, which produced agricultural machinery. Josef was gifted and took an interest in the natural sciences as well as natural philosophy. As a child, he narrowly escaped death several times due to illness or accidents. At the age of 6, he nearly drowned in a rain barrel and later also survived a severe case of blood poisoning. In 1926 he fell ill with osteomyelitis, but managed to recover.

After completing his secondary education, he went to Munich to study medicine at the faculty of philosophy and medicine at the local university. After a year of study, he joined the youth branch of *Stahlhelm*, a nationalist paramilitary organisation that brought together veterans of the First World

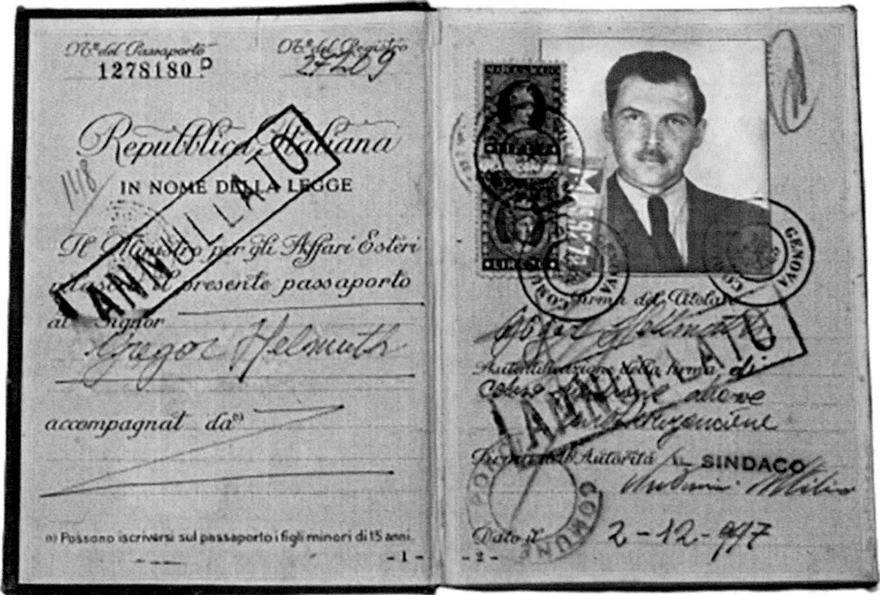

Josef Mengele's identity card. (*Public domain*)

War. During his studies, he also took supplementary courses in anthropology, palaeontology, and medicine. At that time, he came into contact with the Swiss eugenicist Dr Ernst Rüdin, who believed that doctors should destroy 'lives unworthy of life'.

Another of his teachers was Professor Theodor Mollison, who claimed that knowledge of heredity made it possible, on the basis of photographs, to determine whether a given person had Jewish ancestors. These two examples alone show that Mengele, exposed to such bizarre assertions, must have acquired a distorted view of medicine.

Mengele was one of the authors of the Nazi laws on compulsory sterilisation, which came into effect in July 1933. Two years later, in 1935, he received his doctorate in medicine for a thesis entitled *Racial-Morphological Study of the Lower Jaw among Four Racial Groups*. The following year he passed the state medical examination in Munich and took up his first post at the Children's Clinic of the University of Leipzig, where he served as a junior resident. Was it then that he began to take an interest in twins, for which he later became infamous in Auschwitz? Or perhaps somewhat later, when, thanks to the recommendation of Professor

Mollison, on 1 January 1937 he became an assistant at the Institute for Heredity, Biology, and Racial Purity of the Third Reich at the University of Frankfurt am Main? At that time, he joined the research team of the geneticist Professor Otmar von Verschuer, who considered twin studies one of the key elements of his scientific work.

In May 1937 Josef Mengele joined the NSDAP, receiving party membership card no. 5574974. A year later, after a thorough check of his family tree, he was admitted into the SS. In July 1938 he received his diploma of Doctor of Medical Science from the University of Frankfurt am Main. His career was progressing at a pace that satisfied him, yet the looming terror of war was already palpable. The annexation of Austria, the partition of Czechoslovakia, and then the swift defeat of Poland caused nearly every German to believe that the long-desired time of the German Empire ruling the world, or at least over Eastern Europe, had arrived.

In July 1940, the army called for Mengele. As a medical officer he was assigned to a unit in Kassel. After just a month, however, he was promoted to the rank of SS-Untersturmführer and transferred into the Waffen-SS. In June 1941 he was sent to Ukraine, where he first took part in combat. For heroism shown during the evacuation of the crew of a stricken tank, he was awarded the Iron Cross, 2nd Class. Later, in occupied Poland, he worked in a branch of the Genealogical Office for Race and Settlement Affairs (*Rasse- und Siedlungshauptamt*). In January 1942, together with the 5th SS Panzer Division 'Wiking', he returned to the Eastern Front. In the summer of 1942, after the five-day battle of Bataisk, he received the Iron Cross, 1st Class, for pulling two wounded soldiers from a burning tank under fire and administering first aid. He was also awarded the Black Wound Badge and the Medal for the Care of the German People (*Medaille zur Pflege des Deutschen Volkes*).

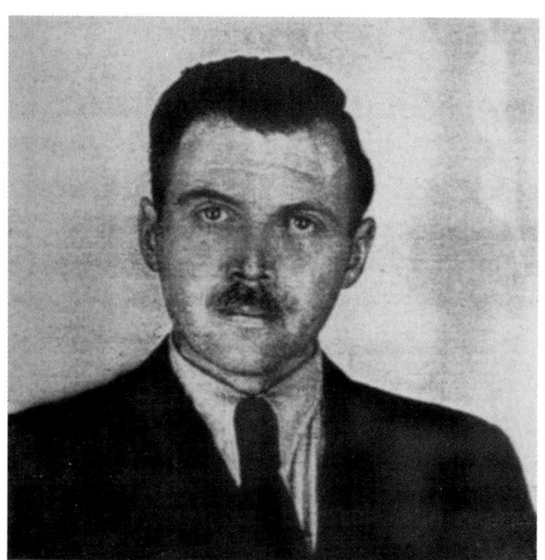

A photograph of Josef Mengele taken in Buenos Aires in 1956 for the issuance of Argentine identity documents. (*Public domain*)

He did not remain long at the front. At the end of the year, he was transferred to the Main Office of Race and Settlement of the SS in Berlin. On 24 May 1943, after another promotion, Mengele was assigned to the Auschwitz concentration camp, where he was to replace one of the sick doctors. At that moment, his true career was just beginning.

At first, he assumed the post of camp doctor in the women's camp at Birkenau. His first decision, made two days after his arrival, was to send to the gas chambers 1,042 Romani women suffering from typhus. From May 1943 to November 1944, Mengele took part in at least seventy-four selections on the ramp, where, together with other doctors, he decided who was to be sent into slave labour in the camp and who was to be sent directly to their death in the gas chambers. According to the British historian Martin Gilbert, Mengele also played an active role in thirty-one selections in the camp hospital, sending to death by shooting, injection of toxic substances, or gassing those whose health had been broken by hunger, forced labour, untreated diseases, or the sadism of the guards. It was at this time, impeccably dressed in a white doctor's coat and white gloves at every selection, that Mengele earned the epithet 'Angel of Death' among the Auschwitz prisoners.[1]

Former prisoner Irena Perkowska-Szczypiorska described him in these words:

> He treated prisoners like dead objects or specimens needed for his criminal experiments. (…) In the camp I met two beautiful 2-year-old twins, cherubic in appearance, whom Mengele 'took care of'. Thanks to this, the children were allowed to remain with their mother in the same block. Mengele often visited them, stroked their heads, brought them candies and chocolate, while the mother, happy that she had not been separated from her children, praised his goodness all around. After some time, when the experiments were completed, the 'kind' Mengele personally took the children to the crematorium. The mother, in her despair, went mad.[2]

Mengele's main interests centred on multiple pregnancies and twins. He searched out twins among the prisoners and subjected them to every possible experiment. About 1,500 twins were tested, of whom fewer than 100 survived. The tests included the simultaneous killing of twins in order to compare their internal organs. Mengele also worked on developing a method to change eye colour, as well as on a disease present in the Romani camp at Birkenau, the so-called noma (*Wasserkrebs*). He was also interested in various biological anomalies, such as dwarfism.[3]

The studies began with precise measurements of skulls, ears, noses, and other external features of children. Then they were taken to the men's hospital, where anatomical tests were conducted. Afterwards, twins and dwarfs were subjected to cruel experiments without anaesthetic. Amputations were performed, lumbar punctures carried out, typhus bacteria injected, wounds deliberately infected. Mengele often ordered complete blood transfusions between pairs of twins. One of the victims of such experiments was the then 10-year-old Eva Mozes Kor and her sister Miriam. The former recalled her encounters with Mengele in these words:

> To this day I do not know what I was infected with in July 1944. I had a very high fever and was trembling all over, even though it was very hot outside. My hands and feet swelled, and red rashes appeared all over my body. I was taken to the camp hospital located right next to the crematoria. The next morning Josef Mengele appeared at my bedside with four other doctors. He looked at the temperature chart and laughed, saying with mockery: 'What a great pity. Such a young girl, and she has no more than two weeks to live…' But I did not allow myself to think that I might die. I promised myself that I would be strong and do everything to get out of the hospital and show that man how wrong he was.

The young girl, despite the absence of medical help and extreme exhaustion, recovered from the illness. As she herself said, she knew she was fighting not only for her own life: 'Had I died then, my sister would have immediately been sent to the mortuary and killed with an injection of chloroform directly into the heart. Mengele would have performed two parallel autopsies on our bodies in order to compare what changes the illness had caused in my organism. Many pairs of twins met this terrible fate.'[4]

Mengele fled Auschwitz ten days before the Red Army entered, taking with him the documentation of his research on twins and dwarfs, which was later most likely destroyed, though it was supposed to serve him in writing his habilitation thesis. From 18 January 1945, he served in the Gross Rosen camp and its subcamps in Lower Silesia. In the final days of the war, he exchanged his SS uniform for that of a Wehrmacht soldier. When captured, the Americans placed him in a prisoner-of-war camp near Munich. As he did not bear a blood group tattoo, he escaped recognition as an SS member.

After his release, he hid in Germany for four years, despite the large-scale manhunt for him. In 1949, with the help of the fascist-leaning Bishop Alois Hudal in Rome (see Chapter 21), he escaped to Argentina. There he was located by the Mossad. He was not abducted, however, since at that time Mossad's priority was Adolf Eichmann, whose capture shook the entire German community in Argentina. Although Eichmann was not under the direct protection of the Nazi underground, the Germans overhauled their entire security system. The abduction of Eichmann, as well as information that Mengele most likely received from his family, caused him to feel less safe in Argentina. Therefore, in 1959 he decided to move to Paraguay. Because of this unplanned emigration, Mengele became rather nervous, and it took a toll on his health. He often fell asleep unexpectedly and became irritable. Another factor prompting him to move was the change in Argentina's presidency.

The move to Paraguay allowed Mengele to devote more time to gainful work. He also planned to purchase land in a remote part of the country. He treated this investment as his 'long-term' plan. In Paraguay, ruled by Alfredo Stroessner, he settled not far from the Argentine border in the Alto Paraná region, on the farm of Alban Krug. Helpful in arranging this accommodation was the former pilot Hans Ulrich Rudel, a staunch Nazi and the head of the local farmers' community.

Mengele did not have much to occupy him there. He looked forward to the weekends, when he took a jeep and drove to Asunción to meet with his old acquaintance Werner Jung, at whose house he bathed in the swimming pool. In his diary he described his host in rather unflattering terms:

> Sometimes they would get up in the middle of the night – at five o'clock – for a solemn ceremony drinking mate [herbal infusion]. Naturally, it would be far better for them, both physically and mentally, to sleep two hours longer instead of wasting time indulging in these senseless and primitive rituals. It is astonishing that early rising makes these people consider themselves morally superior to those who get up a little later.[5]

After several months of residence, Mengele applied for Paraguayan citizenship. On 27 November 1959, the Supreme Court of Paraguay issued Josef Mengele certificate of naturalisation no. 809. At that time, it was already widely known that Mengele was a wanted war criminal. Interestingly, he did not apply for citizenship for his wife or children.

Despite having obtained citizenship, Mengele's situation was becoming increasingly precarious, and he even considered committing suicide. These thoughts intensified after the unfortunate death of Frederico Hasse, to whom he owed many of his connections.

Through trusted friends, increased information reached Mengele about the actions being taken against him in his homeland. As he wrote in his diary, he was embarrassed to read articles about his alleged crimes committed at Auschwitz. He also constantly feared abduction at the hands of Israel. It is in this that one should look for the explanation of why, immediately after obtaining citizenship, he decided to leave his new homeland.

In October 1960, his choice fell on Brazil. He probably chose to settle in São Paulo, as suggested by an entry in his diary dated 27 October 1960:

> The spiritual horizon of this place is as different as its physical horizon. Until now I had travelled mostly through flat plains, but now I am surrounded by 'hills'. The only barrier separating my dwelling from the bustling street, 10 metres away, is a hedge. Street traffic, with its cars, buses, and trucks, increases in the early morning and late evening, when masses of people pour into the streets. Over time, each of the millions of inhabitants of the great city grows accustomed to the tumult and noises of civilization.[6]

In Brazil, a change took place in Mengele's private life. His wife no longer wanted to be the wife of a fugitive and returned to Germany. Until the end of his life, Mengele never stood trial, despite the substantial reward of 10 million marks offered for help in his capture. He died on 7 February 1979, near Santos in Brazil, while bathing in the ocean. He most likely suffered a stroke and drowned.

Chapter 10

Heinz Reinefarth – The Mayor Who Ran Out of Ammunition

'General Reinefarth, you are one of the most hated figures in Poland. Do you know that?'

'I know.'

'Are you aware of your nickname, "the Butcher of Warsaw"?'

'That too is known to me. But are you aware of the fact that the court proceedings in my case lasted twenty years and I was acquitted?'

This was how the conversation began between Polish journalist Krzysztof Kąkolewski and attorney Heinz Reinefarth. In these few words lies everything that German war criminals represented, living peacefully in postwar Germany.

The interview was conducted in 1973. At the time, Reinefarth was a respected resident of the town of Westerland on the island of Sylt. Between 1951 and 1964 he served as mayor of this seaside resort, and never answered for his crimes until the end of his life.

Heinrich Friedrich Reinefarth was born on 26 December 1903, in Gniezno. He was the son of Prussian judge Fritz and Bertha, née Ende. Four years later the family moved to Cottbus. In 1916 Reinefarth began his education at the local Gymnasium, and in 1922 began studying law at the University of Jena. In 1930 he completed his legal clerkship, passing the assessor's examination, and began working as a lawyer and notary. In August 1932 he joined the ranks of the NSDAP, and four months later he applied for admission to the SS.

After the outbreak of the Second World War, Reinefarth fought in the September Campaign, for which he received the Iron Cross, 2nd Class. At the turn of 1939–1940 he entered a non-commissioned officers' school, and soon after, an officers' school. Later, in the 337th Infantry Regiment of the Wehrmacht, he took part in the campaign against France. Still as a sergeant,

SS-Gruppenführer Heinrich Friedrich Reinefarth (1903-1979) was Generalleutnant der Waffen-SS, and a war criminal responsible for numerous atrocities committed by German troops during the Warsaw Uprising in 1944. (*Public domain*)

he captured 3,000 French soldiers with his platoon and, as one of the few non-commissioned officers, was decorated with the Knight's Cross. He left the Wehrmacht with the rank of lieutenant, transferring to the reserve.

Recalled in 1941 once again to the Wehrmacht, to his 337th Infantry Regiment, he took part in the fighting on the Eastern Front. He also began to advance rapidly in the civil SS, and on 20 April 1942, he received the rank of Major General of Police and SS-Brigadeführer. He was then assigned to the staff of the Chief Inspector of the SS in the Protectorate of Bohemia and Moravia.

In September 1943 he was transferred to the SS Main Office of the Order Police (*SS-Hauptamt Ordnungspolizei*). On 29 January 1944, he joined the staff of the Higher SS and Police Leader in the Warthegau in German-occupied Poland. After the outbreak of the Warsaw Uprising, he received from Himmler the order to form a unit composed of sixteen police companies.

It is not entirely clear why this task was assigned to Reinefarth specifically. Available sources are silent on the matter. One may suppose that it was not so much his military experience as a lieutenant of the Wehrmacht, but rather his unwavering ideological stance. By August 1944, only optimists still believed that the war could be decided in favour of the Third Reich. Reinefarth was to set an example that would radiate across the entire Eastern Front. The Germans wanted to show that they were still strong, and that all who offered any resistance would be immediately liquidated. The insane order to eliminate all Poles was stopped only by General Erich von dem Bach-Zelewski, commander of all German forces in Warsaw, to whose command Reinefarth's unit was also subordinated.

From 5 August 1944, Reinefarth's units took part in the fighting in Wola. Within a few days they massacred approximately 50,000 civilian inhabitants of Warsaw in mass executions. In one conversation with General Nikolaus von Vormann, Reinefarth asked: 'What am I to do with the civilians? I have less ammunition than prisoners.'[1] On 19 August he sent a letter to Himmler in which he wrote: 'From our Warsaw war booty I take the liberty of sending you two packets of tea along with my best wishes.'[2]

The children of Wanda Lurie were murdered on the grounds of the Ursus factory. A fragment of her testimony illustrates the scale of the crime:

Since 1937 I had been living with my family in Warsaw, at 18 Wawelberga Street, apartment 30. (…) Until 5 August I remained in the basement of the house with my three children, aged 11, 6, and 3½, and myself being in the last month of pregnancy. On that day, at 11–12 o'clock, German gendarmes and Ukrainians entered the courtyard, ordering the residents to leave the building immediately. (…) Having no husband with me, who had not returned from the city, I delayed leaving the house, hoping they would let me stay. But I was forced to leave. (…) On Wolska Street I joined a group of people from our house. Altogether there were more than 500 of us gathered under the factory. From conversations with fellow sufferers, I understood that in the factory they had assembled residents from Działdowska, Płocka, Sokołowska, Staszica, Wolska, and Wawelberga streets. We stood in front of the gate of the 'Ursus' factory, at 55 Wolska Street. (…) We waited about an hour in front of the gate. From the factory yard came the sounds of shots, pleas, and moans. The Germans let people in – or rather shoved them – through the gate in groups of about 100. (…) We had no doubt they were killing inside the factory, though we did not know if they were killing everyone. I stayed at the back, retreating all the time, hoping that surely they would not kill a pregnant woman. I was brought in with the last group.

In the factory yard I saw piles of corpses 1 metre high. (…) Our group was directed towards a passage between the buildings. Corpses already lay there. As the first four people reached the spot where the bodies lay, the Germans and

Ukrainians shot them in the back of the neck. The dead fell, the next four stepped up to die the same way. (…) I was in the last group of four. I begged the Ukrainians surrounding us to save my children and me; one of them asked if I could pay. I gave him three gold rings. Taking them, he wanted to lead me away, but the German officer – the gendarme directing the execution – noticed and did not allow it, ordering me back into the group destined for execution. I began pleading with him for the lives of my children and mine, speaking of an officer's honour. But he shoved me so that I fell. He also struck and pushed my eldest son, shouting: 'Faster, faster, you Polish bandit!' (…) Thus I stepped forward in the last group with my three children to the place of execution, holding the two younger children's hands in my right hand, the eldest's in my left. The children walked, crying and praying. The eldest, seeing the murdered, cried out that they would kill us too. At some point a Ukrainian standing behind us shot my eldest son in the back of the head; the next bullets struck the younger children and me. (…) The bullet hit my neck on the left side and passed through the lower part of my skull, exiting through my right cheek. (…) But I remained conscious, and lying among the corpses I saw almost everything happening around me. I watched further executions. New groups of men were brought in, their bodies falling on top of me. About four corpses pressed me down. Further groups of women and children were brought in and so, group after group, they were executed until late evening. It was already dark when the executions ceased. In the breaks the perpetrators walked over the corpses, kicking, turning them, finishing off the living, robbing valuables. (…) The next day the executions stopped. Only a few times did the Germans burst in with dogs, running across the corpses, checking if anyone was alive. I heard single shots, probably finishing off the survivors. I lay there for three days, until Monday (the execution had taken place on Saturday).

On the third day I felt the child I was expecting was alive. That gave me strength and suggested the idea of escape. I began to think and search for a way. When trying to get up, several times I vomited and grew dizzy. (…)

Everywhere lay corpses, piled as high as I am tall, across the whole yard. I had the impression there could have been more than 6,000 killed there. (…) After long searching and many attempts, we discovered an exit onto Skierniewicka Street, and through it, together with Ms Staworzyńska, we left the factory. (…) Ukrainians stood on Wolska Street and at first did not realise where we were coming from. They stopped us and, despite pleas and begging to let us go to a hospital as wounded, they drove us towards Wola, gathering more people along the way. Near St Stanislaus church the group was divided into the young and the old. The group of young men and women was taken into some ruined house, from which soon we heard shots. I suppose an execution was carried out there. The rest, among them myself, were driven to St Adalbert's [St. Wojciech's] church on Wolska Street. (…) I lay for several days near the main altar. No help was given. Only fellow sufferers gave me a little water. After two days I was transported by cart with the heavily wounded or sick to the transit camp in Pruszków, from there to hospitals in Komorów and Leśna Podkowa.[3]

SS-Gruppenführer Heinz Reinefarth (left), the 'Butcher of Wola', seen here near Wolska Street during the Warsaw Uprising, 1944. (*Public domain*)

After the suppression of the uprising in Wola, the unit commanded by Reinefarth was moved to the Old Town, and later to Powiśle and Czerniaków. For his role in crushing the Warsaw Uprising, on 30 September 1944 he was awarded the Oak Leaves (*Eichenlaub*) to his Knight's Cross (*Ritterkreuz*).[4]

In December 1944 Reinefarth became commander of the XVIII SS Army Corps, which initially fought the Red Army in the middle Oder region and then defended the fortress of Kostrzyn. After exhausting ammunition, he did not surrender to the Soviets. Leading a detachment of about 600 men, he broke out of encirclement, violating Hitler's explicit order to fight to the last man. For disobeying the order, he was sentenced to death. However, the sentence was never carried out, and Reinefarth continued to command his units, which were renamed the XIV SS Army Corps.

After the war, the '*kat Woli*' (Butcher of Wola) became a prisoner of the Americans. They refused Poland's request for extradition so that he might answer for his crimes before a Polish court. With the Cold War beginning, American military counterintelligence was interested in leading figures of the German Reich who had experience in the eastern territories. Reinefarth was recruited as an informant.

Although the Americans quickly realised that this informant had nothing of value to offer, they continued to protect him, unwilling to hand him over to Poland. First, they were covering up their own blunder, and second, they did not want information about Reinefarth's services to American intelligence to come to light. Officially, they justified it on grounds of 'security'.

Reinefarth even testified as a witness at Nuremberg. In 1948 he was released and settled on the island of Sylt, in the British occupation zone, where his wife's family owned a summer house. Yet he still faced one more trial before a German denazification court. There he displayed extraordinary brazenness or, as he likely saw it, extraordinary cleverness. He claimed that he had joined the police, and that his inclusion in the SS had been automatic, beyond his control. He further emphasised that he had shown 'honour' by not carrying out Hitler's order to defend the Kostrzyn fortress to the last soldier. The court accepted this argument and issued a grotesque verdict, declaring Reinefarth 'a man of honour'.

The denazification proceedings were supposed to be a mere formality. Courts handling denazification assigned every defendant to one of five categories: '*Hauptschuldige*' (main offenders), '*Belastete*' (offenders), '*Minderbelastete*' (lesser offenders), '*Mitläufer*' (followers), and '*Entlastete*' (exonerated). At first, Reinefarth was classified as a *Mitläufer*, but this was not enough for a mass murderer. He appealed, and the court upgraded him to the category of *Entlastete*. This was a blatant insult to the thousands of murdered residents of Warsaw and their families.

Such a verdict allowed Reinefarth to return to practising law and to pursue public office. He joined the Association of Expellees and Disenfranchised (*Bund der Heimatvertriebenen und Entrechteten*, BHE), and after being elected mayor of Westerland, in 1958 he became a deputy to the regional parliament. This, however, was accompanied by scandal first triggered by the film *Urlaub auf Sylt* (Vacation on Sylt), and then by a letter to the *Der Spiegel* newspaper, written by German professor Hans Thieme, who had himself served as an officer under Reinefarth in Warsaw. As the adjutant to a staff officer, he had heard with his own ears SS-Brigadeführer Reinefarth state that he did not have enough ammunition to shoot all the prisoners.

Although Reinefarth died in 1979, it was only in 2014 that the authorities of the federal state of Schleswig-Holstein condemned the crimes committed by their former deputy.

Heinz Reinefarth (centre, wearing the Knight's Cross) during the fighting in Wola, commanding from a staff bus positioned at the intersection of Syrena and Wolska streets. (*Bundesarchiv, Bild 101I-695-0411-01A / Gutermann / CC-BY-SA*)

Chapter 11

Ludolf von Alvensleben, 'Bubi' – Mass Murderer and Uranium Seeker

In 1945 the British arrested Ludolf von Alvensleben, nicknamed 'Bubi', and interned him in the Neuengamme camp. A year later he escaped, and after boarding a ship in Genoa, fled to South America, following the same route as Adolf Eichmann and Josef Mengele. Despite being one of the greatest German criminals, he remains little known to this day.

Ludolf Hermann Emmanuel Georg Kurt Werner von Alvensleben was born on 17 March 1901 in Halle, Germany. At the age of 10 he began his education in a cadet school. In 1912 he became heir to the Schochwitz estate, which was leased out. In 1918 he was promoted to the rank of Fähnrich (officer cadet) and later served in the *Freiwilligenkorps Maercker* (Volunteer Corps Maercker). He joined the NSDAP in 1929 and received membership card no. 149345. In the early phase of his party career, he held many functions, including inspector of the Halle-Merseburg district.

Throughout the entire existence of the Third Reich, he was a member of the Reichstag. In 1934

Ludolf-Hermann Emmanuel Georg Kurt Werner von Alvensleben, 'Bubi' (1901-1970) was a German war criminal and a member of the NSDAP. In November 1943 he was proted to SS-Gruppenführer and served as Lieutenant General of Police, From July 1944 he also served as Lieutenant General of the Waffen-SS. (*Public domain*)

he was transferred from the SA to the SS, where he received membership no. 177002. Between 1935 and 1936, while serving in Halle, he obtained the rank of SS-Standartenführer. Later he became commander of the SS districts of Stuttgart and Schwerin. From November 1938 to 31 January 1941, he served as the first adjutant of Reichsführer-SS Heinrich Himmler. With the outbreak of the war, he was delegated to various assignments in the field. The most important of these was taking command of Selbstschutz Westpreussen.[1] He chose Bydgoszcz as his headquarters, specifically the ground floor of the villa at 10 Wyspiańskiego Street. This is how Teodor Kociński, who lived on the upper floor of the building, recalled the situation:

> About a week or two after the Germans entered the house in which I lived, Alvensleben moved into the ground floor (I lived upstairs). (…) He came from Hanover. He wore a grey-green uniform, the same colour as that used by the SD. He occupied the flat of the pharmacist Kowalewski, who had left before the outbreak of the war, leaving the apartment fully furnished. The flat consisted of four rooms. Immediately upon moving into this house Alvensleben took away my car. (…) He lived there until, I believe, 21 November 1939.
>
> When Alvensleben was in the street near the house, which I often observed, he would stop passers-by, ask them who they were and what they were looking for, and when he realised they were Poles, he slapped them in the face. More than once, I eavesdropped, lying on the floor upstairs in my flat, on conversations Alvensleben conducted over the telephone. I often heard him issuing orders to execute, to kill Poles. (…) In front of the house stood a *Selbstschutz* guard. In the neighbouring house (8 Wyspiańskiego) there were the offices subordinate to Alvensleben. (…) Alvensleben often went out by car. His driver was Stefan Starszak, currently living in Sępólno.[2]

Very little documentation produced by the *Selbstschutz* in Pomerania has survived to this day. Practically all of it burned in a car transporting it to Gdańsk. We can only speculate whether the destruction of the documents took place on Alvensleben's orders.

Photograph showing Alvensleben's handwritten greetings from Bydgoszcz. (*State Archives in Bydgoszcz*)

On 26 November 1939 the *Selbstschutz* was officially disbanded. Teofil Czerwiński, then imprisoned in a camp set up in former army barracks, witnessed important events connected with the destruction of records of crimes committed by the formation. This is what he testified in 1947:

On 27 November 1939 we were ordered to prepare the best car for Gdańsk. Schmitz and Betraun were to drive it to Forster with the papers about murdered Poles. At the appointed hour the above-mentioned men did indeed leave in that car. A few minutes later, news reached me that the car had burned. Starszak went after the car. When he returned, I saw that the car had been shot through, full of bullet holes. Schmitz and Betraun reported to Alvensleben that about 20 km from Bydgoszcz, in the direction of Gdańsk, the car had burned. To this Alvensleben replied that it was good they had done so and patted them on the shoulder.[3]

As is known, Alvensleben received for this feat the *Kreuz von Danzig* (Cross of Gdańsk) from Albert Forster in Gdańsk. Of course, for the sake of accuracy, it should also be noted that there exists another explanation of this alleged accident. Tadeusz Kur, in his work on the Alvensleben family, suggested that the documentation in the car was burned on the direct orders of 'Bubi' in order to conceal from Forster the scale of the looting of Polish property and the appropriation of landed estates.

Alvensleben was also rewarded by Reichsführer-SS Himmler, who placed two estates that had belonged to his family until 1918 under his administration. On 26 March 1940, in justifying the granting of this reward, Himmler wrote to Heydrich: '…to give Oberführer von Alvensleben, who as commander of the *Selbstschutz* played an important role in carrying out executions…'[4]

In 1940 he was promoted to SS-Brigadeführer. From October 1941 he served as SS- und Polizeiführer in Ukraine. In 1943 he became Höherer SS- und Polizeiführer in the operational area of Army Group A. At the end of the war, he commanded the SS *Abschnitt Elbe* (SS Sector Elbe).

Arrested and held for sixteen months in the Neuengamme camp near Hamburg, he escaped from there on 11 September 1946. According to SS-Gruppenführer Karl Wolff, Alvensleben hid in a milk transport tank. Years later, in Argentina, he claimed that he had hidden in a truck. For some time, he stayed in his family estate in Schochwitz, but feeling unsafe there, and with the support of the Evangelical Church, he managed to board a ship and escape.

Alvensleben receiving the Danzig Cross from Gauleiter Albert Forster. (*IPN*)

It is not known exactly when he arrived in Argentina. The first mention of him dates from 15 December 1952, when, together with his wife and two children, he was granted Argentine citizenship. Initially he settled in Buenos Aires, later moving to Córdoba, where he lived under the assumed name of Carlos Luecke until July 1959. At first, he resided in Villa María. On 15 September 1959, he moved to Villa General Belgrano in Santa Rosa de Calamuchita. He lived there until his death, and the house still exists today, located on Route 5, fifteen blocks from the town centre.

His untouchability in Argentina was guaranteed by his friendship with dictator Juan Perón. Alvensleben, under the name Luecke, quickly purchased 80 hectares of land in the inhospitable area of Cañada de las Mulas, 30 kilometres (19 miles) northwest of Santa Rosa de Calamuchita. It was a rather isolated place, with rocky soil and no vegetation. In the middle of the property stood a stone cottage, where Alvensleben liked to lock himself in for several days at a time.

He became an inspector of hunting and fishing in Embalse de Rio Tercero. In addition, he bought a narrow strip of land, 17 kilometres long and 700 metres wide, in Rincon de Luna at the foot of Cerro Blanco. There, with the help of Romanian nuclear physicist Nedo Marinescu, who had been living in Argentina since 1951, he began searching for uranium ore, which was then intended for Argentina's nuclear programme. Argentina has

Reichsführer-SS Heinrich Himmler (centre) during a visit to Crimea. On the left is his first adjutant (1938-1941), Ludolf von Alvensleben. (*USHMM*)

not yet declassified all its archives, so we do not know how great a role Alvensleben played in the Argentine nuclear programme. That, for now, remains a mystery.

Alvensleben brought his entire family – his wife Melitta and their children, Ludovic, Constantino, Erika, and Busso, to live with him in South America. The household was managed by a housekeeper, whose son worked for him as a driver. He owned two boxer dogs and also had a Ford truck, which he used for cattle trading. He practised shooting and became president of the football club Atlético Unión, where he also played himself in veterans' matches as a goalkeeper. Feeling confident in his new homeland, he became politically active, serving as vice-president of the local municipality where he resided. Those who knew him at the time described him as polite and cold, with an excellent command of Spanish.[5]

Meanwhile, in 1948, he was sentenced to death in absentia by a Polish court for the murder of 4,247 people. In 1964, the district court in Munich issued an arrest warrant, but extradition never followed.

Alvensleben died on Wednesday, 1 April 1970, in Santa Rosa de Toay, most likely of a heart attack. His family, however, claimed he had cancer. In the last few weeks of his life, he had been visiting a doctor in Buenos Aires. His funeral was attended by many local Germans and Argentinians, as well as a group of more than twenty Germans from outside the area. Reportedly, the latter appeared visibly nervous. That did not stop them from singing the military march *Deine Kameraden* at his grave.[6] This is how an eyewitness later recalled the events:

> They looked grim. (…) The ceremony was simple and short, but the epilogue was powerful. Men with very light skin, hard faces, and dressed in dark clothes raised their right arms forward, above shoulder height. An exclamation, short and deep, in a foreign language, closed the act, which lasted no longer than ten seconds. Later, the gravedigger said he felt a chill, while the pigeons nesting among the tombs broke off their flight.[7]

Attempts made by the author to trace Alvensleben's family and those who knew him turned out to be relatively easy. However, the only response received to the questions asked was a proposal to abandon the subject and a suggestion to turn to something else.

Chapter 12

Adolf Eichmann – The Secret of the Hidden Treasure

It was a strange and incomprehensible event for other Germans. Indeed, it remains difficult to understand even today. The abduction of Adolf Eichmann by the Israeli Mossad in Argentina, in May 1960, shocked the German community there. For years, efforts had been made to ensure that the Germans living in Argentina felt safe and possessed solid alibis, often supported by false documents. The same was true in Eichmann's case.

His capture caused great agitation and triggered changes throughout the entire security system that had, until then, protected fugitive Nazis. It is not entirely clear why this was the case, since Eichmann himself had not been covered by the elaborate German network of surveillance and protection that had guaranteed safety for so many others in hiding. It should also be noted that the man responsible for deporting millions of Jews to extermination camps was never particularly liked, even among his fellow fugitives.

So, who was this man, about whom people whispered that he was learning Hebrew and studying the history and culture of those he had condemned to death?

SS-Obersturmbannführer Adolf Otto Eichmann (1906-1962), seen here in 1942, was the chief coordinator and executor of the Final Solution to the Jewish Question. Abducted from Argentina by Mossad in 1960, he was sentenced to death in Jerusalem. (*Public domain*)

Adolf Otto Eichmann was born on 19 March 1906 in Solingen, Austria. In 1914 his family moved to Linz. At primary and secondary school, he was never a top student. As he later admitted from his prison cell in Israel: '...I was not one of the diligent pupils...' Physical activities, however, were not foreign to him. In his youth he joined the Austrian scouting movement *Wandervogel*, which included mainly right-wing activists with nationalist leanings and paramilitary ambitions.

After finishing secondary school, he began engineering studies in electrical technology and mechanical construction. However, he did not complete them due to poor academic progress. In 1925 he entered the workforce – at first spending two years in his father's company. From 1927 he worked as a sales representative and later as a procurement agent, responsible for supplying fuel to petrol stations. That same year, he became a member of the nationalist, violently antisemitic organisation *Frontkämpfervereinigung Deutsch-Österreichs* (Combat League of German-Austrian Front-Line Soldiers), led by Colonel Hermann von Hiltl.

The global economic crisis soon caught up with Eichmann. Despite being a competent employee, he was laid off. As severance and compensation, however, he received one month's pay for each of his five years of service. It was then that he turned to politics.

Encouraged by his childhood acquaintance Ernst Kaltenbrunner, in April 1932 he joined the Austrian NSDAP, receiving party card no. 889895. He also entered the Austrian SS. In 1933 he moved to Germany and joined the German SS with membership no. 45326. As a motorcycle owner, he was active in the motor section. He worked to locate Austrian Nazis fleeing across the border into Germany, helping to organise them into a special Austrian Legion.

In January 1934 he was transferred to the Austrian Legion in Dachau, near Munich. He also underwent successive rounds of ideological training. Thanks to his intelligence, he was admitted to the newly established *Sicherheitsdienst* (SD) and assigned to the section dealing with Freemasonry. After some time, with the support of Leopold von Mildenstein, he was transferred to the Jewish Section.

Eichmann threw himself into these new duties with such zeal that he declared his willingness to learn Hebrew – an idea that was not welcomed by his superiors. Still, this did not discourage him. Interested in Zionist ideas, he even met with representatives of Zionist organisations and considered the concept of resettling Europe's Jews to Madagascar.

After the *Anschluss* of Austria in 1938, Eichmann was able to return to his homeland. He set up his headquarters in the Rothschild Palace, where he became the master of life and death for Austrian Jews. He decided who would be sent to a concentration camp and who, for the right price, would be allowed to leave the country. To gain the necessary contacts and establish control over the Jewish minority, he released Jewish Zionist specialists from prison and forced them into collaboration. His chief assistant became Dr Josef Löwenherz, for whom refusal would have meant deportation to Dachau.

In Vienna, Eichmann was doing well enough that he brought his wife to live with him. He created a system in which every Jew wishing to emigrate had to pay for the departure. The wealthy were forced to cover the costs of the poorer emigrants. After the occupation of Czechoslovakia, he established a sister office in Prague to the one in Vienna.

Following changes within the RSHA, the head of the Gestapo, SS-Gruppenführer Heinrich Müller summoned Eichmann to Berlin and appointed him head of the Reich Emigration Office (*Reichszentrale für jüdische Auswanderung*), housed in a former Jewish palace at Kürfürstenstraße 116. The main task assigned to Eichmann was the removal of Jews from the Third Reich and the Protectorate of Bohemia and Moravia.

By November 1941, Eichmann had forced 128,000 Jews to flee the Reich. At that time, he was promoted to the rank of SS-Obersturmbannführer. SS-Gruppenführer Bruno Streckenbach, head of personnel at the RSHA, justified the necessity of his promotion with the following words:

> I submit this promotion on the basis of the exceptionally reliable service rendered by Adolf Eichmann, who previously achieved outstanding results in the process of removing Jews from Austria as head of the Jewish Emigration Office [*Jüdische Auswanderungsstelle*]. Thanks to his work, an enormous number of real estate properties and other assets were seized by the Reich. His activities in the Protectorate of Bohemia and Moravia, carried out with exemplary initiative and the required decisiveness, also deserve recognition. He is currently working on important problems of evacuation and population transfer. In view of the significance of his tasks, I consider this promotion justified and appropriate to his mission.

On 20 January 1942, the Wannsee Conference took place in the Berlin suburb. Its purpose was to discuss the policy of the 'Final Solution' (*Endlösung*) to the Jewish Question among representatives of the most important offices of the Third Reich. Eichmann took the minutes and prepared the statistics and the speech for the head of the RSHA, SS-Gruppenführer Reinhard Heydrich, who outlined the plan for the Final Solution. After the official session, the head of the Gestapo, Heinrich Müller, together with Heydrich and Eichmann, enjoyed a glass of cognac and cigars by the fireplace. Everything went according to Heydrich's design.

After the war, already living in Argentina, Eichmann recounted his role to Wilhelm Sassen, who hoped that after his interlocutor's death he would publish a book that would bring him profit. In one of their alcohol-fuelled conversations, Eichmann recalled his visit to the Auschwitz concentration camp in 1944: 'I remember well that Höss drove me around Auschwitz. He took me to a pit where a high pile of gassed Jewish bodies lay on a metal grate. Höss poured some flammable liquid over the corpses and set them alight. The bodies suffocated like meat. Twelve years have passed, and I still remember that mountain of corpses, and I still have in my nostrils the stench of burning flesh.'[1]

Eichmann was active everywhere a need arose or where problems mounted. Having direct access to Himmler, he often managed to resolve issues quickly. His next step in the mission of annihilating the Jews was to be Hungary.

On 19 March 1944, Operation *Margarethe* began, consisting of the occupation of Hungary, which until then had been a loyal ally. By that time, in the face of the looming defeat of the Third Reich, Eichmann had already begun to explore escape routes from the sinking ship.

Nevertheless, until the end, he strove to exploit the Jews as much as possible for forced labour, leading to death through overwork and starvation. He organised marches of over 200 kilometres (124 miles) from Budapest to Vienna. For this reason, he soon found himself even in opposition to Himmler, who advocated the mildest possible treatment of Jews. The Reichsführer knew that this was his only bargaining chip in peace negotiations with the Allies.

Eichmann, however, fell into nervous breakdown, became unbearable, drank heavily, and shouted at his protégés. He displayed increasingly severe signs of psychosis. On Christmas Eve 1944, just hours before the Red Army entered Budapest, together with his driver, under heavy artillery fire, he left the city on Ernst Kaltenbrunner's orders, heading first to Sopron on the Austro-Hungarian border and later to Berlin. At the Gestapo headquarters, SS men were planning escapes and preparing false documents. Meanwhile, Eichmann began fortifying his office as if he intended to engage in guerrilla operations. He destroyed documents, sending them to Theresienstadt, where they were burned, erasing the traces of the Final Solution. According to SS-Hauptsturmführer Dieter Wisliceny – Eichamnn's deputy, he delivered a speech to his subordinates in which he spoke of the peace of his own conscience and of how he could, with a smile on his face and a sense of extraordinary satisfaction, lie down in his grave knowing that 5.5 million 'enemies of the Reich' had been eliminated with his participation.[2]

It might have seemed that Eichmann would meet his end in Berlin. However, he first received from Himmler the order to evacuate 1,000 influential Jews from Theresienstadt and hold them as hostages. Then, upon learning that his chief and childhood acquaintance was in Austria, he wished to see him one more time, but his car broke down on the journey. Kaltenbrunner, at the time in a drunken frenzy, ordered that members of the SD and other SS men in the area be gathered to form a partisan unit.

Eichmann assembled the detachment, and SS-Obersturmbannführer Otto Skorzeny procured ammunition and vehicles. They hid in mountain cabins, where they were reached by a messenger with Himmler's order not to fire upon the Americans or the British. By then, Eichmann was already concealing his true identity.

Adolf Eichmann (circled) in Argentina. (*Public domain*)

After the capitulation of the Third Reich, he left his companions – among them the leader of the Romanian Iron Guard, Horia Sima – and, together with his adjutant, SS-Sturmbannführer Rudolf Jänisch, planned to disguise themselves in Luftwaffe uniforms. However, Eichmann, who bore a tattoo of his blood type, realised he could not convincingly pose as an airman. He decided instead to wear the uniform of an SS-Untersturmführer from an SS cavalry division, and assumed the name Otto Eckmann.

Both men were detained by an American patrol on the road to Ulm, with Eichmann being held in Weiden in the Upper Palatinate until August 1945, when he was transferred to a prisoner-of-war camp in Franconia. He remained there until January 1946.

In February, having obtained false papers, he escaped from the poorly guarded American camp and made his way to Prien, where he met the sister of one of his fellow SS inmates. Posing as a married couple, they travelled north to Hamburg. Soon afterwards, however, Eichmann moved to the sparsely populated and heavily forested region around Eversen, near Bremen. There he met the brother of another SS man held in the American camp. He took work as a lumberjack and saved money. The business he founded eventually went bankrupt, and Eichmann was forced to seek new employment. He purchased a chicken farm in the same area, but in 1950 he abandoned it, spreading the story that he was heading to Scandinavia for engineering work. In truth, his destination was entirely different. He made his way to Rome, where, with the assistance of Bishop Alois Hudal, he obtained a passport and visa, enabling him to board a ship in Genoa.

In June 1950, the *Giovanni C* departed the port. On board, one of the passengers took a black-and-white photograph. It shows Eichmann smiling, dressed in a black coat, a white shirt with a dark bow tie, sunglasses, and a black hat. Two men accompanied him. One was SS-Obersturmbannführer Herbert Kuhlmann, then travelling under the name Geller. The other was Luftwaffe ace Hans Ulrich Rudel.

On 14 July 1950, Eichmann disembarked on Argentine soil under the name Ricardo Klement. He contacted former comrades, who provided him with lodging and a forged identity card. Former SS-Hauptsturmführer and intelligence officer Horst Carlos Fuldner employed him in his construction company, Capri, in the province of Tucumán, where he worked until April 1953. He resided in a small mountain village.

Upon arriving in Argentina, Klement contacted his wife by letter. In 1951, Veronika Liebl, who had officially divorced him and reverted to her maiden name, came to Buenos Aires with their three children. Waiting for them was 'Uncle Ricardo'. None of the children recognised their father, as even during the war they had rarely seen him. In 1953, they moved permanently to Buenos Aires. In 1959, Eichmann took a job as a mechanic and welder at the Mercedes-Benz factory, where many other former SS men also worked. In 1953, Veronika gave birth to a fourth son, who was named Ricardo Francisco.

Eichmann maintained contact with many former comrades, including SS-Obersturmbannführer Otto Skorzeny, who introduced him to the Dutch journalist and Nazi sympathizer Willem Sassen. Sassen, in turn, presented him to Josef Mengele. Sassen offered Eichmann paid recording sessions, during which the SS man would seek to exonerate the elite of the Third Reich, especially Hitler. Eichmann agreed. He provided detailed accounts, often under the influence of alcohol. He confided hidden details and his own role in the Final Solution to the Jewish Question.

A total of sixty-seven tapes and nearly 700 pages of transcripts were recorded, plus eighty pages of Eichmann's personal commentary, which later became evidence in his trial in Israel. Eichmann was dissatisfied with most of the recordings and attempted to recount his version again, this time by himself and in writing. With money from Sassen, he purchased land in the Bancalari district.

However, the name Eichmann never left the front pages of European newspapers. German prosecutor Fritz Bauer and Nazi hunter Simon Wiesenthal, having received numerous reports both from Argentina and Altaussee, launched investigations and searches to find the fugitive. An agent dispatched to Argentina located Eichmann's new home, took photographs of him working in his garden, and immediately returned to Israel.

Mossad decided to take the risk. A team dispatched to Bancalari abducted Eichmann as he walked towards his secluded home after stepping off a bus. The agents held him for eight days in a specially prepared safe house and confronted him with his SS and Nazi Party membership numbers. When the El Al aircraft carrying Israeli diplomats was ready, the agents smuggled a drugged Eichmann aboard.

The plane landed in Israel on 22 May 1960. Eichmann's wife raised the alarm about her husband's disappearance only several days later. Within weeks, newspapers around the world reported that the architect of the Final

Solution was in an Israeli prison, where he would stand trial for crimes committed during the Second World War.

For the next nine months, Eichmann was held in the same cell, which he pedantically cleaned every day. The initial interrogations yielded no desired results, as the prisoner pretended to remember nothing or simply lied. In June, he handed his 'memoir', similar to the one he had fabricated for Sassen, to the chief investigator Awner W. Less. In 2001, the text of these memoirs was published in Polish under the title *Bożyszcza. Wspomnienia z celi śmierci* (*Idols: Memories from Death Row*). In it, Eichmann declared that he did not belong to those who, after the lost war, suddenly cast everything aside and opportunistically committed themselves wholeheartedly to democratic re-education, presenting themselves as people who had been enslaved and seduced. 'Even today I consider the form in which this was carried out to be nonsense, surely not devised by anyone intelligent.'[3]

The main line of defence he adopted before the court was to present his role as that of a minor cog in a gigantic machine. He also claimed that he was compelled to follow orders without question. He denied many facts, some of which could not be directly used against him, but denying deeds that were clearly proven did not make his testimony credible.

The indictment to the District Court in Jerusalem was delivered on 2 February 1961. Eichmann was charged under Section I (a) of the *Nazis and Nazi Collaborators (Punishment) Law, 5710/1950*, an Israeli law that criminalised crimes against the Jewish people, derived from Article II of the 1948 Convention. The court held that there was no doubt that genocide during the Second World War had been recognised as a crime under international law *ex tunc*, that is, retroactively, thus establishing universal jurisdiction over such crimes.

On the day the trial opened, 450 journalists listened to the opening speeches. American television filmed the entire trial, later broadcasting it across the Atlantic. Eichmann, along with two guards, was placed in a special glass and bulletproof booth visible from every point in the courtroom. The proceedings were simultaneously translated into three languages. The presentation of evidence and the testimony of as many as 112 witnesses lasted fifty-six days.

During the trial itself, Eichmann argued that antisemitism in the Third Reich had been merely a secondary matter, and that he himself was a great supporter of Zionism. His defence attorney, Dr Robert Servatius, likewise sought to emphasise his client's allegedly subordinate role in the entire criminal machinery of the Third Reich.

The reading of the 211-page reasoning of the verdict took the three judges fifteen hours. Before that, Eichmann had heard his sentence: he was found guilty of crimes against the Jewish people, war crimes, crimes against humanity, and membership in criminal organisations, and was therefore sentenced to death. The court found no mitigating circumstances. Eichmann wrote a letter by his own hand to the President of Israel, Yitzhak Ben-Zvi. In it, he reiterated his line of defence that he had been merely an instrument in the hands of the leadership and did not feel guilty.

The executioner of the death sentence by hanging was chosen from among the prison guards by drawing lots. The lot fell upon Shalom Nagar, a Yemenite Jew.

Moments before the sentence was carried out, Adolf Eichmann spoke his last words: 'Sieg Heil Germany! Sieg Heil Argentina! Sieg Heil Austria! These are the three countries with which I was most closely connected and which I shall never forget. I greet my wife, my family, and my friends. I am ready. We shall meet again soon, for such is the fate of all men. I die believing in God.'

At midnight, between 31 May and 1 June 1962, Nagar pressed the button that released the trapdoor. Eichmann's body was hastily cremated in a prepared crematorium near the beach. His ashes were scattered over the international waters of the Mediterranean Sea.

With Eichmann's death, the opportunity to solve one of the mysteries connected to his activities in hiding Nazi treasures was buried as well. For that, we must go back to April 1945. At that time, Eichmann, accompanied by a detachment, once again arrived in the town of Altaussee, using the alias 'Dr Müller'. He commanded a group of trained Waffen-SS soldiers and 150 members of the *Hitlerjugend*. At his disposal was a large quantity of weapons and other military equipment.

In addition to organising an armed underground, he had probably received another secret mission from his friend, Ernst Kaltenbrunner. Eichmann's detachment was to secure valuables looted from the occupied territories. The entire cache was transported on several trucks, with witnesses and participants in this operation later recalling that it consisted primarily of large quantities of gold and currency.

At first, the crates containing the precious deposit were stored in the Kremsmünster monastery, where the detachment established its headquarters. Later, the load was transferred to the Park Hotel in Altaussee, and preparations began for its concealment. Ultimately, the crates of valuables were transported in the direction of Blaa Alm, a small village near Salzburg. Over the following days, the soldiers busied themselves with hiding and securing the previously transported treasures. On 8 May 1945, American troops entered Blaa Alm. They knew nothing about the hidden valuables, and the matter was never raised during the Israeli investigation.

Is it therefore possible that the crates of treasures hidden by Adolf Eichmann still lie buried in the ground? For now, that remains a mystery.

Chapter 13

Franz Stangl – The Organiser
of the Death Machinery

On 22 December 1970, twenty-five years after the end of the Second World War, the former commandant of the Sobibór and Treblinka concentration camps was finally sentenced. He did not serve much of his life sentence; on 28 June 1971, he died of a heart attack. Who was this man, one of the greatest mass murderers of the twentieth century?

Franz Paul Stangl was born on 26 June 1908 in Altmünster, Austria. In 1931 he joined the police. Shortly thereafter, captivated by the ideas of National Socialism, he applied for membership in the local structures of the NSDAP, and subsequently also in the SS. It was only after the *Anschluss* in 1938, however, that his career began to accelerate, and he was appointed overseer of the T4 programme; the campaign of killing the mentally ill and the disabled, whose centre was located at Hartheim Castle. He must have fulfilled the expectations placed upon him, for in April 1942 he was appointed commandant of the newly established camp in Sobibór. This was the second extermination centre, after Bełżec, created as part of *Aktion Reinhardt*.[1]

The first transports to Sobibór most likely arrived at the end of March or the beginning of April 1942. In May, the systematic process of extermination began, lasting until the end of June. At that time, Jews from parts of the Lublin district were brought there. Simultaneously, transports also began to arrive from Austria, Germany, and Czechoslovakia.

The camp functioned without fault. Stangl proved to be an efficient organiser of the machinery of death; thus, in September 1942, he was transferred to the newly established extermination camp Treblinka II. His predecessor, SS-Untersturmführer Dr Irmfried Eberl, had failed to cope with the influx of prisoners. The gas chambers had broken down, meaning transports with victims waited for weeks on railway sidings to be killed,

SS-Hauptsturmführer Franz Paul Stangl (1908-1971) was one of the principal perpetrators of the Holocaust. (*Public domain*)

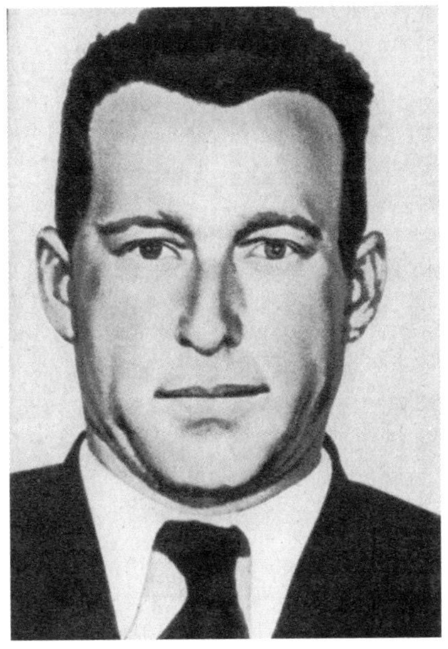

and a terrible stench of decomposing bodies spread around the camp.

Stangl was tasked with increasing the efficiency of the camp. To this end, he ordered the construction of a wooden mock railway station at the camp ramp, so that future victims would not suspect what awaited them. He also had new gas chambers built, capable of holding up to 3,000 people.

The first transport arrived at the camp on 23 July 1942, bringing Jews from the Warsaw ghetto. From that day onwards, victims were brought mainly from the territories of occupied Poland, but also from Czechoslovakia, France, Greece, Yugoslavia, and the Soviet Union, as well as Germany and Austria. Roma and Sinti from Poland and Germany were also sent there.

It is estimated that more than 800,000 people perished in Treblinka II. To erase the traces of the crime, the corpses were burned on specially constructed pyres. After Stangl was dismissed from his position as commandant and transferred to northern Italy in August 1943, a prisoner uprising broke out in the camp. Of the 840 inmates, only about 200 managed to escape. At most 100 could have survived until the end of the war. After the uprising, the camp was gradually dismantled.

After the war, Stangl returned to Austria. There, as a former SS-Hauptsturmführer, he was arrested by the American army and placed in the internment camp at Glasenbach, near Salzburg. In 1947 he was transferred to the investigative prison at the regional court in Linz. Classified as a prisoner who did not require strict surveillance, he worked clearing rubble from areas destroyed by bombings.

At the end of May 1948, one day Stangl did not return to prison after work. His disappearance, however, did not cause much commotion, nor were the American authorities notified. Around the same time, one of the most renowned Nazi hunters, Simon Wiesenthal, began searching for him. He later recalled that time:

> I learned that he was staying in the American internment camp in Glasenbach, near Salzburg. When I went there, it turned out that Stangl had been handed over to the Austrians and imprisoned in the investigative prison in Linz. In the very same city where I was working and where my office was located. As bad luck would have it, a week earlier this man, thanks to the help of his wife Teresa and the Nazi organisation 'Odessa', had escaped from prison. There was nothing more I could do at that time.[2]

By then, Stangl was already in Rome, where he received help from Bishop Alois Hudal.

The choice of Stangl's further escape route from Europe remains a mystery. Unlike most of his comrades, he did not immediately decide to set out for South America. Within a few weeks, he found himself in Damascus, Syria. It is not known exactly what he was doing there; from the scarce accounts available, it is known only that he became an expert for the Syrian secret services. He worked together with another German war criminal, Alois Brunner, who presented himself as Dr Fisher, alias Ali Mohammad.

Stangl felt secure enough in Damascus that he attempted to bring over his family, but what happened that made him decide, in 1951, to leave this friendly country and continue his journey to Brazil where, for the following years, he worked as a mechanic at Volkswagen plants, remains a mystery. Living in São Paulo, he kept his surname, but changed his first name to Paul.

In the early 1960s, Wiesenthal once again picked up the trail of the former commandant of Sobibór and Treblinka. A man was said to have approached him, demanding a specific sum of money in exchange for revealing Stangl's home address:

> He told me then that he was in trouble and wanted to make a deal with me. Right after that, he asked whether I was interested in Franz Stangl, because he had information about his whereabouts. When I confirmed, he said it would cost me $25,000. We began bargaining, and he came up with an

outrageous proposal. He said he wanted one cent for every person murdered by Stangl – a total of $7,000. I thought to myself at that moment that no decent man would ever provide me with this address, so I would have to strike a deal with a rogue. And so I did.

More vigorous efforts then began to gather evidence of Stangl's guilt and to prepare a plan for his capture. This was achieved only at the beginning of 1967. On 28 February, after leaving work, Stangl received a phone call informing him that his daughter had been in an accident and taken to a hospital. Without hesitation, he got into his car and drove to the indicated clinic, where the Brazilian police were waiting for him. Despite his arrest, when he realised at the police station that it had not been carried out by Israeli services, he breathed a sigh of relief.

Soon after, Poland requested his extradition, where he could expect the death penalty. However, he was handed over to the authorities of the Federal Republic of Germany, and on 13 May 1970, his trial began. During the proceedings, Stangl did not admit his guilt, claiming that he had been 'only following orders'. Nevertheless, on 22 December 1970, he was found guilty of the murder of nearly 900,000 people and sentenced to life imprisonment. As mentioned at the start of this chapter, he died six months later.

Chapter 14

Walther Rauff – The Creator of the Mobile Gas Chambers

During one of his inspections at the front, Himmler noted that the mass executions of Poles and Jews, which had been carried out practically since the very first day of the war, could eventually result in members of the SS being regarded as mentally disturbed and, on that basis, excluded from society. Walther Rauff, the creator of the mobile gas vans, provided a solution to these concerns. In 1972, already in exile, Rauff referred to this task in one of his letters: 'Whether at the time I had any reservations about the use of mobile gas vans, I cannot say. For me, what mattered most was that the shootings represented a significant burden for those who carried them out, and that this burden was removed once the mobile gas vans were used.'[1]

Rauff was born on 19 June 1906 in Köthen. In 1924 he joined the Reichsmarine, but was forced to leave the service in 1937 due to a moral scandal: it came to light that he had a mistress, and his wife filed for divorce. He then tied his further career path to the SS. In September 1939 he became responsible for the technical equipment and preparation of the *Einsatzgruppen*, carrying out mass murders of Poles.

It is not known why, but in 1940 he returned to service in the Kriegsmarine, where in April 1941 he was even promoted to the rank of Korvettenkapitän (lieutenant commander). At the same time, he headed Office Group I G (Technical Matters) in the Reich Main Security Office (RSHA). In 1942 he became head of Groups III D (Technical Matters) and VI F (Technical Auxiliary Means for Foreign Intelligence Service). He also served in Tunis, where he commanded a hastily created SS *Sonderkommando*. SS-Obersturmbannführer Rauff led seven officers and seventeen NCOs, all of whom had gained experience in the *Einsatzgruppen*.

Heinrich Himmler, recovering from the shock shared by other Germans caused by the capture of Tobruk by the Afrika Korps under Erwin Rommel, sensed an opportunity to implement his plan to liquidate the Jews of Palestine. The 'Desert Fox', however, ultimately disappointed him. Instead, Rauff 'made up' for this failure on the local Jews. In Tunisia, he even left behind a legend of a hidden treasure somewhere on the island of Djerba, consisting of dozens of kilograms of looted gold and valuables.

In Milan, as a member of the Gestapo, Rauff commanded the SS. At the end of the war, he was arrested by American soldiers. It is not entirely clear how he managed to escape custody, but in 1949 he was living in Syria, where he co-organised a group of German military experts working for that country. He was even appointed by Husni al-Za'im as security commissioner, with his main task being to reform Syrian intelligence.[2]

In August 1949 a bloodless coup d'état was carried out in the Syrian Republic by Sami al-Hinnawi. Most of the Germans employed by the previous government were expelled from the country, and thus Rauff also lost his position.[3] Thanks to the help of Catholic priests, however, he managed to obtain false documents, enabling him to leave for Ecuador.[4] He soon found himself on the payroll of the BND intelligence service. As is now known, this service was created with the consent of the Americans by the Gehlen Organisation, about 8% of whose roughly 1,000 members were former SS men. One of those responsible for recruiting Rauff was

SS-Standartenführer Walter Rauff (1906-1984) was an also an officer of the Reichsmarine, later the Kriegsmarine. (*Public domain*)

Rudolf Oebsger-Röder, operating under the pseudonym 'Kleist', who in September 1939 had commanded *Einsatzkommando* 16, responsible for mass shootings in Bydgoszcz.

Rauff did not stay in Ecuador long, as information about his crimes began to surface from all sides. He moved to Punta Arenas in Chile, where he became the manager of a canned king crab factory. He continued to carry out secret assignments for the BND, for example gathering intelligence on Fidel Castro's cooperation with the USSR.

In 1963 he was arrested in Santiago, but the following year he was released by court decision. In 1973, Chile saw a change of power, when a military Junta led by Augusto Pinochet seized control. Rauff proved very useful to the new regime and served the secret political police DINA, providing advice on the use of torture and on the planning of concentration camps.

After living under the radar for several years, in 1979 he was tracked down in Los Pozos, Santiago, by William Bemister, who conducted an interview with him. On the basis of this interview, the documentary film *The Hunter and the Hunted* was produced.

A wrecked Magirus-Deutz truck found in 1945 in Koło, near the Chełmno extermination camp. This model was used as a mobile gas van. (*Public domain*)

Rauff also gave an interview to the Argentine weekly *Somos*. In it, he explained that: 'One must find oneself in wartime conditions in order to understand the real meaning of words such as: to murder, to massacre, to kill. They only reflect the fact of an action undertaken in a situation when there is no time for emotions, and the only thing that matters is the gravity and urgency of the task received.'

Walther Rauff died of a heart attack in Santiago on 21 October 1984. He never answered for his numerous crimes.

One of the mysteries, unresolved to this day, connected with Rauff's postwar intelligence activity, concerns his links with Poland. As is known, the RSHA archives largely disappeared at the end of the war. Is the hypothesis correct that these files were taken over by the Gehlen Organisation and subsequently handed over to the BND, which buried them deep in its archives and has not disclosed them to this day? In Poland, in the area of Lubiąż and Wołów, RSHA deposits were supposedly hidden, containing items from the Führer's Chancellery, paintings, valuables, and files. After the war, companies established by Rauff attempted to gain access to these caches. Did they succeed? That remains unknown, just as in the case of many other places where valuables were hidden. What is known, however, is that Nazi enclaves in South America, including Colonia Dignidad, where Walther Rauff stayed, suddenly, and in unexplained fashion, came into possession of significant financial resources.

Chapter 15

Otto Skorzeny – The Führer's First Commando

After Italian dictator Benito Mussolini (il Duce) was stripped of power, he was imprisoned and held in secrecy. No one was to learn where he was being kept. Hitler, remembering Mussolini's consent to the *Anschluss* of Austria into the Third Reich, ordered a search for the place where his Italian friend was being detained. When German intelligence, thanks to numerous bribes learned that il Duce was being held in the Gran Sasso complex, his liberation was ordered. Responsibility for the success of the operation was to rest, among others, with Hitler's favourite commando, Otto Skorzeny.

When the Fieseler Storch plane took off from the mountain slope at Gran Sasso, it almost crashed. The machine was not designed to lift such a heavy load. On board, next to the pilot, sat the former Italian leader, and squeezed into the cabin beside him was Otto Skorzeny, who later recalled the event:

> In the plane, tilting onto its left wing and plunging towards the abyss, I waited for the crash, closing my eyes for a moment. I opened them when I felt that Gerlach had managed to pull up his 'Storch' slightly – we were flying 30 metres above the rocks, the aircraft gliding out of the Arezzano valley. I couldn't help but place my hand on Mussolini's shoulder. Just as pale as Gerlach and myself, he turned his head and smiled. He was aware of the danger but did not say a word.[1]

Skorzeny had been in commanded of a unit of twenty-six commandos and was operating under the orders of General Kurt Student, who had an additional 108 soldiers at his disposal. The Germans were to be transported to the site by gliders. On board the glider carrying Skorzeny was also

General Fernando Soleti, commander of the Italian Carabinieri, whose task was to prevent the Italians guarding il Duce from opening fire on the attackers or from killing Mussolini themselves.

On 12 September 1943, around 2:00 pm, the gliders began their silent descent. As soon as they touched down, General Soleti ran towards the Campo Imperatore hotel, shouting in Italian: 'Don't shoot!' The absence of resistance from the Italian guards allowed the Germans to seize the area within moments. Entering the building, Skorzeny burst into the radio operator's room, kicking over his chair and smashing the radio with the butt of his submachine gun.

The search for the Italian dictator began. His suite was room number 201. When the Germans stormed in, il Duce was standing with two Italian officers and a civilian. One commando shoved the officers against the wall and quickly led Mussolini away. Skorzeny greeted him with the words: 'Il Duce, the Führer has sent me, you are free!' Mussolini replied: 'I knew that my friend Adolf Hitler would not abandon me in my hour of need.'

The next challenge was to secure an escape route. The road down the mountain appeared risky. A Fieseler Storch was supposed to wait near the hotel, but it had been damaged. The situation seemed deadlocked. The only option left, and the one that was chosen, was to use another Storch, circling over Gran Sasso, piloted by Heinrich Gerlach.

After Gerlach had landed, Mussolini boarded the plane, followed, despite the pilot's protests, by Skorzeny, who forced himself in. For a moment the aircraft disappeared beyond the cliff's edge, only to reappear moments later above the Avezzano valley. It was now about 3:00 pm, and two hours later Gerlach landed safely in Rome. Mussolini and Skorzeny transferred to a Heinkel He 111 and, after receiving congratulations from General Student's envoy, flew on to Vienna. From there, the entire group proceeded to Munich, where they reunited with Mussolini's family, also freed that same day.

Skorzeny suddenly found himself the centre of worldwide attention. The German press, controlled by Joseph Goebbels, published numerous photographs of him; a development that did not please the commando himself, who now had good reason to fear that he might become a target.

Otto Skorzeny was born on 12 June 1908 in Vienna, although his family originated from Skorzęcin in Poland. In 1926 he began engineering studies at the Technical University in Vienna, with a focus on motorisation and engine construction. In 1931 he received his engineering diploma. While

SS-Sturmbannführer Otto Skorzeny with the Knight's Cross of the Iron Cross, 1943. (*Bundesarchiv, Bild 101III-Alber-183-25*)

a student and a member of a student corporation, he was obliged to duel. In one of these encounters, he was wounded in the face, leaving him with the distinctive scar he bore for the rest of his life.

In 1932 he joined the Austrian branch of the Nazi Party. In March 1938, during the *Anschluss*, he protected Austrian President Wilhelm Miklas in the palace on Reisnerstraße. Hitler wanted Miklas alive, but members of SA militias, seeking revenge for the repression of Nazis after the 1934 putsch in which Chancellor Engelbert Dollfuss was murdered, were plotting to kill him. At that time, 4,000 members of the Austrian NSDAP were imprisoned, and thirteen were executed by hanging.

At the outbreak of the war, Skorzeny volunteered for service in the Luftwaffe, but at the age of 30, he was rejected. He then turned to the newly created Waffen-SS. In February 1940, he was transferred to the 2nd Company of the SS *Leibstandarte Adolf Hitler* Replacement Battalion in Berlin-Lichterfelde. He took part in the invasion of the Netherlands and France, but because of misconduct and excesses, his promotion was suspended.

As part of the *Das Reich* Division, he participated in the Balkan campaign and in the USSR, where he worked on the maintenance of artillery weapons. At the end of 1941 he was seriously wounded in the head, and at the beginning of 1942, after further injuries, he was evacuated from the front. After being released from the hospital and withdrawn from combat, he was sent to repair works in Berlin, where he worked for several months. Later he volunteered for the tank warfare school and was transferred as an officer-engineer to the Waffen-SS *Totenkopf* Division. In 1943, within the Waffen-SS, special units began to be formed. Responsible for them was RSHA chief Ernst Kaltenbrunner, who recommended his fellow Austrian Otto Skorzeny to command the *Friedenthaler Jagdverbände* unit.

After the Gran Sasso Raid, Hitler was deeply impressed by Skorzeny's achievements, and personally telephoned the commando to thank him for the liberation of il Duce.

> The phone rang; I paid no attention, but Querner said to me: 'The Führer wants to speak to you personally.'
>
> I picked up the receiver. I heard Hitler's voice very clearly: 'Skorzeny, you have accomplished not only a great and unparalleled feat in the history of warfare, but you have also restored to me my friend Mussolini. I knew that if anyone could succeed, it would be you. I have promoted you to Sturmbannführer of the Waffen-SS and awarded you the Knight's Cross.
>
> 'I know you are already wearing it, for I gave the order for it to be presented to you immediately.'[2]

He then conveyed his gratitude. Skorzeny had the impression that Hitler was truly happy that Mussolini was alive and unharmed.

The liberation of Mussolini, to whom Hitler had once sworn help under any circumstances, launched Skorzeny into a meteoric career. The Führer entrusted him with control over all special forces of the Third Reich, and his

The Hotel Gran Sasso Campo Imperatore, where Mussolini was imprisoned. This photograph was taken by the Germans on the day of his rescue, 12 September 1943. (*Bundesarchiv, Bild 1011-567-1503A-05/Toni Schneiders/CC-BY-SA 3.0*)

unit began attracting adventurers and fortune-seekers of all kinds. Under his command were also placed the existing special units of the Luftwaffe and Kriegsmarine.

Skorzeny was given numerous special missions. Not all ended in success, such as Operation *Rösselsprung* in the spring of 1944, which attempted to destroy the headquarters of Josip Broz Tito in Bosnia. Successful operations, however, included *Mickey Mouse*, aimed at kidnapping Miklós Horthy Jr., the son of Regent and de facto Hungarian dictator Admiral Miklós Horthy; and Operation *Panzerfaust* in October 1944, during which power in Hungary was seized. As a result, Hungary fought at Germany's side until the end of the war, and Skorzeny received a promotion from Hitler to Obersturmbannführer.

Skorzeny's unit also carried out sabotage operations during the Ardennes Offensive under Operation *Greif*, conducted by soldiers disguised in American uniforms. Some of his special forces also fought in Pomerania in 1945, including during the defence of Malbork.

Otto Skorzeny was captured by American soldiers near Salzburg, ten days after the end of the war. In 1947 he stood trial in Dachau, accused of crimes committed during the Ardennes Offensive. He was charged with violating the laws of war by wearing enemy uniforms and plotting to assassinate General Dwight Eisenhower. The charges were soon dismissed, and on 9 September 1947, Skorzeny was acquitted.

His freedom did not last long, however, as he was arrested again and placed in a prisoner-of-war camp, from which he escaped in July 1948. After his release, he contacted General Reinhard Gehlen, the former head of *Abteilung Fremde Heere Ost* (Foreign Armies East, German military intelligence), who was then working for the CIA. With his assistance, Skorzeny opened a company involved in design and, above all, work in the steel and machinery industries.

In 1950 he arrived in Madrid, where he operated as an entrepreneur under the name Rolf Steinbauer. In the 1950s he trained commandos for Egyptian President Gamal Abdel Nasser. Interestingly, one of his trainees was Yasser Arafat, the future leader of the Palestine Liberation Organisation.

During this time, Skorzeny's memoirs were published, exposing him further to public attention. In Spain, at the beginning of the 1960s, he was located by agents of the Israeli Mossad, who, guaranteeing him immunity from Israel, requested his help in their rivalry with Egypt, where many German scientists were working. His cooperation with Israeli intelligence

Above: Benito Mussolini and Otto Skorzeny surrounded by German soldiers in front of the Gran Sasso Hotel, where il Duce had been held. (*Bundesarchiv, Bild 101I-567-1503C-15/Toni Schneiders/CC-BY-SA 3.0*)

Right: Otto Skorzeny as a witness during the Nuremberg Trials. (*USHMM*)

remains not fully documented and is one of the many mysteries of the postwar activities of Nazi war criminals. The Israelis feared Egyptian technological dominance, who, with the help of German scientists, had built the Al-Zafir and Al-Kahir rockets, modelled on the V-2. Skorzeny was tasked with sabotaging the Egyptian missile programme and with obtaining and delivering information on German scientists working in Egypt.

The Austrian's assistance proved invaluable. Soon the Egyptian programme for weapons of mass destruction had to be abandoned because of the lack of German specialists, who had been enticed away by the West German government. It was precisely their data that Skorzeny supplied to the Israelis. He collaborated with the CIA, West German, and Austrian intelligence.

Skorzeny remained a staunch Nazi until his death in Madrid from cancer on 5 July 1975. His body was cremated, and his ashes interred at the Döblinger Friedhof cemetery in Vienna.

Chapter 16

Léon Degrelle – Hitler's Dream Son

Hitler once said that if he were to have a son, he would want him to be like Léon Degrelle. To this day, the Belgian figure is revered by neo-Nazi groups, who see in him a kind of romantic warrior fighting against communism. In his homeland, however, he was sentenced to death in absentia after the war.

Léon Degrelle was born on 15 June 1906 in Bouillon, Belgium, into a deeply Catholic family. He attended secondary school run by Jesuits in Namur. Beginning in 1925, he studied law at the University of Louvain, and during this time became active in Catholic Action, a lay Catholic movement whose goal was to infuse public life with Christian values.

After five years, he abandoned his studies without obtaining a degree and travelled to Mexico, which was then engulfed in the Cristero War. There, he wrote articles about the persecution of Catholics. Degrelle's writing was marked by style and passion, showing his deep personal involvement in the causes he embraced. Upon returning from Mexico, he received an offer to work for the Catholic publishing house *Christus Rex*.

Under the same name, in 1935 Degrelle founded a nationalist movement which, in the following year, won 271,491 votes in the Belgian parliamentary elections – 11.5% of the total vote. This result secured his party twenty-one seats in the lower house and eight in the senate.

Despite cultivating strong ties with both the Third Reich and fascist Italy, and despite his loud proclamations of support for the Church, the Belgian primate declared before the next election that Degrelle represented 'a threat to both the country and the Church' and urged the faithful not to vote for his party. The effect was devastating. In the 1939 election, *Christus Rex* obtained only 103,636 votes, translating into just three seats.

When the Wehrmacht invaded Belgium in 1940, Degrelle was among the thousands swept up in the turmoil. He was immediately arrested and handed over to the French, who tortured and imprisoned him in no fewer than nineteen different prisons. The fear was not unfounded that he might

SS-Standartenführer Léon Degrelle (1906-1994) was a Belgian politician who commanded the 28th SS Volunteer Panzergrenadier Division 'Wallonien'. He was sentenced to death in absentia. (*Public domain*)

collaborate with the occupiers. And indeed, once released, that is precisely what he did. The Germans recognised *Christus Rex* as the only legal party in Wallonia. Other parties could either merge with it or face dissolution.

In July 1941, within the structures of the Wehrmacht, the 373rd Walloon Infantry Battalion was formed, better known as the Walloon Legion (*Légion Wallonie*). Since Degrelle had no military experience, he could not become an officer; instead, he enlisted as a common private. In August 1941, he joined the Legion for exercises in Meseritz, Brandenburg, before being deployed to the Eastern Front.

After only a year, in recognition of his courage, he was promoted to lieutenant. In 1943 he returned from the front to Belgium, where he turned his attention to seizing Jewish property and assets. With the profits he acquired in this way, Degrelle purchased real estate in Cannes. He also founded the newspaper *L'Avenir*, which brought him substantial income.

His growing popularity, however, did not change the opinion of the Church hierarchy, and in July 1943 Degrelle was excommunicated. Father Michel Poncelet refused to administer the sacrament of the Eucharist to him, so in retaliation, Degrelle's supporters beat the priest, expelled him from the Church, and locked him inside a crypt. By December 1943, however, the excommunication was lifted.

A key moment for Degrelle came in May 1943, when he met Reichsführer-SS Heinrich Himmler. During their discussions, it was agreed that the Walloon Legion would be reorganised into the SS-*Sturmbrigade 'Wallonien'* (Assault Brigade Wallonia) and formally incorporated into the Waffen-SS.

Himmler was intent on building up the power of his SS units, expanding them with new brigades, legions, and divisions composed of so-called 'Aryans' who were not necessarily German. Degrelle, as a fervent nationalist, a devoted supporter of Hitler, and a man already celebrated for his service on the Eastern Front, fitted perfectly into Himmler's vision as a propaganda figurehead for the Reichsführer's quasi-private army.

On 22 October 1943, the Walloon Legion was reorganised and expanded into the 5th SS Volunteer Assault Brigade 'Wallonien' (5. SS–*Freiwilligen Sturmbrigade 'Wallonien'*), which was sent to Ukraine in November 1943, where it fought alongside the 'Wiking' Division. Among its ranks was Degrelle, now serving as the commander of one of the units.

Crushed in heavy fighting in the Cherkassy pocket, the brigade was withdrawn to Germany in the winter of 1944. Degrelle took part in all the battles on the Dnieper and in the Battle of Cherkassy, for which he was personally awarded the Knight's Cross by Adolf Hitler. In July, the brigade was sent to Estonia, from where its remnants were evacuated to Germany in October, as preparations began to transform it into a division.

Degrelle was in Berlin at this time, and for his actions in Estonia and Courland in September–October 1944 he received the Knight's Cross of the Iron Cross with Oak Leaves. It was then, when presenting him with this decoration at the beginning of 1945, that Adolf Hitler declared: 'If I had a son, I would want him to be like you.'

After the war, in his memoirs from the Eastern Front, Degrelle described this visit as follows:

> The Führer occupied a modest wooden cottage. We entered
> a square vestibule. To the right was a cloakroom. To the left,
> at the far end, wide doors separated us from Hitler's office.

We waited a moment. Himmler recalled a few words of French that he had in his repertoire. The doors opened. I had no time to see anything or even to think: the Führer came up to me, took my right hand in his, and shook it warmly. The room lit up with flashes of magnesium. Film cameras captured the meeting.

And I saw only Hitler's eyes, I felt only his hands pressing my right hand, I heard only his voice, somewhat hoarse, greeting me and repeating: 'I was very worried about you...' We sat down in wooden armchairs before a massive fireplace. With astonishment I looked at the Führer. His pupils still carried that strange fire, direct and captivating. But four years of war had lent him an extraordinary dignity. His hair had turned grey. His back had bent slightly from constant stooping over maps and from bearing the burdens of the entire world.[1]

Yet the war was drawing to an end, and the Red Army was approaching Berlin. Degrelle suffered a blow from his homeland. For his collaboration with the Germans, he was sentenced to death in absentia. As part of collective responsibility, his parents were imprisoned and his brother was executed. If he wanted to go on living, he had to choose exile. So what did his escape route look like?

After his final meeting with Heinrich Himmler, Léon Degrelle decided it was time to look after his own skin. He first made his way to Denmark and then to Norway, which at that time was still under German occupation. On Sunday, 6 May 1945, Degrelle was received in Oslo, at the castle of Crown Prince Olav, by the German governor, Dr Josef Terboven. The following day, the Walloon met with Norway's prime minister, Vidkun Quisling.

Thanks to Albert Speer, he was given the use of a Heinkel He 111 aircraft, in which he set out for Spain, then under the rule of Francisco Franco. During the landing on the beach at San Sebastián in northern Spain, the plane was destroyed and Degrelle was seriously injured. He later recalled it this way:

From a distance I could see the white curves of the Pyrenees on the horizon at the mouth of the Bidassoa. But the plane could no longer go on. It skimmed along, almost brushing the waves. We would perish 20 kilometres from the Iberian coast. We had

The Heinkel He 111 bomber that brought Léon Degrelle to Spain, wrecked after an emergency landing on La Concha beach in San Sebastián. (*Wikimedia Commons/Vicente Martín*)

to fire red distress flares: two small boats coming from the French side of the coast turned in our direction. Disaster! And to think that just then, in the distance, a lighthouse shone forth, a Spanish lighthouse! It was a strange thing to see beneath us the sharp crests of the waves and the churning sea, ready to swallow us whole… Yet still we had not gone down. The coast drew nearer, thrusting towards us its surf, its coastal rocks, and the black-green mountains rising from the darkness.

Suddenly the pilot pulled the plane upwards, set it vertically, almost flipped it, the engine roaring terribly as he drained the last drops of fuel, and then hurled it with a dreadful howl over the rocky rise towards a cluster of red roofs. We didn't even have time to think.

For the briefest instant we saw a small strip of sand. The Heinkel, which had not even lowered its landing gear, skimmed across the ground at a speed of 250 kilometres an hour. I saw the right engine explode into a ball of fire. The machine spun, veered towards the water, and plunged into the waves. Water rushed into the shattered cockpit and rose up to our waists. I had five fractures.

On the beach at San Sebastián, anxious Guardia Civil officers in black bicorn hats were running back and forth in front of houses and hotels. Some Spaniards, half-naked like Tahitians, swam out to our wrecked plane. They hauled me onto the wing, then into a canoe. An ambulance pulled up.

This time the war was truly over...[2]

The Belgian authorities requested Degrelle's extradition from Spain, but permission was denied on account of his poor medical condition.

Once he had recovered, Degrelle's escape from the military hospital *Mola* was arranged. From that point on, he had to live in hiding and under false names. At first, he was known as Juan Muñoz, and later he adopted the identity of León José de Ramírez Reina. He settled in the Spanish capital, where he operated as a businessman. In 1954, he attempted to return to Belgium to clear himself of the charges against him, but the Belgian authorities refused to reopen his trial.

He remained in exile until the end of his life, dying in Spain on 31 March 1994. In a 1977 interview he declared: 'I was a Hitlerite, I still am, and I will remain so until my death.'

Chapter 17

Kidnapping the Pope!

Despite the many years that have passed since the end of the Second World War, and despite the declassification of Vatican archives concerning the role of Pope Pius XII during the conflict, he is still widely regarded as 'Hitler's Pope'. One of the arguments cited for this statement is the signing of the so-called *Reichskonkordat* on 20 July 1933, which, in exchange for bishops taking an oath of loyalty to the state, granted the Church freedom of worship and the right to teach religion. The agreement, on behalf of Pope Pius XI, was signed by the Apostolic Nuncio Eugenio Pacelli – the future Pope Pius XII.

In the contemporaneously recorded *Table Talk*, Hitler referred to this concordat. He said:

> One has to consider: is it not easier to govern after having signed a concordat? After thorough reflection, the answer we receive is this: it is a surrender of the authority of the state into the hands of a third power, a power on which it is uncertain how long we can rely. The Anglican Church, nominal as it is, yes, England can rely on it. But the Catholic Church? Do we not run the risk that one day it will change its course, even though at first, in the name of preserving its influence, it placed itself at the service of the state? If one day the Church or the priests no longer agree with state policy, they will turn against the state. We are seeing something like that right now, and discouraging examples can also be found in the past.[1]

Pope Pius XII is also commonly accused of passivity, or even of tacit approval of the Holocaust. Yet it is rarely mentioned that Hitler issued an order to kidnap the Pope and occupy the Vatican. The operation, codenamed Operation *Rabat*, was intended as punishment for the Church's efforts to

SS-Obergruppenführer Karl Friedrich Otto Wolff (1900-1984) was a Police Leader in Italy and organised the deportation of Jews to the Treblinka extermination camp. (*Bundesarchiv, Bild 146-1969-171-29/ Friedrich Franz Bauer/CC-BY-SA 3.0*)

save Jews. At the same time, the abduction of the Pope was to serve as retaliation for Benito Mussolini's loss of power in Italy, something Hitler partly blamed on the Pontiff himself.

On 8 September 1943, the new Italian government under Pietro Badoglio signed an armistice with the Allies. The Italian armies, long underestimated by the Germans, switched sides and began fighting their former ally. In response, the Wehrmacht occupied the country, disarmed the Italian army, and deported about 600,000 Italian soldiers to forced labour in Germany and the occupied territories.

To carry out the mission of kidnapping the Pope, Hitler did not choose his new favourite commando, Otto Skorzeny, instead appointing SS-Gruppenführer Karl Wolff. To present him with the plan, Hitler summoned Wolff to a direct meeting at the Wolf's Lair. According to notes taken by Wolff shortly after the conversation, Hitler explained that he was forbidden from mentioning the mission to anyone without his permission, and that the only other person who was aware of it was the Reichsführer-SS, Heinrich Himmler. He then went on to explain what Operation *Rabat* would involve:

> I want you, as quickly as possible, to occupy the Vatican with your troops, secure its archives and works of art, and deport the Pope and the Curia to the north. I do not want him to fall into the hands of the Allies or come under their political influence and pressure. Even now, the Vatican is a nest of spies and a centre of anti-Nazi propaganda. Depending on the political and military situation, I will arrange for the Pope to be transported either to Germany or to neutral Liechtenstein.[2]

It might seem that Wolff, upon hearing his leader's plans, would be stunned. Yet he knew perfectly well why he had been summoned. A few hours earlier, Himmler had already given him a preliminary briefing on the secret mission. Both men realised that the kidnapping of the Pope would weigh heavily on the list of crimes for which they would be held accountable in the course of the war. Such an act, in the eyes of the Allies, would constitute a moral crime and would have destroyed any chance of initiating potential peace negotiations.

Reichsführer-SS Heinrich Himmler arrives with his adjutant, SS-Oberführer Karl Wolff, for a session of the newly opened Reichstag, 12 December 1933. (*Bundesarchiv, Bild 183-H0226-501-003/CC-BY-SA 3.0*)

Wolff had already prepared his answer to Hitler in advance. He explained the necessity of bringing additional Waffen-SS and police forces into Italy, arguing that in order to secure the archives and works of art, he would need specialists familiar with Greek and Latin. Ultimately, Wolff stated that he could not provide a specific timetable for carrying out the mission.

This reply did not satisfy Hitler. The Führer knew that every day counted in the execution of this plan. Rome could fall into Allied hands at almost any moment, and once that happened, the kidnapping of the Pope would become impossible. Hitler had nothing left to lose, unlike the man to whom he entrusted this difficult task.

Wolff feared that such an operation would irreparably stain his reputation. Moreover, he believed that shielding the Pope from the Führer's grasp could bring far greater benefits in the face of the now-predictable end of the war and the inevitable punishment awaiting the highest-ranking German officials among whom he, as the plenipotentiary of northern Italy, was certainly counted. The blessing of Pius XII might protect him from a possible death sentence, but saving the Pope would mean open betrayal, which itself carried the penalty of death. Karl Wolff realised he had to walk a dangerous tightrope, where a single misstep meant death. But he had no choice.

At the Wolf's Lair meeting, Hitler ordered Wolff to report on the progress of preparations for the mission every two weeks. Each time the moment came for him to present his report, the general distorted the truth, a tactic that infuriated the Führer.

At the beginning of December 1943, the SS-Gruppenführer was once again summoned to the Wolf's Lair. Hitler was growing impatient and demanded concrete information about the resources necessary to storm the Vatican and abduct the Pope. Wolf explained what would be needed: 'Two thousand men to encircle and seize the Vatican, a group of German professors who would quickly identify and prepare the most valuable documents and works of art for removal, a team of officials from South Tyrol to serve as interpreters, and buses and trucks to transport the Pope, his entourage, the politicians who had fled from the Germans into the Vatican, as well as the looted Vatican archives and works of art.' He also used the meeting to plant a seed of doubt in the Führer's mind, saying:

> I am indeed capable of carrying out this operation in the Vatican
> swiftly and effectively with these forces, mein Führer, but

afterwards I will not be able, with such insufficient numbers, to keep the Italian population under control. They will surely react with outrage at our actions. Based on my assessments so far, I must then reckon with widespread strikes and mass demonstrations which, though I could suppress them by force, would nonetheless paralyse the armaments and production so vital [to Germany] and shift the overall situation in Italy to our disadvantage.[3]

At the end of the meeting, Hitler declared that Wolff should do whatever he deemed necessary. He was expected to know best which methods would be most effective.

Meanwhile, Allied advances on the Italian front were becoming significant. Wolff, unwilling to allow the Pope to be abducted, also could not afford to let his role in preventing such a plan go unnoticed. Although the details of his mission were supposed to remain under the highest level of secrecy, within a short time several people became aware of the Germans' intentions.

After arriving in Italy, Wolff immediately shared his knowledge with Ambassador Rudolf Rahn, who recalled after the war:

> Shortly after my arrival in Rome in September 1943, General Wolff informed me of his conversation with Hitler concerning the plan to abduct the Pope. We agreed that carrying it out would have disastrous consequences and must be prevented at all costs. Therefore, I decided to seize the first opportunity to discuss the matter with Hitler and volunteered to present a report on the political situation at his headquarters. When I arrived, I was surprised to find a large circle of leading figures in Hitler's office, who were also to listen to my report.[4]

News of the alleged abduction of the Pope was even broadcast by a British radio station posing as a German opposition broadcaster. This report was immediately reprinted by the press in Italy and Great Britain, this reaching the eyes and ears of the Pope himself.

There was no time left to waste. Wolff decided to meet the Pope in person. To do so, he had to disguise himself in civilian clothing, and since he never parted with his uniform, he was forced to borrow some. On 10 May 1944,

Karl Wolff, dressed in a tight-fitting suit, went to a private audience with the Pope. He sat across from Pius XII, who in excellent German expressed his concern about reports of incidents at the Gestapo torture chamber located on Via Tasso in Rome. He also asked for the possible release of his friend, the socialist activist Giuliano Vasselli. Wolff promised to intervene in the matter. Pius XII also assured his guest that, whatever might happen, he had no intention of voluntarily leaving Rome.

At the end of the audience, the Pope gave Wolff his blessing. Wolff clicked his heels together and raised his right hand in the Nazi salute. In his exhilaration, he barely restrained himself from shouting 'Heil Hitler!' Soon afterwards, the Allies marched into Rome, and on 8 June, American General Mark Clark met with the Pope. The plan to abduct the Pontiff had finally collapsed.

Chapter 18

The Mythical Fortress

The defeat at Stalingrad in February 1943 marked the beginning of Germany's slow march towards ultimate defeat. The disaster was compounded by the loss at the Battle of Kursk later that summer, the largest tank battle in history. From that moment onwards, the Wehrmacht on the Eastern Front was forced into a permanent defensive stance. Many Germans still clung to hopes of news about the *Wunderwaffe* - the miracle weapon. Hitler repeatedly promised that it would not merely change the course of the war, but immediately bring about the long-awaited victory.

The *Wunderwaffe* label encompassed more than 150 different projects, though only a handful offered any genuine hope of tipping the balance in the air or on land. The closest were the jet fighter Messerschmitt Me 262 Schwalbe and the *Vergeltungswaffe*-2 (retaliatory weapon 2), better known as the V-2 rocket. When even these projects failed to deliver, Germans began to fantasise about fighting from an 'ultimate redoubt' that would serve as the starting point for a victorious counteroffensive. Thus, the idea of the Alpine Fortress was born. In reality, it fulfilled a few minor functions but never achieved the primary goal for which it had been conceived. Yet the question remains, did the Germans truly invent the Alpine Fortress?

The first reports of the possible establishment of a fortified zone in the Alps, specifically in the Berchtesgaden region, actually came from… the Swiss. By late 1944, American intelligence services were preparing assessments of possible scenarios for sustained German resistance. While analysing southern Germany, they pointed to the Berchtesgaden area, especially since, according to information gathered from Switzerland, the Germans had been surveying the terrain there for opportunities to establish some kind of defensive redoubt that could significantly prolong the war. Berchtesgaden, after all, housed the private residences of the most important figures of the Third Reich. It was therefore reasonable to assume that this difficult-to-access terrain would be heavily fortified. With the deployment of sufficient military forces, the area could, in theory, become almost impregnable.

As it turned out, not only did American intelligence predictions fail to materialise, but their very existence contributed to the fact that the Soviets were the first to enter Berlin.

The intelligence received from Switzerland triggered a wave of hysteria among American military circles at the end of the war. Commanders were deeply unwilling to prolong the fighting and to incur heavy losses in mountainous, fortified terrain. Ironically, these same reports reached the Germans themselves. Gauleiter of the Tyrol-Vorarlberg region, Franz Hofer, seized on the idea and tried to persuade Hitler of the necessity of building fortifications in the area described by the Swiss. In his report to the Führer, he argued:

> If the report correctly predicts the course of military developments in 1945, then the creation of the 'Alpine Fortress' will become not only a military necessity but also the sole opportunity to open diplomatic negotiations, provided it is skilfully and quickly exploited.
>
> If, on the other hand, the report incorrectly assesses military developments, then the creation of the 'Alpine Fortress', with its underground factories, equipment depots, and food stores, will ensure the sense of 'having an ace up one's sleeve' and will undoubtedly have a positive influence on the continuation of the struggle.[1]

As Hofer pointed out, panic within American ranks could also allow the mythical Alpine Fortress to be used as a bargaining chip in peace negotiations.

However, Hofer's memorandum never reached Hitler's desk. As with everything else in the final months of the war, the report first had to pass through the hands of Martin Bormann, who, after reading it, quietly filed it away in his personal archive. He feared that submitting such a defeatist document might provoke the Führer's wrath, which might easily turn against Bormann himself.

From a military standpoint, the time that could have been used for actual preparations, fortifications, supplies, and equipping of the fortress in any meaningful form was wasted. Yet the rumours of the so-called Alpine

Redoubt did reach the Minister of Propaganda and Public Enlightenment, Joseph Goebbels. As a master of demagoguery, he immediately recognised the possibilities that even the illusion of such a stronghold offered.

On Goebbels' order, the ministry established a Special Department 'Alpine Fortress'. It had only one task: to convince public opinion that the Alps had become an armed super-fortress, manned by elite troops, perfectly supplied, and practically impregnable. The officials fulfilled this mission with remarkable efficiency, and even received unexpected assistance from none other than Joseph Stalin, who was keenly interested in sowing panic among his American allies. Stalin hoped that the Americans, frightened by the spectre of months of bloody fighting in the mountains and thousands of dead American soldiers, would divert most of their forces toward the Alps, weakening or even abandoning their advance on Berlin altogether.

In the dying days of the war, on 9 April 1945, Hitler summoned Gauleiter Franz Hofer to report on the Alpine Fortress project. During the meeting, Hofer urged the Führer to relocate to the Alps, where he would be far safer than in the Berlin bunker. As a potential headquarters, Hofer even offered his own manor house, equipped with an underground shelter. But Hitler had no intention of taking up the offer. His destiny, he had already decided, would be fulfilled in Berlin.

Still, during Hofer's visit, on 12 April Hitler issued an order for the inspection and expansion of an 'inner Alpine fortress'. Only from that moment can we speak of a genuine intent to create such a defensive redoubt. Yet the concept was almost immediately ridiculed by Wehrmacht officers, who derisively labelled Hofer a 'saboteur of authority'. Valentin Feurstein, commander of the 5th Mountain Division, slated for redeployment into the not-yet-existent stronghold, did not hold back his biting remarks about Hitler, Hofer, and the entire plan:

> Was Hitler still even capable of assessing the situation of the country? (…) These musings about the Alpine Fortress were a laughable illusion. (…) The mountains themselves cannot stop the enemy, and it was already far too late to construct effective defensive positions. Comparisons with the First World War or even with the Wars of Liberation cannot be made. After Italy left the Triple Alliance in 1915, the spirit of Andreas Hofer was revived, and the Tyroleans steeled themselves with the will to endure.

According to Feuerstein, in 1945 there was also a kind of Hofer – one granted by Hitler's favour. It seemed that the last effort wrung from a population that had already lost all hope was completely crushed by the Party and the Allies. The former hero of freedom did not come back to life.[2]

On 24 April 1945, Adolf Hitler signed an order that sanctioned the creation of the Alpine Fortress as one of the three areas not yet occupied by Allied forces. Meanwhile, reports about this fortress paralysed General Eisenhower, the Supreme Commander of the Allied Forces. His decision to abandon the advance on Berlin and redirect the main forces toward the Alps infuriated Field Marshal Montgomery and British Prime Minister Churchill. Both knew that the war would be won by whoever captured the German capital. Montgomery, whom Eisenhower referred to as a 'prima donna', was stripped of command over the 9th Army. The American sent him a radiogram in which he wrote: 'You will surely notice that I did not mention Berlin at all. That city is for me only a geographical concept, and such things have never interested me. My goal is to destroy the enemy's forces and break his will to resist.'[3]

Stalin could barely contain his delight, applauding Eisenhower's misguided decision while suggesting that he, too, attached little importance to the German capital and would assign its capture only to second-rate units. In reality, the Battle for Berlin had become a race between the fronts of marshals Ivan Konev and Georgy Zhukov, who had been given command of the best units the Red Army could muster. On 16 April, Zhukov, ultimately chosen by Stalin to take Berlin, gave the order to attack. Meanwhile, the Americans still waited along the Elbe for their eastern ally…

Chapter 19

Hitler's Werewolves

From 1943 onwards, the Wehrmacht on the Eastern Front was in constant retreat. Nothing indicated that the situation could radically change. Yet much of the German leadership insisted these were merely temporary setbacks and that the war would inevitably end in the ultimate victory of the Third Reich. After all, the 'superior [Aryan] race' could not be defeated by the 'subhumans'.

Reichsführer-SS Heinrich Himmler saw an opportunity to support the German army through sabotage operations carried out directly behind enemy lines, already on territory occupied by the foe. Soon, however, as the situation continued to deteriorate, the plans had to be modified.

On 16 September 1944, at Himmler's headquarters, a meeting was held during which a plan was devised for underground resistance in the event of German territory itself falling under occupation. Under this new plan, the chief of the RSHA, Ernst Kaltenbrunner, 'was tasked with taking over the organisation and command of resistance movements in France, Flanders, Wallonia, Finland, across the entire occupied East (and later in Estonia, Latvia, and Lithuania), as well as in Romania, Transylvania, Bulgaria, Greece, and other areas occupied by the enemy.'[1]

SS-Obergruppenführer Hans-Adolf Prützmann (1901-1945) was a Police Leader in the occupied territories of the USSR and organised the Werwolf units. (*Public domain*)

Generalmajor Reinhard Gehlen, head of the *Fremde Heere Ost* Division, also attended the meeting. Based on the files of the Polish Home Army seized after the suppression of the Warsaw Uprising in August 1944, he created a structure built around small strike groups, placing particular emphasis on the decentralisation of the organisation.

The development of the concept of guerrilla warfare was also influenced by SS-Obergruppenführer Richard Hildebrandt, head of the Main Office of Race and Settlement in the RSHA. He wrote a nine-point memorandum to Himmler. The most important were the first three demands:

1. In all the frontline provinces of the Reich, bases and hideouts must immediately be prepared in the form of a network in places difficult to locate. The bases must be equipped with explosives, weapons, ammunition, food supplies, and clothing. They should allow for overwintering and be equipped with means of communication (radio sets).

2. The civilian population may go underground only on the condition that it involves members of leading families of the Party, the State, and the Wehrmacht. All those who do not hold prominent positions must remain in public life, in order to form a base for the continued activity of our partisan units and to ensure the preservation of the German character of the landscape.

3. All men and women remaining in hiding to carry out combat missions must be equipped with false passports. The leadership of these combat groups, down to the smallest units, must rest in the hands of Higher SS and Police Leaders, or alternatively such Führers and men who have been specially selected and, if possible, have gained experience in the East. Numerous SS Führers and men who have lost their assignments and are free due to withdrawals on all fronts would be particularly suited to this task. Some units should be equipped with anti-tank weapons in order, as far as possible, to prevent the enemy from moving freely with tanks.[2]

SS-Obergruppenführer Hans-Adolf Prützmann was appointed as the man responsible for creating the *Werwolf*. That was the name given to the organisation that was supposed to be responsible for sabotage operations after the front had passed.

Prützmann was born on 31 August 1901 in Tolkemit, near Elbląg. After the end of the First World War, he joined the Freikorps, in which he fought against French troops occupying the Ruhr and the Rhineland. In 1930, he joined the NSDAP and simultaneously the SS, becoming a commander of an SS-*Standarte* in Gelsenkirchen, and later in Königsberg. He must have proven himself, since by 1933 he was appointed commander of an SS sector in Stuttgart. Afterwards, until 1937, he served as commander of SS-*Oberabschnitt Südwest*. From 1937-1941, he commanded the SS-*Nadregion Nordsee*, and from 1938-1941 held the position of Higher SS and Police Leader for the Nordwest region, headquartered in Hamburg.

Following the German invasion of the Soviet Union, on 29 June 1941 he was appointed Higher SS and Police Leader for the Ostland and Northern Russia region, with headquarters in Riga. From May 1941 to May 1945, he served as Higher SS and Police Leader in the Nordost region and commander of the SS-*Nadregion* of the same name. Then, from December 1941, he replaced Friedrich Jeckeln as Higher SS and Police Leader of *Russland-Süd*. During this period, he was also commander of the SS-*Nadregion Ukraine*. He held both positions until 1944.

On 29 October 1943, a new position of Supreme SS and Police Leader for the Ukraine region was created, and it was Prützmann who assumed the post. After he was entrusted with tasks related to the organisation of partisan operations, on 5 December 1944 he was also appointed Special Plenipotentiary of the Reich for Croatia. In May 1945 he was captured, and while held at a villa in Lüneburg, on 21 April 1945 he is said to have committed suicide, allegedly fearing extradition to the Russians. Interestingly, Prützmann was guarded by the same soldier who, a few days later, was present at the supposed suicide of Heinrich Himmler.

The organisation of *Werwolf* also involved – unsurprisingly – the 'First Commando of the

The 'Wolf's Hook' was the symbol of the Werwolf organisation. (*Public domain*)

Third Reich', Otto Skorzeny. Yet he was rather sceptical about the entire operation:

> What was I supposed to do in that situation? Everyone around me was putting on serious faces, and Schellenberg, as always, was nodding eagerly. I simply could not awaken any faith in the effectiveness of this so-called *Werwolf*, for the very good reason that a resistance movement must be present throughout the entire country, have realistic and constructive political goals, and above all be very strongly supported materially, including from the outside. Suitable terrain conditions are also essential. The *Werwolf* strategy would certainly have proven effective in the Balkans or in Iran, in Russia or China. Some tactical benefits could surely have been achieved. But not in a country with the largest concentration of population on a limited area, with railways, highways, and roads, when there was no hope whatsoever of any help from the outside.
>
> We could, admittedly, have made use of a similar resistance movement within a limited period of time in the mountains and forests of the so-called 'Alpine Fortress', had it actually been organised, in order to continue the struggle toward a political goal – that is, to gain time for the evacuation of our soldiers and civilians from east to west. Otherwise, *Werwolf* would have inevitably provoked cruel acts of retaliation, and our country could not have derived the slightest benefit from such a resistance movement. A guerrilla war of that kind would only have made sense if it had been conducted for the necessary period in the necessary territory. It would then have had to combine the actions of a resistance movement with an uprising of all the European nations that had already fallen under Soviet domination or were directly threatened by Bolshevism.[3]

Skorzeny, in his memoirs, greatly embellished certain events. He certainly could not have been considered as a potential candidate to take on the role of organizing *Werwolf*, since that position had already been assigned to Hans-Adolf Prützmann.

According to its guiding principles, *Werwolf* members on German territory occupied by the Allies were supposed to carry out acts of sabotage, engage in guerrilla warfare, and mete out justice to Germans who had committed treason or collaborated. In western and northern Germany, however, virtually no operations targeting the enemy were recorded. Neither the broadcasts transmitted over the special *Werwolf* radio station, nor the proclamations issued to 'attack the enemy wherever possible', similar to those directed at Lower Silesian members of the Hitler Youth, proved effective. 'Every weapon and every method is justified. Every harm inflicted on the enemy on German soil helps bring us closer to victory! No special training, technique, or weapon is needed. To wield the weapons of our resistance, only courage, readiness to act, swiftness, prudence, and fanatical hatred are required!'

Instructions were given on how best to carry out acts of sabotage. It was suggested, for example, that railway operations could be disrupted by jamming a switch with a stone or by placing a brake shoe on the tracks, which would result in the derailment of a train.[4]

To better illustrate the activities of the *Werwolf* at the time, and how they were perceived by young boys, it is worth citing the testimony of 14-year-old Hans-Joachim von Leesen, from Flensburg:

> One night in early May 1945, I was awakened in the middle of the night. A comrade from the *Deutsches Jungvolk* brought me an order from Standortführer DJ Hans-Werner Nissen that I was to report immediately to the Harbor Square, and on my way there, wake up and bring along another *Jungzugführer* from our unit. That is what I did. Upon arriving at the Harbour Square, we met a group of somewhat older leaders from the DJ and HJ in civilian clothes, some of whom I recognised. Gradually, younger boys than myself also arrived, and like me, they had no idea what it was all about.
>
> The older boys had brought to the Harbour Square several carts, so-called Scottish carts, apparently taken from shops in Flensburg. They were piled high with crates and boxes. The boys needed help transporting them out of the city. After binding us to secrecy, they told us this was part of preparations for *Werwolf* operations. The older ones had been recruited – some even showed us their military service books – and had

volunteered for the Waffen-SS. They were tasked with building dugouts in which weapons, ammunition, and provisions would be stored for *Werwolf* units. If the Allies occupied all of Germany, a secret signal would trigger a popular uprising unleashed by *Werwolf* units to sweep the enemy from the country. We now belonged to the *Werwolf* Flensburg group. The task was to push the carts loaded with Panzerfausts, hand grenades, small arms, ammunition, and canned provisions up Kappelner Strasse, transporting them toward Satrup in the Hürup area (about 5-6 km away). There, in the forest, hiding places and dugouts had been prepared for storing weapons and provisions. We pushed the carts with all our strength – often uphill, or so it seemed to us – towards Hürupholz. When fatigue overcame us, we were given coffee beans from a small box to chew; these revived us. After several hours, we reached the forest. A few older DJ leaders appeared, among them Standortführer Hans Werner Nissen. Some carried pistols.

They had unpleasant news to deliver: a man from Hürup had been caught when, having stumbled upon the prepared underground caches, he tried to carry off the canned food. The loot was taken back from him. Now, as punishment, he was to help with the construction of further dugouts. We, the younger ones, were sent home; the point was to keep the hiding places secret from us. Orders regarding further actions were to be given in the following days. Since British units were quickly approaching Flensburg, we were alerted already the next day. We were to take over heavily loaded carts at Südermarkt and once again push them through Angelburger Strasse/Harbour Square toward Hürup. When our convoy of handcarts tried to cross Süderhofenden Street, we had to stop. Our way was blocked by a column of military trucks heading north. Only after looking more closely did we realise they bore painted white stars. The Americans or the British were already here. After we crossed the street, we pushed the carts (...) to the edge of the forest near Hürupholz.[5]

The situation of the *Werwolf* looked somewhat different in the East. Here there was a stronger will to fight against the Red Army, but also a greater fear of possible reprisals. It was also much harder to distinguish genuine actions attributable to members of the *Werwolf* from mere acts of disobedience or revenge for the looting, murders, and rapes committed by Soviet soldiers. According to a report by Ivan Serov sent to Stalin, in the territories occupied by the Red Army thousands of underground activists were captured, which in turn prevented the execution of a significant number of sabotage operations and allowed the seizure of large stockpiles of ammunition and weapons accumulated by the *Werwolf*.

The reality, however, was quite different from what the reports claimed. Most Germans from territories overrun by the Red Army had already evacuated before its arrival. Others fled after the front had passed. The majority of those who remained in lands annexed to Poland still hoped for peaceful coexistence. Yet it quickly turned out that some were locked up in temporary camps, where hunger and disease caused mass deaths. Others were deported to the East. Of course, this does not mean that there were no instances of *Werwolf* activity or actions by other groups of fanatical Germans. For example, on 14 August 1945 a group of armed Germans in Nowa Ruda attacked local Polish inhabitants. One of them was abducted into the forest, where, under torture, he was forced to reveal the layout of a nearby militia post.

Werwolf bands revealed themselves near Jelenia Góra, in Wałbrzych, and in Oleśnica, while the most decisive partisan activity took place in Silesia. In other regions of Poland, the activity of German partisan bands was either not recorded at all or occurred only sporadically. By the second half of 1945, any German activity in these areas had apparently come to a complete halt.

Chapter 20

Hitler's Atomic Bomb – Truth or Myth?

There is no doubt that the use of the atomic bomb by the United States against Japan in August 1945 became a turning point not only by ending the war in the Pacific, but also in global military history. The dropping of nuclear devices on Hiroshima and then Nagasaki opened an entirely new chapter in the arms race between the two emerging world superpowers. For decades, historians and researchers have debated what might have happened if Germany had been the first to produce an atomic bomb. For just as long, scholars have argued over whether the Third Reich's atomic programme had advanced far enough to conduct a test of a low-yield nuclear weapon, or whether the project never reached such a stage.

Early scientific work and experiments describing and presenting the process of nuclear fission had already been taking place at European universities since around 1935. However, the true breakthrough came shortly before Christmas 1938, when Otto Hahn, together with his assistant Fritz Strassmann, conducted the first successful laboratory experiment splitting the uranium nucleus at the Kaiser Wilhelm Institute for Chemistry in Berlin.

In April 1939, a report was produced on the potential military use of energy released from nuclear fission, which immediately drew great interest. At this early stage, two main concepts of uranium enrichment crystallised: through the use of heavy water or through graphite. As it later turned out, erroneous calculations led to the rejection of graphite. Did this decision bury Germany's chances of acquiring an atomic weapon?

For many years after the end of the Second World War, this view could be found in nearly every publication addressing the subject. Most researchers also tended to focus on a single research centre working on the atomic bomb, while in fact there were at least several such centres in Germany. Apart

Otto Hahn (1879-1968) was a German radiochemist and Nobel Prize laureate in Chemistry (1944), who was regarded as the father of the German nuclear programme. (*Public domain*)

from the *Uranverein* (Uranium Club), which has been studied most extensively, work on nuclear weapons was also being pursued by the army, the navy, the Luftwaffe, the SS, the Reich Research Council, and even the Reich Postal Service. To these must be added several major German industrial enterprises. However, documentation concerning much of their activity ended up in Soviet archives.

In 2005, Rainer Karlsch published his groundbreaking book *Hitler's Atomic Bomb: The History of Secret German Nuclear Weapons Tests.*[1] In the introduction, he wrote:

> Parallel to our archival research, together with Heiko Petermann, we commissioned several institutes specializing in the detection of even the slightest traces of radioactivity to examine the area where nuclear tests were supposedly carried out and to collect soil samples for analysis. The research involved physicists under the direction of Prof. Arthur Scharmann of the Justus Liebig University in Giessen, Prof. of Radiochemistry Reinhard Brandt of the Philipps University in Marburg, and scientists from the Physikalisch-Technische Bundesanstalt in Brunswick, headed by experimental physicist Prof. Uwe Kayser. If nuclear explosions had indeed taken place in the presumed area, the concentrations of artificial isotopes such as cesium-137 and cobalt-60 in the collected samples should significantly exceed the normal values for the region. Later analyses also showed above-average levels of uranium-235 and lithium-6.[2]

Returning, however, to the research conducted at the beginning of the war, it is worth noting that Germany's early military successes did not encourage investment in the atomic bomb project. In the first weeks after the invasion of the Soviet Union, it seemed that the war would soon be won. Plans were even being made for a victory parade on Red Square. As a result, costly scientific research was scaled back.

It appeared that a fundamental shift in attitude within the highest circles of the Third Reich came at the end of 1941. The Wehrmacht, bogged down first in Russian mud, then in snow, meant German soldiers began to taste defeat. At the same time, in December of that year, Japan entered the war against the United States by attacking Pearl Harbor. In fulfilling his obligations, Hitler also declared war on the American colossus.

The rapid construction of an atomic bomb could have decided the war almost immediately in Germany's favour. However, both the German economy and its armed forces had been structured for a short war. With Japan and the

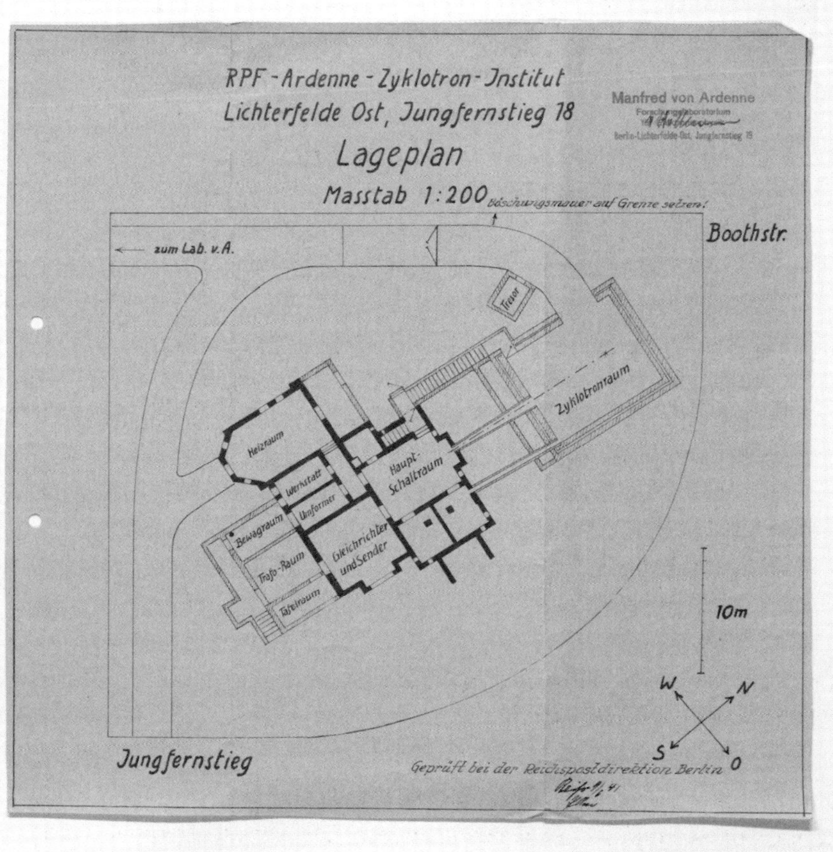

Plans for the construction of a bunker for the cyclotron at the von Ardenne Institute. (*Bundesarchiv, ref. R/4701/25895/0719*)

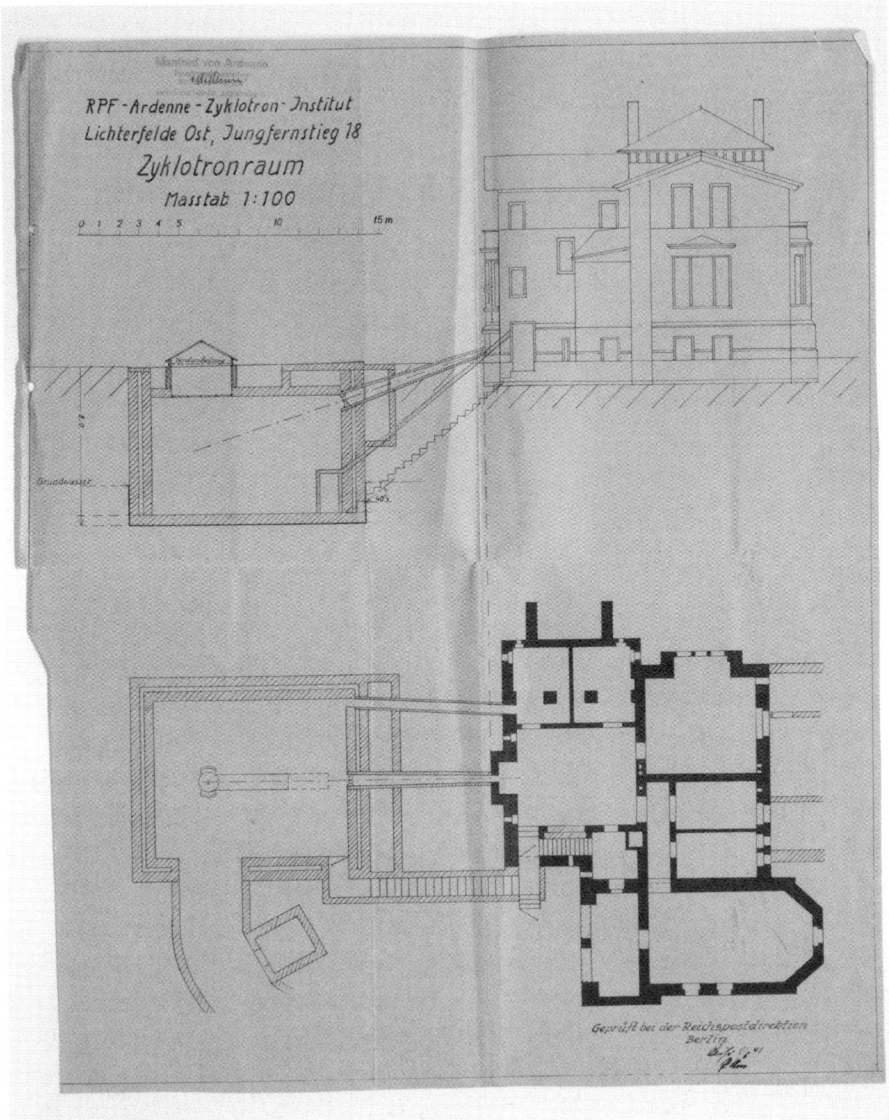

The visible difference in levels between the cyclotron bunker and the von Ardenne villa. (*Bundesarchiv, ref. R/4701/25895/0719*)

United States now involved, the conflict expanded into a truly global struggle – already the second in just a few decades. This forced a reorganisation of the war economy, which in turn brought significant changes to both industry and scientific research. The atomic programme was no exception.

The army, and later the Reich Postal Service, withdrew from further participation. Progress was further hampered by disputes among scientists from competing centres, as well as intrigues by high-ranking officials seeking to seize control of the project. Heinrich Himmler, leveraging his vast pool of cheap forced labour, factories, and access to scientists, sought to extend his influence. An alliance with Postal Minister Wilhelm Ohnesorge gave the SS access to valuable knowledge about the ongoing research. According to SS-Obergruppenführer Hoffmann, Himmler declared: 'It is difficult to say how long the war will last, and this will likely not be the last war. Future wars will certainly not begin with lengthy declarations or with air raids that can be detected in time. (...) Thanks to technological progress, charges will suddenly appear that will be so effective and so rapid that they will eclipse the explosives of our latest reprisal weapons.'[3]

The SS pursued the atomic programme both openly and clandestinely. Secret nuclear research facilities and production plants were established. One such facility operated in the uranium mine at Kowary in Lower Silesia. Others were located in Thuringia and Austria. Within the SS Main Command Office, a new branch called 'Office T' was created, headed by Waffen-SS Brigadier General Dr Otto Schwab, a physicist. However, due to difficulties in obtaining heavy water, the office's activity was severely limited.

Himmler sought to compensate for these failures in other ways. According to Karlsch, in November 1944, under SS supervision, the Ohrdruf proving ground was adapted for testing a special weapon. Such a test was reportedly conducted on 3 or 4 March 1945. A local resident of Ohrdruf, Clara Wehrer, claimed to have witnessed the event. She testified: 'I saw a fiery sphere, as bright as hundreds of lightning flashes. It was red in the centre and yellow on the outside. You could read a newspaper by its light. It all lasted very briefly, and then we could see nothing more. We only felt a powerful blast of air, and then everything became calm again.'[4]

Another witness allegedly assisted in the cremation of 700 prisoners from a Buchenwald subcamp located near the test site. However, death records point to the deaths of 'only' thirty-five people, not 700.

Himmler, it was said, was pleased with the outcome of the new weapon test. In the presence of a small circle of trusted men, and with a glass of champagne in hand, he delivered a short speech. His adjutant, Werner Grothmann, later recalled it as follows:

> When Himmler was later with us in a smaller group, he
> ordered champagne to be served and gave a short speech
> (...) I do not recall the exact words, but he said that the
> enormous amount of work and the incredible sacrifices
> made in recent years had finally brought the long-awaited
> result, and that the critics would soon be proven wrong
> when it all began (...) In any case, Himmler stressed
> that no one would be able to withstand this new weapon
> (...) German science, and with it all of us, had achieved
> something utterly impossible.

Both this speech and the words he once confided to his masseur, Felix Kersten, would suggest that Himmler still saw a chance for victory. Yet, as mentioned in an earlier chapter, at the very same time the SS chief was secretly conducting talks with the Allies regarding a ceasefire and a possible capitulation in the West. At no point did he mention the existence of such a deadly weapon – an omission that, had he raised it, might have made a profound impression.

Ultimately, the war ended before Germany was able to deploy its long-awaited *Wunderwaffe*; the atomic bomb. But was its use only a matter of time? Considering the sheer number of inventions and the pace of technological progress achieved by German scientists during the war, one might assume they were capable of producing and using an atomic weapon. Nonetheless, despite the passing decades, many aspects of the German atomic bomb project remain purely speculative.

In the final days of the war, the Allies launched an operation codenamed *Epsilon*. Its goal was to capture and intern the most prominent German scientists involved in the nuclear weapons project. Between 1 May and 30 June 1945, several researchers were apprehended and held at Farm Hall, a secluded facility in Godmanchester near Cambridge.

Among them were Erich Bagge, assistant at the Kaiser Wilhelm Institute in Berlin and collaborator of Werner Heisenberg; nuclear physicist Kurt Diebner, former head and administrator of the German Nuclear Programme and Heisenberg's rival; nuclear physicist Walter Gerlach; Otto Hahn, regarded as the father of the German nuclear programme, who in 1944 was awarded the Nobel Prize (collected in 1946); physicist Paul Harteck, author of numerous works in nuclear physics and chemistry; and Werner Heisenberg himself, Nobel laureate and Germany's leading nuclear physicist, who arguably did more harm than good to the project not by sabotage, but by leading it down blind alleys.

Also interned at Farm Hall were physicist Horst Korsching; Nobel Prize winner Max von Laue; Carl Friedrich von Weizsäcker, a specialist in X-ray physics; and the distinguished chemist and mathematician Karl Wirtz.

From the published transcripts of their conversations spoken in the belief that they might be under surveillance, though they could not be sure, it is clear that the scientists were deeply shaken by the news of the American atomic bombings of Hiroshima and Nagasaki.

Chapter 21

ODESSA – Truth or Myth?

Public interest in secret organisations of former SS men exploded after the 1972 publication of Frederick Forsyth's novel *The Odessa File*. Two years later, the book was adapted into a film, which further amplified the subject. Many began to wonder: did such an organisation really exist? And what if the truth turned out to be far more fascinating than fiction?

Organisation der ehemaligen SS-Angehörigen (Organisation of Former SS Members, or ODESSA) was allegedly created in late 1944 on the orders of Reichsführer-SS Heinrich Himmler. Its supposed goal was to transfer capital to South America, and, after the war, to smuggle SS members and leading Nazis out of Europe.

In recent years, however, more and more scholars have leaned toward the view that ODESSA never existed as a structured organisation. Instead, they argue, it was a myth, a useful cover story that masked the real networks of escape and support established after the war. These, in contrast, appear to have been carefully planned and meticulously executed.

Information that could help someone escape from Europe could be obtained in Rome and was passed on only in the strictest confidence. You had to be lucky or have the right connections to know where, and from whom, you could get it. The route to the Italian capital led through the Alps. The first stopover was South Tyrol and specifically, the monastery of the German Teutonic Order in Merano, followed by the Capuchin monastery near Brixen and the Franciscan monastery near Bolzano. Some Nazis tried to cross this path alone, while others relied on hastily specialised guides who, for a fee, pointed out safe trails. These escape routes became known as the 'ratlines' or sometimes the 'monastery road'.

Upon reaching Rome, fugitives were to go to the seminary for German-speaking clergy, Santa Maria dell'Anima, near Piazza Navona. There, the rector of the institution, His Excellency Bishop Alois Hudal, awaited them. The clergyman was born on 31 May 1885, in Graz, and had been ordained a priest in 1908 and served as a chaplain during the First World War. In 1923 he became rector of the Roman theological college *Collegio Teutonico di Santa Maria dell'Anima*, and received episcopal consecration in 1933.

Three years later, he published a controversial work titled *Foundations of National Socialism*. Pope Pius XI intended to place this Hitler-dedicated book on the Index of Forbidden Books, but this was prevented by the Secretary of State, Eugenio Pacelli. Despite Hudal's attempt to curry favour with the Nazis, the publication did not gain approval in Germany. Chief Nazi ideologue Alfred Rosenberg particularly condemned it, claiming it was an attempt to subordinate National Socialism to the Church. The book was officially banned in Germany, and after the *Anschluss* in 1938, it disappeared there as well.

After the war, Hudal began extensive efforts to aid Germans fleeing Europe. Those who reached him could count on receiving new identity documents, passports, and even support in purchasing tickets for ships bound for South America. He himself described this activity in his memoirs: 'After 1945, all my charitable work was aimed at helping former members of the National Socialist and Fascist parties, especially the so-called war criminals (...) subject to persecution, who were often completely innocent. (...) Thanks to false documents, I saved many of them. They could slip away from their persecutors and escape to happier countries.'[1]

On 31 August 1948, the bishop wrote to Argentine President Juan Perón requesting 5,000 visas for German and Austrian 'soldiers' who had defended Europe against 'Soviet domination'. Due to pressure from other bishops, in 1952 Hudal was forced to resign as rector of Santa Maria dell'Anima and withdraw from active church life. He settled in Grottaferrata near Rome and devoted himself to writing his memoirs, which were published posthumously in 1976.

It should be noted, however, that upon arriving in Rome, many Germans often had no idea what their next step should be. They moved about blindly, asking questions of other Germans then living in Rome. Such was the case with Franz Stangl, who inquired about the possibility of escaping the continent.

Once the necessary documents, ship tickets, and some start-up money were secured, fugitives usually went to the port of Genoa, from where they sailed to South America.

While ODESSA proved to be a fictional creation deeply rooted in popular culture and in the minds of those hungry for sensational stories, the existence of the organisation *Stille Hilfe* was entirely real. What is more, it was informally headed by Gudrun Burwitz, daughter of Heinrich Himmler himself. *Stille Hilfe für Kriegsgefangene und Internierte* (Silent Help for Prisoners of War and Interned Persons), as the group was formally known, was founded in 1946 by Princess Helene Elisabeth von Isenburg. However, it only began operating legally in 1951. Its registration allowed it to organise fundraising campaigns, which were then used to rescue and support Nazis threatened with imprisonment, and later to provide care for them in old age after their release from prison.

Another organisation dedicated to supporting former SS comrades was *Hilfsgemeinschaft auf Gegenseitigkeit der Angehörigen der ehemaligen Waffen-SS* (HIAG) (Mutual Aid Association of Former Waffen-SS Members). This structure was founded in 1951 on the basis of the *Notgemeinschaft* organisation, which had been active for two years.

Among HIAG's founders were:

- SS-Oberstgruppenführer and Colonel General of the Waffen-SS Josef 'Sepp' Dietrich
- SS-Obergruppenführer Gottlob Christian Berger, chief SS racial selection expert, head of the SS Main Office, and one of the creators of the Waffen-SS concept
- SS-Gruppenführer Heinz Lammerding, commander of the 2nd SS Panzer Division *Das Reich*, responsible for the massacre of civilians in Tulle and Oradour-sur-Glane
- SS-Obergruppenführer and General of the Waffen-SS Herbert Otto Gille, commander of the 5th SS Panzer Division *Wiking*.

HIAG members organised aid for their former comrades-in-arms, many of whom, deprived of pension rights, fell into extreme poverty. The association also engaged in informational and propaganda activities. Under its patronage, journals such as the monthly *Der Freiwillige* and numerous books were published, glorifying SS formations.[2]

At the height of its influence, HIAG gathered as many as 70,000 members, all former Waffen-SS soldiers. However, public hostility toward its activities grew steadily, ultimately leading to its dissolution in 1992.

Chapter 22

The Mystery of Adolf Hitler's and Eva Braun's Deaths

The mystery of Adolf Hitler's and Eva Braun's final moments occupied newspaper front pages for many years. Practically to this day, speculation continues about their possible escape from the Berlin bunker and eventual flight to South America. After 1945, at least several hundred articles, dozens of books, and just as many documentaries attempted to prove that a safe exit from the shelter and escape to a distant location was possible. These insinuations were repeatedly advanced by the Russians, who claimed Hitler must have fled Berlin since his body was never conclusively found.

But what is the truth? Can we, once and for all, cut through the speculation and, relying solely on facts, answer the question about the fate of Hitler and his alleged wife in the final days of the Third Reich? Let us begin with how the last two days inside Hitler's bunker unfolded.

Sunday, 29 April was yet another regular day in the Führerbunker. No one expected Hitler to change his mind and decide to leave the shelter. That decision had already been made irrevocably. But there was another 'irrevocable' decision he had long proclaimed: that he would never marry. As he so often said, driving German women into rapture, he was 'married to Germania' and would remain faithful to her until the end of his days.

So why, on the day before his death, did he marry the woman who had faithfully stood by his side, living in his shadow, for fourteen years?

Eva Braun had always been hidden from the public eye. The German people, especially German women, were never to know of her existence. During visits by foreign diplomats to the grand Berghof residence, she had to remain locked in her room, peeking only through the curtains at what was happening outside. Maintaining this secrecy was of utmost importance.

136

Adolf Hitler and Eva Braun at the Berghof, the Führer's Alpine residence in Bavaria. (*Bundesarchiv, B 145 Bild-F051673-0059/CC-BY-SA*)

Did Hitler, by deciding to marry her, wish to compensate Eva for those years of humiliation? Shopping trips to foreign designers, especially Italian ones, certainly were not enough for her.

That day in late April, from the early morning, she began her preparations. Her personal maid, Liesl Ostertag, arranged her hair, fastening in it a barrette designed by Albert Speer with the monogram 'EB' shaped like a four-leaf clover. She wore little makeup, as her chosen one preferred her to look natural. She put on a long black silk-taffeta gown, complemented by her favourite diamond-studded watch, a gold bracelet set with pink tourmalines, a topaz necklace, and black suede shoes by the Italian designer Ferragamo.

While Eva Braun was selecting her outfit, Adolf Hitler remained in the conference room. There, he dictated his final reflections and orders to his secretary, Traudl Junge. He also dictated his personal will, as well as his 'political' testament: 'Together with my wife, I choose death in order to avoid the disgrace of overthrow and capitulation. I desire that our bodies be immediately burned at the place where I carried out the greatest part of my daily work in twelve years of service to the nation.'

'My heart pounded in my chest as I wrote down what Hitler was saying,' Junge later recalled after the war, while Hitler continued in a calm, almost monotonous tone, stripped of the former magnetism with which he had once enthralled thousands of Germans during his speeches:

> It is not true that either I or anyone else in Germany wanted war in 1939. This war was desired and incited exclusively by those international statesmen who had Jewish origins or who worked for Jewish interests. I made too many proposals for disarmament, proposals which future generations will not be able to deny for centuries, for anyone to place responsibility for the outbreak of this war on me.
>
> I also have no doubt that as soon as the nations of Europe are once again treated as nothing more than shares of stock by those conspirators of international finance, the people who will be held jointly responsible will be precisely the ones who are the true culprits of this murderous struggle: the Jews!
>
> I shall not fall into the hands of enemies who wish to stage a new spectacle, organised by the Jews, for the amusement of hysterical masses. Therefore, I have decided to remain in Berlin and to choose voluntary death at the moment when I realise that the Führer's residence and the Chancellery can no longer be defended.

It is clear that until the very end, Hitler blamed the Jews, whom he claimed dominated international finance, for starting the war. He also foreshadowed his own end, stating for the last time that he intended to give his life in the struggle.

In the latter part of the document, he appointed Grand Admiral Karl Dönitz as his successor and the new Führer. The head of the Luftwaffe, Reichsmarschall Hermann Göring, and the Reichsführer-SS Heinrich Himmler were formally expelled from the party and stripped of their positions, once it became known that they had secretly attempted to negotiate peace with the Allies.

In one of the rooms of the bunker, the wedding guests were already waiting. Walter Wagner, an official from the ministry run by the crippled Goebbels, had been brought in. Shortly after performing the ceremony, he would die on the streets of Berlin as a member of the *Volkssturm*. The reception resembled more a wake than a wedding feast. No one wished the young couple happiness or good fortune on their new path in life, for that path simply did not exist. From time to time, Hitler would leave the room to confer with Bormann and Goebbels.

Interestingly, however, not everyone present in the bunker confirmed that the wedding had taken place. Pilot Hanna Reitsch and Field Marshal Robert Ritter von Greim, appointed as Göring's successor, both claimed after the war that no marriage ceremony ever occurred. Upon leaving the shelter, Reitsch received letters from Eva Braun, which she proceeded to tear up. According to historian Hugh Thomas, Reitsch may have been jealous and angry that Hitler had lowered himself to a relationship with such a simple woman as Eva Braun.[1]

Over the next several hours, Hitler held a few short conferences and dictated a letter to Field Marshal Wilhelm Keitel, in which he explained that it was Germany's duty to secure *Lebensraum* in the East. He also said farewell to the women who remained in the bunker. He finally gave permission to dispatch couriers to General Wenck, who was supposed to come to Berlin's relief. This was the last fragile hope to which those still in the bunker desperately clung. Yet General Wenck was still far away. Even if he had moved with all his meagre forces, it was doubtful he could have reached Hitler, let alone effectively resisted the Soviet onslaught.

Thus passed the final hours in the life of the Chancellor and Führer of the Third Reich. The next morning, 30 April, Hitler rose, shaved, and dressed carefully. His hands were trembling more than ever, but he knew this condition would torment him for only a few more hours. He had resolved to take his own life at precisely 3:00 pm. Summoning his ever-present shadow of recent years, Martin Bormann, along with his adjutant Major Otto Günsche, he informed them of his final decision. Günsche was to ensure that the suicide attempt would succeed. If anything went wrong, the adjutant was to enter the room and deliver the coup de grâce, then secure gasoline to burn the bodies of both Hitler and Eva Braun. 'I do not want my corpse to be displayed to the public in some future sideshow,' he declared.

After the meeting, the Führer once again walked down the main corridor, bidding farewell to his fellow sufferers. A sobbing Magda Goebbels, the wife of the propaganda minister, begged him not to end his life. For many years she had lived only for him, and with his death, her own existence lost all meaning. Soon after Hitler's suicide, she gave poison to her own children and, together with her husband, followed in the footsteps of her beloved Führer. Hitler, however, remained unmoved, reconciled with his fate.

He and Eva Braun then entered the small study, its walls covered in white and green tiles. They sat down on a narrow sofa. Eva slipped off her shoes while Hitler glanced at the portrait of his mother and the painting of Frederick the Great hanging opposite. Almost simultaneously, they took from their brass cases the glass phials of poison previously tested on Hitler's beloved German shepherd, Blondi. Eva rested her head on her husband's shoulder and bit through her capsule, her knees jerking upward in death's convulsion. At the same moment, Hitler bit down on his own capsule while pressing the trigger of his Walther pistol against his temple. Or perhaps, as some 'witnesses' later suggested, he had placed the barrel into his mouth? Either way, for a man afflicted with advanced Parkinson's disease, both were acts of extreme difficulty.

The British historian Hugh Trevor-Roper, writing on assignment for British intelligence, described the events following the fatal shot: 'A single shot was heard. A moment later, those nearby entered the room. Hitler was lying on a sofa spattered with blood. He had shot himself in the mouth. On the couch beside him lay Eva Braun, also dead. At her side rested a revolver, but it had not been used; she had died from swallowing poison. This took place at half past three.'[2]

What, then, became of Hitler's and Eva Braun's bodies? In this matter we must rely solely on the testimonies of those who were present in the bunker. In his account, Trevor-Roper concluded that anyone who undertakes this kind of investigation soon comes to realise one crucial truth: 'how utterly worthless eyewitness testimony can be.' By penning that statement, the British agent was attempting to mask certain shortcomings in his book. Yet in the case of Hitler's death, this observation proves to be exceptionally accurate, just as it does when analysing the final moments of Heinrich Himmler's life, as discussed earlier.

The Germans who testified after the war generally altered their stories multiple times. Those captured by the Soviets had the chance, after their release, to study the testimonies already published and adjust their own accounts accordingly. Few had any real interest in disclosing the full truth. Some, by contrast, were eager to cast themselves in the role of key witnesses, claiming knowledge of every detail – a strategy that all but guaranteed their memoirs would sell well. Others, however, sought to downplay their involvement altogether, avoiding testimony whenever possible, or, when compelled, entangling their stories in contradictions until they ceased to make sense.

Untangling this web of truth, lies, and countless half-truths can be compared to cleansing the mythical Augean stables. The task was made no easier by the Soviets who, led by Stalin, insisted they had never found Hitler's body and continuously accused their Western allies of either letting him escape or concealing the truth. In Stalin's narrative, the Führer had revealed himself to be a coward who fled Berlin while condemning his own people to a fight to the death. Facts were irrelevant when propaganda demanded proof of one's version of events, while investigations were subordinated to justifying attacks on the Americans and British, regardless of whether the conclusions bore any resemblance to reality.

In one of his testimonies, Heinz Linge, who claimed to be the first person to see Hitler's corpse, recalled that he slowly opened the door. Overwhelmed by strong fumes, he had to squint his eyes. As he began to choke, he stepped back and shut the door, bolting it. Then he went to fetch Bormann. 'To be honest, I was shaking all over. I simply didn't have the courage to go in there alone it was too overwhelming,' he later recounted.[3]

According to other witnesses, Bormann, together with the Hitler Youth leader, Artur Axmann and Günsche, stood by the door, straining to hear sounds from the room where their leader had locked himself away. They then entered together – although some accounts claim Axmann joined slightly later – only to find the space still thick with the acrid stench of prussic acid.

By contrast, Hitler's personal pilot, Hans Baur, stated that he had already been inside the room for some time. Apparently, he alone seemed unaffected by the irritating fumes.

Linge went on to describe his observations as follows:

On his [Hitler's] right temple there was a small hole about the size of a silver Reichsmark, with a thin trickle of blood running down his cheek. He was dressed in the uniform I had carefully prepared for him just a few hours earlier. The uniform was only slightly wrinkled. One pistol – a 7.65 calibre Walther – lay on the floor where Hitler had dropped it from his hand. About a metre away lay another pistol, a 6.35 calibre.

The body of Eva Braun, the only woman who had ever truly mattered in Hitler's life from the time I had known him, was lying beside my master. I believe she had died a few minutes before the Führer, whose wish it had been that they die together, just as they had spent so many years of life together. There were no marks on Eva Braun's face; she seemed merely to be asleep. She had swallowed a capsule of poison, one of a dozen given to Hitler by a military physician for just such circumstances. These capsules had been intended for the women assigned to his staff and for Dr Goebbels' wife, but above all, they had been meant for Eva Braun.

Linge's account was supplemented with further details by Major Günsche:

A small Dresden vase, in which earlier that morning a bouquet of hothouse tulips and white narcissi had been placed, had fallen over, spilling water onto Eva Braun's blue chiffon dress just above the hip. The vase rolled onto the carpet without breaking. Linge, the faithful valet, picked it up, checked that it was not cracked, gathered the scattered flowers, and placed them back into the vase, which he set once again on the table. At least two minutes – two long minutes – passed before any of us could say a word; we simply watched what Linge was doing with the white vase.

As can be seen, both accounts left by the SS men contain virtually no substantive detail. The descriptions of the overturned vase, the gathering of flowers, and Eva Braun resting on Hitler's shoulder seem intended to lend a kind of romantic aura to the scene, one entirely at odds with reality. Both men claimed Hitler shot himself in the temple, yet neither noticed an exit wound. Axmann and Kempka, an SS-Obersturmbannführer who, from 1934, served as Adolf Hitler's personal driver and head of his motor pool, who were said to have inspected the body, insisted instead that Hitler shot himself in the mouth. They, too, however, failed to note any exit wound or blood spattered across the wall, something that would have been inevitable in the case of a gunshot to the head.

For this reason, the oft-repeated claim that Hitler simultaneously bit down on a poison capsule while firing a shot seems inconsistent with the facts. In 1968, Lev Bezymenski announced that fragments of glass had been found in Hitler's remains. In doing so, he publicly admitted that the Soviets had indeed recovered his body and had 'taken care' of it accordingly.

The revelation of information about the fragments of glass found in Hitler's remains profoundly altered what had previously been believed about the Führer's death. Few still raised the question of a gunshot to the temple or the mouth; instead, explanations emerged to argue that taking poison in no way diminished his honour. Once again, witnesses' testimonies were reshaped to fit the prevailing narrative. Western historians continued to select those accounts most convenient for their purposes, tailoring them to match their adopted theories.

Amid all this confusion, the attitude of Hitler's chief of security, Johann Rattenhuber, was particularly striking. He did not believe in the suicide theory, and it took considerable effort to persuade him otherwise. After all, the ingestion of potassium cyanide would not have left two corpses serenely seated on a sofa, Eva resting her blonde head on her lover's shoulder, frozen in peace. Cyanide poisoning causes violent convulsions, facial contortions, foaming at the mouth, and the bitter-almond stench of escaping gas.

Could it be, then, that these contradictory testimonies were meant to conceal the fact that someone helped Hitler across the threshold of death? That a third party crushed the capsule in his mouth and then arranged the body so that nothing appeared suspicious, creating a death scene more reminiscent of a frame from a romantic film? Over eighty years later, this idea remains shocking to many.

After their deaths, Hitler's body, wrapped in a thin blanket, was carried outside. The same was done with Eva Braun's body, dressed in a blue dress. After being released from Soviet captivity, Heinz Linge altered his testimony once again, this time claiming that Eva Braun's body had been covered with a second 'thick blanket'. Where this blanket suddenly came from remains unclear. If we accept its existence as true, perhaps it was the very coverlet Eva had used to drape over her legs just before her suicide. But was that really the case?

The corpses, carried into the garden of the Reich Chancellery, already scarred with numerous bomb craters, were placed side by side, faces upward, in a previously dug pit. Most likely, one of the existing craters had simply been widened. It seems doubtful that anyone, with shells still whistling overhead, would have risked their life to dig a completely new grave. For the sake of safety, the location was chosen close to the bunker's entrance. The bodies were then set on fire, doused with gasoline that had been procured for the purpose. Hitler's driver Erich Kempka, after returning from captivity, claimed that 180 litres of fuel were used for the cremation, poured gradually to ensure proper burning. By 6:00 pm, the process of adding gasoline was stopped.

Eva Braun's once slender body, according to Linge, bent in half under the effect of rigor mortis, but now sat upright, 'as if riding a horse'. Both arms were stretched out before her, as though she were holding invisible reins. The claim about Eva Braun's rigor mortis, however, seems highly dubious. At other times, Linge insisted that the bodies had burned completely, leaving only small fragments behind.

Before midnight, Rattenhuber ordered three SS men, led by Harry Mengershausen, to bury the bodies. Another crater was widened, into which the charred remains were dragged. Günsche, on the other hand, testified that nothing of Eva remained except ashes, which were collected into a box. The remains were then supposedly covered with rubble, while the edges of the crater were camouflaged, though rather poorly.

It is worth pausing to consider the conditions necessary for cremating human bodies. Today, cremation requires 50-60 minutes, with the body exposed to a temperature of around 800°C. Afterwards, the remains must be cooled before further handling. To achieve such a temperature, far more than 180 litres of gasoline would be needed.

So, what is the truth about Hitler's death? As has become clear, virtually none of the testimonies conveys the full reality. The repeatedly altered and embellished accounts served disinformation more than clarification. If Hitler did not shoot himself in the temple or mouth, and if he did not ingest poison by his own hand, then what happened? What was the true cause of his death? If we eliminate the versions involving poison and a gunshot, what remains? The answer seems simple.

In the final hours before Hitler's death was announced, while he was still alive, the atmosphere in the bunker was tense. Nervousness consumed everyone. Most were concerned with their own survival, as the Soviet encirclement tightened. Yet no one could decide to attempt escape while Hitler still lived. Thus, three possibilities remained: wait passively for the Soviets to storm the bunker, wait for Hitler to commit suicide, or murder him.

The first option was virtually unthinkable. No one intended to sit idly and hand themselves over to the Soviets, whose actions could not be predicted. Waiting for Hitler's suicide could amount to the same if he never acted, the Soviets would arrive first. After all, even for Hitler, taking one's own life required great resolve.

That left the third, most logical option: Hitler's closest associates helped him depart this world, thereby increasing their own chances of escape.

The individual most likely to have committed the act was Heinz Linge, who was closest to Hitler at the moment of the supposed suicide. As he himself claimed, he was the first to enter the lounge where Hitler and Eva Braun were. After a gunshot was fired, he could have placed a cyanide capsule into Hitler's mouth, crushed it, and then stepped out, locking the door behind him before summoning Bormann. Later, the group entered together.

Chief of security Johann Rattenhuber, who had not been informed of any such plan, reportedly shouted through the bunker after learning of his leader's death: 'They killed Hitler!' He was eventually calmed down with the official story of suicide. Initially sceptical, he ultimately accepted – or at least publicly endorsed – that version, perhaps out of fear for his own life.

But what about Eva Braun? Did she truly commit suicide? Or was she, too, murdered?

The official testimonies of those who entered the room where Hitler and Eva Braun were said to have committed suicide consistently state that Eva ingested poison. For safety, however, she also had a small pistol within reach. All witnesses claimed that Eva was seated with her head resting on the shoulder of her lifelong partner, her legs tucked up. Yet one must ask: what does a body look like after ingesting potassium cyanide? Almost immediately after the substance enters the body, hydrogen cyanide is released, leading to tissue hypoxia. Within seconds, the victim loses consciousness and dies. The body usually twists into unnatural positions, saliva flowing from the mouth. Nothing of the kind was observed in Eva Braun's remains. In fact, it was noted that she appeared almost as if she were peacefully asleep.

Hugh Thomas suggested that Eva Braun may have attempted suicide earlier by cutting her veins. She was then supposedly discovered in time and moved to a different location. Later, after Hitler's murder, the body of another woman – dressed in Eva Braun's blue gown – was brought in from outside. During the removal of the bodies to the surface, which was done in front of witnesses, most of her body, including her head, was covered with a blanket. The only thing visible to observers was the blue dress; a flimsy basis on which to confirm that the body was Braun's. Meanwhile, other details point towards the likelihood that the corpse was not hers at all.

When the Red Army discovered the bodies, one was completely burned, the other only slightly charred. Inside the woman's body, they found a cyanide capsule. At a temperature of about 180°C, such a capsule should have melted, but it had not. This can only mean it was planted and crushed after the fire had already gone out. Was someone concerned that a melted capsule would leave no trace of suicide? This was not the only mystery.

In the corpse they also found a new, undamaged dental bridge allegedly belonging to Braun. Her dentist testified that two bridges had been made for her, but only one had ever been used and that the second was unnecessary. The unused bridge, perfectly intact, had simply been inserted loosely into the mouth of the corpse. This suggests it, too, had been planted, to increase the likelihood of identifying the body as Eva Braun's. Evidence also showed that the woman had bled: she had suffered a severe shrapnel wound and been burned. The injury was clearly visible.

Dental examination revealed cavities. It is difficult to imagine that the unofficial First Lady of the Third Reich would have had untreated tooth decay. All of this suggests that the body attributed to Eva Braun was not hers. So what became of the real Eva Braun? That question remains unanswered.

Most likely, under pressure from Moscow, Soviet troops, eager to satisfy Stalin's demands, reported that they had found Eva Braun's body by substituting the remains of another woman discovered near the bunker entrance, a woman killed by artillery fire. Eva Braun's real corpse would no longer have shown signs of bleeding.

The most probable scenario, supported by blood traces found on the sofa and bed in her room, is that Eva Braun committed suicide by slitting the veins of her right arm. Although she was liked within Hitler's inner circle, her burial was not carefully attended to. Most likely, her body was placed in one of the nearest shell craters in the garden of the Reich Chancellery. Once Hitler had been murdered – a fact known only to a select few – the priority was to escape from the bunker before the Soviets arrived.

When Soviet troops took control of the site, they dug through the grounds in search of Hitler's and Braun's bodies. What they found, they hastily and uncritically identified as the burned remains of the pair. These bodies were later reburied in an unmarked site in the forest near Rathenow, about 60 km (37 miles) from Potsdam. Finally, in 1970, Yuri Andropov, then head of the KGB, ordered the exhumation, cremation, and scattering of the ashes of Adolf Hitler and Eva Braun into a German river.

Chapter 23

Where Is Bormann?

Martin Bormann was probably the most hated man in Hitler's inner circle. Ever since Rudolf Hess's solo flight to Britain in May 1941, he had practically taken full control over access to the Führer. Hitler valued him for the fact that, as he often said, even the most complex matters could be summarised by Bormann in just a few simple words. With the overwhelming number of issues Hitler had to handle, this was certainly a significant advantage.

But let us go back to the beginning. Martin Bormann was born on 17 June 1900, in Wegeleben. His parents were Theodor Bormann, a postal worker, and his second wife, Antonie Bernhardine Mennong. Young Martin studied at an agricultural school, but interrupted his education in June 1918 to take part in the war, where he served as a gunner in the 55th Field Artillery Regiment. His dreams of fighting, however, never came true. Until February 1919, he remained stationed in the garrison before returning to civilian life and becoming the manager of a large, landed estate in Mecklenburg.

In 1922, he joined the Freikorps unit commanded by Gerhard Roßbach, where he served as head of a section and treasurer. On 17 March 1924, Bormann was convicted for participating in the murder of Walter Kadow and sentenced to one year in prison. He served his sentence in Elisabethstrasse Prison, which he left in February of the following year. Immediately after regaining freedom, he joined the *Frontbann*, a paramilitary organisation of the Nazi Party created to replace the *Sturmabteilung* (SA), which had been disbanded following the failed Beer Hall Putsch in Munich.

In May 1926, Bormann moved with his mother to Oberweimar. A year later, he joined the NSDAP, a natural consequence of his political choices up to that point, and received party membership card number 60,508. Years later, on 1 January 1937, he also entered the SS, which was systematically being transformed into an elite order. His membership number was initially 278,267, but in 1938, on Himmler's orders, it was changed to 555, a number more fitting for a so-called 'Old Fighter'.

Martin Bormann (1900-1945?) was an honorary SS officer with the rank of SS-Obergruppenführer. As the head of the NSDAP Chancellery, he was also the Führer's secretary, Reichsleiter, and one of the principal leaders of the Third Reich. (*Bundesarchiv, Bild 183-R14128A/CC-BY-SA 3.0*)

At first, within the Party, Bormann sought to serve as a regional press spokesman, but he lacked talent as an orator. Instead, he applied his organisational skills as a commercial manager. In October 1928 he moved to Munich, where the NSDAP headquarters were located, and dealt with insurance policies for SA members. Soon he created a relief fund, for which every Party member was obliged to pay dues, in return for which they could receive compensation for injuries sustained while carrying out Party activities, mainly involving brawls with communists. Payments from the fund, however, were made solely at Bormann's discretion.

After the NSDAP seized power in 1933, Bormann abandoned management of the fund and successfully applied for the post of chief of staff in the office of Hitler's deputy, Rudolf Hess, becoming Hess's personal secretary; a post he held until 1941. On 10 October 1933, Hitler appointed Bormann a *Reichsleiter* of the NSDAP. The following month, he became a deputy in the Reichstag.

From 1935 onwards, Bormann oversaw the expansion of Hitler's estate at Obersalzberg. He ordered the construction of SS barracks, roads and walkways, garages, guesthouses, staff quarters, and other amenities. He also commissioned the construction of the *Kehlsteinhaus* (Eagle's Nest), a teahouse built high above the Berghof as a fiftieth birthday present for Hitler. The building still stands today.

Step by step, Bormann won Hitler's increasing trust, which he used to cut off other Nazis, including his immediate superior, Rudolf Hess, from access to the Führer. Hitler even entrusted Bormann with his personal financial affairs. On 12 May 1941, abolishing the office of Deputy Führer, Hitler transferred Hess's former duties to Bormann, granting him the title of *Parteikanzlei* (Chief of the Party Chancellery).

Additionally, on 29 May Bormann replaced Hess on the six-man Reich Defence Council, which functioned as a kind of war cabinet. Hitler became practically dependent on his secretary. When Hitler moved permanently into the bunker beneath the Reich Chancellery in early 1945, Bormann moved in with him. On 29 April, he was named executor of Hitler's political testament. He was also to serve as a witness at the marriage ceremony with Eva Braun. However, much evidence suggests that the ceremony may never have actually taken place, and that the story was fabricated by those who had a hand in Hitler's death (see Chapter 22).

Martin Bormann, together with several others, left the bunker on the night of 1/2 May 1945. The group soon split, and he remained with SS doctor Ludwig Stumpfegger. From this point on, all trace of him disappears.

Artur Axmann, leader of the Hitler Youth, who was in the first group of escapees, testified that on Invalidenstrasse, north of the River Spree, he stumbled upon the bodies of Bormann and the SS doctor. Seeing no visible wounds, he assumed they had committed suicide. Axmann had no doubt that one of the corpses was that of the head of the NSDAP Chancellery. Another escapee, Erich Kempka, claimed that when he and Bormann were near a damaged tank, an explosion occurred. He himself lost consciousness, and when he awoke, Bormann was nowhere to be found. Since he could not find a body, he assumed that Bormann had perished in the blast.[1]

State funeral of Colonel Werner Mölders, Inspector of Fighter Aviation, who was killed in a crash near Wrocław on 22 November 1941. In the centre, next to Adolf Hitler, is the head of the Reich Chancellery, SS-Obergruppenführer Martin Bormann. (*Bundesarchiv, Bild 183-H0422-0502-001/CC-BY-SA 3.0*)

The absence of a body quickly gave rise to theories that Hitler's secretary had survived the war and had fled Germany. But where to? Here, accounts diverged wildly: Argentina, Italy, Spain, Africa or even a secret base in Antarctica! It is worth noting that searches were carried out at the supposed site of Bormann's death, but they yielded no results.

Then, in December 1972, the post office near Berlin's Lehrter station ordered repairs to underground telephone cables. On 7 December, workers digging in the area near the earlier search site discovered two male skeletons. One measured 190 cm in length, the other 168 cm. It was the latter that was believed to be Bormann. Identification was made through dental evidence by his dentist, Fritz Echtmann, who recognised a gold bridge he had fitted in 1942. Between the teeth, fragments of glass from a poison ampoule were also reportedly found.

On 4 April 1973, a Frankfurt prosecutor, relying on the dental expertise of Reidar Sognnaes, officially declared Bormann dead. His remains were handed over to the family, but with the stipulation that they were not to be cremated. The authorities wanted to preserve them for possible future testing.

In 1998, Dr Wolfgang Eisenmenger of the Institute of Forensic Medicine in Munich carried out DNA testing, which conclusively confirmed that the bones were indeed those of Martin Bormann. Only then were the remains cremated at a facility in Bavaria, and the ashes scattered in Kiel Bay, beyond German territorial waters.

Naturally, the announcement that Bormann's skeleton had been found did not convince all proponents of conspiracy theories. Periodically, claims still surfaced that Hitler's secretary had been spotted in England or Argentina. Some even speculated that he had been in Moscow, working as a KGB operative.

Bormann had long been suspected of being in the service of Soviet intelligence throughout the war. According to journalist Louis Kilzer, he allegedly operated under the codename 'Werther' and leaked vital information, including details of the German offensive at the Kursk Salient. Such insinuations were echoed by Reinhard Gehlen, who, during the war, commanded *Fremde Heere Ost* (Foreign Armies East), and who after 1945 became the founder and first director of West Germany's intelligence service, initially organised as the so-called Gehlen Organisation and later as the *Bundesnachrichtendienst* (Federal Intelligence Service).

And yet, despite careful analysis suggesting that only Bormann fit all the conditions to be identified as the legendary agent 'Werther', Gehlen's hypothesis failed to convince many sceptics.

Chapter 24

How 'Amerika' Became 'Brandenburg'

During the Second World War, the Führer of the Third Reich had numerous headquarters, including several on the territory of present-day Poland. Yet one of them stood out significantly: Hitler's special train (*Führersonderzug*), known as *Amerika*.

As early as 1933, Hitler ordered the construction of several specially designed railway cars intended for the highest-ranking state and military officials. By the outbreak of the war, at least six such special trains were in service.

The ministerial trains (*Ministerzug*) included: *Asien* – Göring's; *Afrika* – Field Marshal Wilhelm Keitel's; *Heinrich* – Reichsführer-SS Heinrich Himmler's; *Westfalen* – Foreign Minister Joachim von Ribbentrop's; and *Atlas* – two staff trains of the Wehrmacht High Command. Once the war began, additional staff trains were organised for the different branches of the armed forces: for the OKH (*Ostpreussen, Sachsen, Schwaben, Würtenberg*); for the Luftwaffe (*Pommern* I and II, *Robinson* I and II, *Rheinland* I and II, *Enzian*); and for the Kriegsmarine (*Atlantik*).

The most information, however, has survived about Hitler's personal train, *Amerika*. Although its configuration changed depending on circumstances, the core composition remained fairly constant. It consisted of two locomotives (BR 50 or BR 52), followed immediately by an armoured flak wagon armed with two anti-aircraft guns, then a baggage car, one of which could house a diesel generator. Next came Hitler's personal coach, where history itself was shaped. Following it was the command coach with a conference room, a telephone and telex exchange (connected to rail networks when stationary), and a radio station. On special occasions, an additional communications coach was attached, equipped with its own power generator, a Telefunken S 406 shortwave transmitter (200-400 watts), and cipher machines.

Joachim von Ribbentrop and Adolf Hitler in front of the special train *Amerika*. (*Public domain*)

Further down were the security coach for *Reichssicherheitsdienst* (RSD) officers, two dining cars (one for dignitaries and officers, the other for staff and guards), two guest coaches, a bathing car, two sleeping coaches for members of the Führer's escort battalion (*Führerbegleitbataillon*), and finally, the press car.

The wagons of Hitler's special train were built by three firms: Wegmann & Co. of Kassel, Gebrüder Credé of Kassel-Niederzwehren, and Linke-Hoffmann of Breslau (now Wrocław). Interior fittings were designed in Munich. Each coach was equipped with air conditioning, remarkable for the time, and armed with 20 mm, later 30 mm, steel plates to protect passengers from shrapnel, aircraft fire, or small arms fire.

The 340-metre-long train could accommodate 141 people, including crew, senior officers, communications staff, and flak gunners. During station stops, the train was guarded by *Bahnschutz* (railway police). Hitler's personal guard included a detachment of twenty-two men from his escort battalion (FBB) and an SS unit. Along the tracks, soldiers were posted every 100 metres. Train operators were warned hours in advance of its approach, while stations were informed only at the last possible moment.

Wherever Hitler travelled, his armoured car and personal aircraft, a Focke-Wulf 200 *Immelmann 3* followed, allowing him to quickly switch to a bunker or front-line headquarters if necessary.

In 1941, the train's name was changed from *Amerika* to *Brandenburg,* after Germany declared war on the United States. With the completion of the *Wolfsschanze* (Wolf's Lair) headquarters in East Prussia, the train ceased to serve as Hitler's mobile command centre and instead became primarily a means of transport.

Between 1940 and 1941, Hitler hosted key meetings aboard the *Amerika* coach, including with figures such as Vichy premier Pierre Laval, Marshal Philippe Pétain, Spanish dictator Francisco Franco, and Italian Duce Benito Mussolini. From 12-25 April 1941, while stationed at Mönichkirchen, near Vienna, Hitler directed the invasions of Yugoslavia and Greece (Operation *Marita*) from his train – its last function as a true command centre.

On 7 May 1945, after Germany's surrender, Hitler's train stood at the small Austrian station of Mallnitz, guarded by twenty-four SS men of the *Begleitkommando.* Aware that the Führer's luxurious coach must not fall into enemy hands, they detached it, moved it to a siding, doused it with the last available fuel, and set it ablaze. Grenades were thrown inside to ensure its destruction. The charred remains were later scrapped, leaving nothing of Hitler's train.

A conference in one of the carriages of the *Amerika* train, April 1944. Besides Hitler, it is attended by Field Marshals Walther von Brauchitsch and Wilhelm Keitel. (*Bundesarchiv, Bild 183-L18678 / CC-BY-SA 3.0*)

Chapter 25

Hitler the Drug Addict?

The Führer was extremely meticulous about controlling information. He monitored what Germans were allowed to know, as well as what could potentially be used by his enemies against him. He was reluctant to admit doctors into his inner circle, so it may therefore seem surprising that he placed such great trust in Theo Morell. But who was this man?

Theodor Gilbert Morell was born on 2 July 1886 in Trais-Münzenberg. An excellent student, it is unclear whether he dreamed of a medical career at the time, but ultimately, he chose medicine as his path of study. He pursued parasitology, immunology, psychiatry, otolaryngology, and gynaecology at universities in Heidelberg, Grenoble, Paris, and Munich. In 1913, he obtained his doctoral degree, along with a licence to practise as a gynaecologist in Bavaria.

He began his medical practice as an assistant at a hospital in Bad Kreuznach. After this brief episode, he worked as a ship's doctor for the Woehermann Lines and later joined Norddeutscher Lloyd. Following the First World War, he opened a modest medical practice in Berlin. In 1933, like many Germans who sensed the political tide turning, he joined the NSDAP. His lack of 'true belief' in the Nazi cause is confirmed, for instance, by the records of his medical practice, which show that he continued to treat Jewish patients until as late as 1938.

In 1936, at his new practice on Kurfürstendamm 216, he was visited by Heinrich Hoffmann, Adolf Hitler's friend and personal photographer. Hoffmann, due to his carefully concealed homosexual contacts, was suffering from gonorrhoea. Morell's effective and discreet treatment led to his introduction to the leader of the NSDAP, who soon appointed him as his personal physician. Morell would serve in this role until 22 April 1945, when the Führer declared that he would no longer be needed.

Morell then departed for Berchtesgaden, where he was captured by the Allies. Over the following three years, he suffered from steadily worsening

Theodor 'Theo' Gilbert Morell (1886-1948) was Adolf Hitler's personal physician. He remained with Hitler until practically the very end of the war. (*Public domain*)

mental decline, personality disintegration, and severe arteriosclerosis, while being held in various internment camps, including the former Dachau concentration camp. He was released on 30 June 1947 and transferred to a hospital in Tegernsee. There he lived in poverty and isolation, without contact with his wife, until his death from a stroke on 26 May 1948.[1]

It is worth noting that both Morell himself and his elevated position in Hitler's 'court' aroused considerable jealousy among other prominent figures. Shortly after the war, Dr Karl Brandt described him in the following way: 'Morell comes from near Darmstadt, he is about 56 years old, bald and corpulent, with a round and exceedingly full face, dark complexion, and dark brown eyes. He is nearsighted, wears glasses, has very hairy arms and chest. He stands about 170 cm tall.'[2]

Indeed, Morell was far from popular within Hitler's inner circle. His obesity was mocked, as was his lack of attention to personal hygiene. Aware of these jibes, the Führer once told Dr Hanskarl von Hasselbach: 'Morell is not here to be smelled, he is here to take care of my health.'

The Führer also seemed completely indifferent to the suggestions of other physicians that the concoctions he was receiving were poisoning him more than they were helping. Even during his Berlin practice, Morell had become known for administering strange preparations of his own making to patients. With Hitler, it was no different.

Theodor Morell and Adolf Hitler. (*US National Archives*)

Morell prescribed pills and tablets, stimulants and sedatives, leeches and bacterial cultures, hot compresses and cold poultices, as well as thousands of injections. Every year, he pumped litres of mysterious fluids into the muscles and veins of the gullible Führer. Indeed, in his introduction to *The Secret Diaries of Hitler's Doctor*, having uncovered the entirety of Morell's documentation, David Irving claimed that Hitler's arms bore so many marks from the constant injections that, in the end, his doctor had nowhere left to insert the needle.

While keeping Hitler's medical file, Morell was obliged to maintain the strictest confidentiality. Thus, in the doctor's records, Hitler did not appear under his own name but as 'Patient A'. When beginning his assessment, Morell prepared the following description of his psyche:

- Orientation in time and space, as well as recognition of persons – excellent.
- Memory of events, both recent and distant – excellent.
- Ability to memorise numbers, statistical data, names, etc. – excellent.
- Lacks a formal higher education, but has compensated for it by acquiring broad general knowledge through reading.
- Evaluation of temporal and spatial relationships – excellent.
- Responses to environmental factors – normal.

- The patient displays a changeable nature; at times he shows impatience, at others a tendency toward eccentricity, though communication with him is easy; he is not often distracted.
- He expresses his likes and dislikes strongly. High emotional instability.
- Thought process normal and continuous. He does not speak either too slowly or too quickly, but always to the point.
- Symptoms of *globus hystericus* (hysterical lump in the throat) not observed. No amnesia noted. The abdominal pains he complains of may have a hysterical origin.
- The patient exhibits no phobias or compulsions.
- I did not observe that he suffered from hallucinations, illusions, or any paranoid tendencies.[3]

Hitler, or 'Patient A', complained of numerous illnesses and ailments, many of which were purely imaginary. The Führer of the Third Reich was a hypochondriac. To ease his pain or provide immediate stimulation, Morell administered a wide variety of substances. According to a report compiled by the Americans after the war, more than seventy different preparations were identified. In the notes published by David Irving, sixty-four different kinds of remedies are listed. The truth, however, is that today we would hardly classify them as 'medicines'. For example, among the substances administered was Eukodal, now better known as oxycodone, a powerful opioid analgesic and a semi-synthetic derivative of morphine produced from thebaine. Its potency is approximately twice that of morphine.

In urgent situations, such as Benito Mussolini's visit in July 1943, Morell injected Hitler with glucose, which he eventually began mixing with amphetamine to enhance the effect. He also administered hormones. For various infections, he prescribed massive doses of sulphonamides; for bloating and cramps, strychnine and atropine; and for sinus pain, cocaine. Today, the use of such narcotic substances may seem shocking, but at the time they were regarded as ordinary medicines.

Can Hitler, then, be considered a drug addict? The answer must be an unequivocal no, if only because he was unaware of any possible dependence.

Among other bizarre substances, the Führer also received injections of bull semen extract, intended to boost his libido and help him appear as a vigorous leader. On occasion, even Eva Braun requested that Morell provide her with some form of aphrodisiac.

He also took belladonna for constipation, bromide for nervousness, and quinine for colds. The narcotic Dolantin (pethidine) was used as a painkiller; an extract of deadly nightshade soothed tremors and muscle tension; and another preparation from the same plant was administered for the symptoms of Parkinson's disease. Homoseran, an extract from placentas, was given to strengthen him, while mercury chloride was applied in enemas. Luminal helped him sleep, Mutaflor (a preparation of *E. coli* bacteria) aided his digestion, and castor oil served as a laxative. For tonsillitis he was given Lugol's solution; for depression, testosterone; and for various infections, ultraseptyl.

His lifestyle, the stress brought on by the burdens of leadership and war, and the enormous amounts of medication he consumed meant that by the end of the conflict, Hitler was little more than a shadow of his former self. Both in appearance and demeanour, he no longer stirred the masses. Yet it would be an exaggeration to say that he ceased to exert an almost paralysing pressure on those around him.

Only a handful of people knew the Führer's true state of health. To the German nation, this information was carefully concealed. Not even a single photograph of Hitler wearing glasses was ever published.

Chapter 26

Lebensborn – A Factory of Nazis?

It is quite widely believed that the centres run by the Lebensborn organisation were nothing more than brothels, where deserving SS men went before leaving for the front so that, before giving their lives for the Fatherland, they could leave behind 'good blood'. But what is the truth about this organisation?

Lebensborn e.V. (*Lebensborn eingetragener Verein*), or the Registered Association 'Fountain of Life', was founded by order of Reichsführer-SS Heinrich Himmler on 12 December 1935. The purpose of the institution was to create suitable conditions for increasing the population of 'German' blood. Lebensborn was also intended to curb abortions: if a woman did not wish to care for her child after birth, she could hand it over to one of the centres without facing any consequences, provided she met the Aryan standards of blood purity.

The role and tasks of Lebensborn were clearly defined by Hitler in a speech delivered on 14 October 1943: 'It is our duty to take Polish children, to tear them out of their Polish environment, even if we have to rob or abduct them. (…) Either we acquire good blood, which we will use for our purposes, or this may seem cruel to you, but nature is cruel we shall destroy that good blood.'

Lebensborn essentially had two faces:

The first, official and statutory, presented the organisation as a social and charitable institution.

The second, criminal, involved the abduction and Germanisation of children taken from occupied countries. The youngest could be adopted by German families. This procedure culminated in a ritual that served as a secularised Nazi counterpart to baptism. The child was touched with a dagger engraved with the SS runes and given a new Germanic name. Those who were not adopted were sent into forced labour, where many perished.

The headquarters of Lebensborn were originally located in Berlin at Hedemannstrasse 23/24, but was later moved to Munich, to Herzog-Max-Strasse 3-7.

The first direct head of the organisation was SS-Obersturmführer Guntram Pflaum, and from 15 May 1942, SS-Standartenführer Max Sollmann.

The central office was divided into several departments:

- The Main Department of Admissions to the Homes (which combined the Welfare Department and the Ancestry Records Department, headed by Engesar).
- The Main Labor Department.
- The Main Personnel Department (headed by SS-Sturmbannführer Herbert Friedrich).
- The Main Finance Department (headed by SS-Sturmbannführer Alfred Lenner, later replaced by SS-Untersturmführer Decker).
- The Main Administrative Department (headed by Wehner).
- The Main Legal Department (headed by Dr Tesch).
- The Main Health Department (headed by Dr Gregor Ebner).

The first Lebensborn facility was opened on 15 August 1936 in Steinhöring, near Munich. Afterwards, eight more homes were established within the so-called Old Reich, including in Achern-Baden and Niederaltreich-Oberbayern.

Lebensborn significantly expanded its activities after the outbreak of the war, as the Wehrmacht occupied more territories. In Poland, the first facility was established in 1940 in Bydgoszcz. It operated for two years and collaborated in the plundering of Polish property. Further homes were opened in Helenówek near Łódź, in Otwock under the name *Ostland – Heim*, in Połczyn-Zdrój, and in Smoszew near Krotoszyn. In Smoszew, there were plans to build an entire settlement called *Lebensborn-Siedlung-Heimstätte*, consisting of 500 houses, though by the end of the war only twenty-four had been completed.[1]

According to various estimates, Lebensborn abducted anywhere from several tens of thousands to as many as 200,000 children with 'Aryan features', primarily from the occupied countries of Eastern Europe, all through organised operations. These children were then forcibly Germanised and handed over to German families.

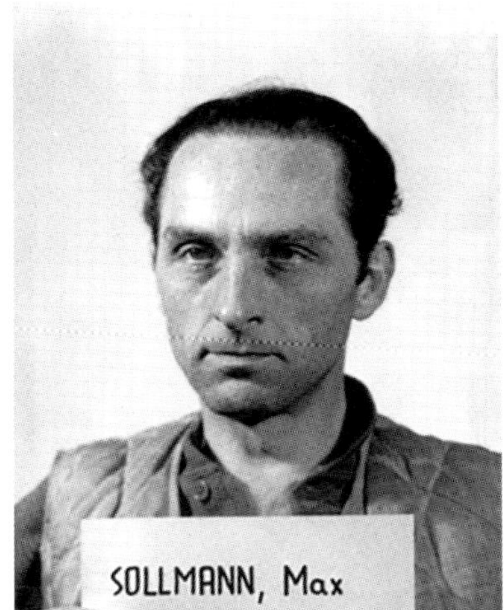

Above: SS-Standartenführer Max Sollmann, head of Lebensborn. (*USHMM*)

Right: A nurse caring for infants in one of the Lebensborn centres. (*Bundesarchiv, Bild 146-1973-010-11 / CC-BY-SA 3.0*)

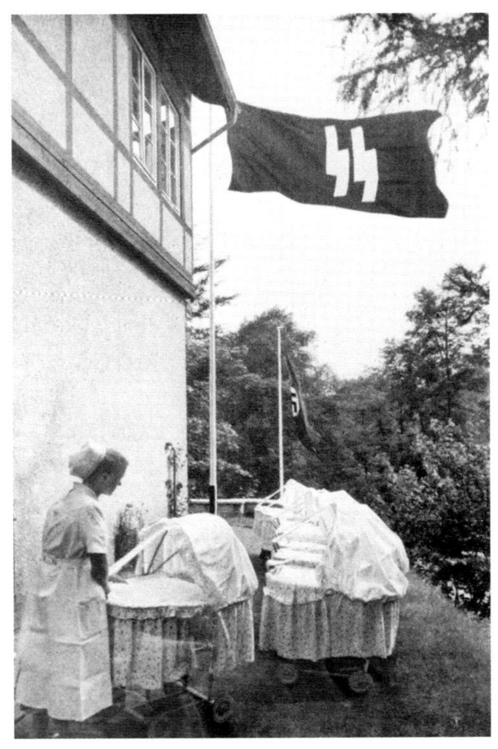

The activities of the organisation were examined during one of the trials before the American Military Tribunal in 1947-1948. Officially, the case was called 'United States vs. Ulrich Greifelt et al'. In the verdict delivered on 10 March 1948, Lebensborn was declared a 'welfare institution'. The entire leadership of the organisation, including Max Sollmann, Gregor Ebner, and Günther Tesch, was released from serving any sentence, while the only woman brought before the court, Inge Viermetz, received a second-class acquittal 'for lack of evidence'.

Chapter 27

Operation *Paperclip*

The photograph of a smiling Wernher von Braun, his arm in a cast, surrounded by several men surrendering to the Americans, became and remains to this day the very symbol of Operation *Paperclip*.[1]

During the Second World War, Wernher Magnus Maximilian Freiherr von Braun was a co-developer of the V-2 ballistic missiles, a member of the NSDAP, and an SS officer.

The end of fighting in Europe in May 1945 did not mean the end of all wartime-related activities. The Allies pursued a two-track policy: on the one hand, they hunted down prominent figures of the Third Reich who were to be put on trial, and on the other, they often recruited actual war criminals – such as Klaus Barbie – into their service. The Soviets, of course, acted in much the same way. The Americans were well aware that their former ally was eager for further territorial gains and would strive to assert its primacy as a global superpower.

It can be said that acquiring German scientists and the documentation they had created on the construction of ballistic missiles such as the V-2 turned out to be far more important than recovering hidden valuables and works of art. The true prize for the Americans and Europeans was gaining a technological advantage over the enemy now lurking behind the Iron Curtain. For the Germans, working for the United States was, of course, a far better option than offering their services to their main adversary, the Soviet Union. Today, it is estimated that under Operation *Paperclip*, more than 1,000 individuals found refuge in the US, including scientists, Hitler's collaborators, members of the NSDAP, intelligence operatives specialising in the Soviet Union, and even outright murderers.

American efforts to secure scientists and other specialists from Germany and Japan were initiated by the Office of Strategic Services (OSS) in late 1944 under the codename *Overcast*. In a secret memorandum from the US War Department dated 6 April 1945, it was stated that certain specialists

(Left to right): Magnus von Braun, two American soldiers, Walter Dornberger, Herbert Axster, Wernher von Braun, Hans Lindenberg, and Bernhard Tessmann surrendering to the Americans in 1945. (*Public domain*)

could be used 'to increase our war potential against Japan and to support postwar research in the military field.'

The number of German specialists was limited to 450, and their stay in the United States to six months. Officially, the document also stipulated that it was forbidden to bring over war criminals or those suspected of war crimes. However, American intelligence services proved adept at concealing undesirable information. In the case of Wernher von Braun, for instance, details about his SS rank did not come to light until eight years after his death, in 1985.

After Japan's surrender in August 1945, the codename *Overcast* was changed to *Paperclip*. The primary targets of the continuing operation became the scientists working on the V-2 rockets, led by Wernher von Braun. The Washington-based Joint Intelligence Objectives Agency (JIOA) carefully whitewashed the problematic biographies of von Braun and other participants in *Paperclip*. Their wartime 'achievements', which included the exploitation of concentration camp prisoners in weapons factories, where hundreds died every day, were deliberately ignored.

The Allies knew that the V-2, which had been touted as a *Wunderwaffe* (wonder weapon), represented a deadly threat to them. The proof of this came in Antwerp, where on 16 December 1944, a V-2 rocket struck the

Rex cinema, where 1,200 people were watching the film, *The Plainsman* starring Gary Cooper. A total of 567 people were killed, including 296 soldiers, making it the single deadliest strike from a single missile in the entire Second World War.

The launch of one of the *Wunderwaffe*: the Aggregat 4 (A-4) rocket, better known as the Vergeltungswaffe 2, or the V-2 (Retribution Weapon No. 2). (*Bundesarchiv, Bild 141-1880 / CC-BY-SA 3.0*)

That same day, Wernher von Braun and General Walter Dornberger received the highest non-combat decoration of the Third Reich, the Knight's Cross of the War Merit Cross, at Varlar Castle. Alongside them, Walther Riedel from the design office and Heinz Kunze, a representative of the Reich Ministry of Armaments, were also decorated.

'It seems likely that if the Germans had managed to perfect this new weapon and deploy it six months earlier, our invasion of Europe would have been extremely difficult, if not impossible,' remarked General Eisenhower, commenting on the existence of the German rockets. Such a weapon could not be ignored, nor could the Allies allow the Russians to capture the most important German scientists. Both von Braun and the aforementioned General Dornberger, therefore, found themselves at the top of the list of individuals who had to be located and persuaded to cooperate.

As it turned out, this was not difficult at all. Von Braun, together with Dornberger and a dozen or so technicians and scientists, had planned to surrender voluntarily to American soldiers. They were utterly convinced of their own value.

After leaving the Nordhausen facility, the Germans hid in the Bavarian Alps, in the ski resort of Haus Ingerburg, located 1,178 metres above sea level. The place was lavishly stocked with food and all kinds of liquor. After the war, von Braun recalled that the vast majority of those staying there did absolutely nothing except drink alcohol and lounge on the terrace: 'In that elegant hotel on the plateau I lived like a king. Below, to the west, were the French, and to the south the Americans. Nobody suspected that we were sitting up there.' It was only the announcement on 1 May that shook the Germans out of their lethargy, when the radio reported that Hitler, 'fighting to his last breath against Bolshevism, died this afternoon for Germany in his command post at the Reich Chancellery.'

Von Braun and Dornberger agreed that, under these circumstances, they had to attempt negotiations with the Americans. They knew they held strong bargaining chips and so to open talks with the soldiers stationed at the foot of the mountain, they sent Magnus von Braun, who until recently had been responsible for overseeing the production of gyroscopes for the rockets and, of the entire group, the one with the best command of English.

On the morning of 2 May, Magnus got on a bicycle and sped down the slope. He came across sentry Fred Schneikert of the 44th Infantry Division. His knowledge of English must have been somewhat overrated, however, because when he tried to explain that he wished to make a deal concerning his brother, Wernher, and the V-2 rockets, Schneikert understood that he wanted to *sell* him his brother.

Schneikert escorted Magnus further down to Reutte, where the headquarters of the American Counter Intelligence Corps (CIC) was stationed. The CIC then contacted SHAEF, which in turn reached out to the CIOS command, the body holding the list of over 1,000 German scientists who were to be interrogated and ideally persuaded to work for the United States. At the very top of that list, of course, was Wernher von Braun.

The Americans, however, may have suspected that someone was trying to set a trap for them. They therefore remained cautious. Magnus von Braun was released with the suggestion that his brother should come down from the mountain and surrender himself. There was no other choice.

Soon, a small group of scientists emerged from the mountain to negotiate on behalf of the rest. At the head of the delegation stood Wernher von Braun and Dornberger, joined by Magnus von Braun, Herbert Axster Dornberger's chief of staff Hans Lindenberg, a propulsion specialist, as well as engineers Dieter Huzel and Bernhard Tessmann. The latter two were responsible for hiding the V-2 documentation.

After packing their personal belongings, the group set off in three grey vans to meet the Americans. They arrived in the evening and were received rather cordially. They were served eggs, coffee, and bread with butter. After dinner, each man was given his own room and fresh bedding. The following day, journalists were brought to the site, taking numerous photographs. The Germans, confident in their own importance, demanded a meeting with General Eisenhower. The scientists were transferred to barracks in Garmisch-Partenkirchen, where they awaited their fate in fairly luxurious conditions.

What they did not realise was that they had, at least in part, already lost some of their bargaining power: the 14 tons of documents hidden in a salt mine. They were unaware that Dieter Huzel and Bernhard Tessmann, who had been responsible for concealing the material, had shared the information with Karl Otto Fleischer, the former director of the weapons factory in Nordhausen. Fleischer had already passed on this knowledge to Major Robert B. Staver, who recovered the entire archive just before the Red Army seized the area and kept it secret from the British.

Staver, in addition to forwarding the documentation, also pushed for the transfer of German scientists to the United States. At that time, however, this was not yet an obvious step. Various military agencies clashed with one another, with some seeking to punish war criminals, and others eager to secure their cooperation.

Once permission was granted, Staver travelled to Garmisch-Partenkirchen to meet with von Braun and Dornberger. Both men were now to help him rapidly evacuate German scientists from the Harz region. Time was of the essence: the area was about to fall into Soviet hands. In great haste, German scientists, technicians, and their families were located and given a stark choice: pack up and leave immediately or remain at the mercy of the USSR.

At the nearby railway station, more than 1,000 Germans quickly gathered, waiting to be transported. Among them, ordinary civilians also tried to slip into the crowd, desperate to escape the advancing Red Army. American soldiers were forced to intervene. Just before boarding the train, Dornberger revealed to Major Staver that five additional crates containing important documentation still needed to be taken along. It was now a race against time.

Faced with no other choice, Staver headed to the nearest unit, the 332nd Engineer Regiment, stationed over 100 kilometres (60 miles) away in Kassel. Armed with pickaxes, shovels, and mine detectors, and supported by three soldiers, they made their way to a field in Bad Sachs. Only a few hours remained before the Red Army's arrival. After extensive searching, they finally uncovered the crates containing 120 kilograms of documents, complete with technical drawings. These were successfully transported, along with roughly 100 fully assembled V-2 rockets. Unfortunately, the

A group of 104 German rocket scientists, including Wernher von Braun, who were brought to the United States under Operation *Paperclip*, photographed at Fort Bliss, Texas, 1946. (*Public domain*)

Soviets were left with an almost intact factory in Nordhausen, where production lines still held parts ready for assembly. It looked as if the prisoners might return at any moment to resume their work.

Von Braun, together with eighty of the most important scientists, was placed in a multi-story school building in Witzenhausen. Soon, a rather curious situation was to unfold. The British, having learned that the Americans intended to employ a large group of German scientists, requested permission to independently carry out two research programmes – a request to which the Americans agreed. What is more, they even temporarily made available to the British a group of detained scientists and technicians, led by von Braun, Dornberger, and Arthur Rudolph. The British conducted the launches of four captured rockets, with Rudolph playing the leading role in the experiments.

Interestingly, Dornberger was not allowed to work with the rockets and was also kept isolated from the rest of the German personnel. The situation seemed rather odd. Soon, however, it became clear that his expertise was not required. The British had entirely different plans for him: they wanted him to answer for his war crimes. Consequently, they had no intention of returning him to the Americans once his 'loan' period was over.

Dornberger and von Braun were taken to England for interrogation. While von Braun was eventually handed over to the Americans, Dornberger was not. He was classified as a prisoner of war, dressed in a brown uniform with large 'PW' letters on the back, and transferred to the London Cage camp. After a thorough interrogation there, he was moved to a castle in Wales and later, on 9 January 1946, to Special Prisoner of War Camp XI at Island Farm. A guard from the camp, Ron Williams, later recalled: 'Walter Dornberger was certainly the most hated man in the camp. Even his own people hated him. Unlike the others, he never went out to work on the nearby farms.'[2] It was also recalled that he was always guarded by three sentries, who feared that some of the Germans might try to kill him. After being cleared of charges, it was only on 9 July 1947 that the British finally handed him over to the Americans.

Meanwhile, von Braun and the rest of his companions were still waiting for transport to the United States. On 12 September 1945, together with six other Germans, he was loaded onto a truck and taken to Paris. There, after being joined by a group of scientists from the Hermann Göring Research Institute, the entire party, which also included pilot Karl Baur, boarded a C-54 transport aircraft. In heavy rain, the plane lifted into the air.

The first compulsory landing necessitated by the need to refuel took place on the island of Santa Maria in the Azores. The next stop was Newfoundland. On 20 September, the Germans set foot on American soil. Yet this was not the end of their journey. They were loaded onto a smaller aircraft, which after a few hours carried them from Delaware to the US Navy base at Squantum in Quincy, Massachusetts.

There, they were transferred onto a transport ship that set out on a short voyage. Once out of sight of people who might have observed the suspicious group, they were moved aboard a whaling vessel from Boston. The journey, during which all the passengers suffered from seasickness, ended at Fort Strong, an island situated in the middle of Boston Harbor. Although the fort was still under military control, it had been practically unused for nearly thirty years.

In addition to the German scientists, prisoners of war were also brought to the site, as they could be useful in adapting the camp and ensuring its continued operation. Translators, bakers, cooks, and tailors all had the opportunity to apply their skills. The Americans now had to handle all the necessary procedures and coordinate with the FBI.

The daily routine was interrupted only by the arrival on the island of Major James P. Hamill from the Ordnance Department, who was tasked with taking six scientists with him to the Aberdeen Proving Ground. This group included Eberhard Reese, Erich Neubert, Theodor Pöppel, August Schulze, Wilhelm Jungert, and Walter Schwidetzky. All six were assigned to sort and translate the documentation discovered in the Dörnten mine.

Then, on 6 October 1945, Hamill took von Braun by train to Fort Bliss, Texas, where he encountered Native Americans for the first time. To him, it felt as if he were living inside a Karl May novel. He even began writing a novel himself, with the theme centred on a space journey to Mars.

Work progressed slowly. Funding did not flow as freely as it had in the Third Reich. Nevertheless, at the beginning of April 1946, they succeeded in launching a rocket from the White Sands proving ground. It reached an altitude of 5 kilometres (3 miles), and afterwards von Braun prepared a memorandum addressed to Robert Oppenheimer, head of the Los Alamos Laboratory, in which he suggested equipping his rockets with nuclear material.

In the following years, von Braun built a dazzling career in the United States, even accepting US citizenship in 1956 and declaring himself an American patriot. Dornberger, too, after being released by the British, pursued a career in the United States. The Americans were untroubled by the information reaching them about their involvement in war crimes. Nor did they acknowledge the criminal experiments conducted by men such as Hubertus Strughold. During the war, Strughold had served as a physician in Dachau, where he carried out experiments on humans, testing, among other things, their reactions to extreme cold and simulating high-altitude falls.

Hubertus Strughold was born on 15 June 1898 in the town of Westtünnen im-Hamm in Westphalia. He studied medicine and natural sciences at the Ludwig Maximilian University of Munich and the Georg August University of Göttingen, later receiving his doctorate in medicine from the University of Münster. Increasingly, he devoted his attention to aviation medicine and worked with Robert Ritter von Greim, who assisted him in studying the effects of high-altitude flights on the human body.

In 1928, Strughold travelled to the United States on a one-year Rockefeller Foundation research fellowship. He pursued specialised studies in aviation medicine and human physiology at the University of Chicago and Case Western Reserve University in Cleveland. Upon returning to Germany, he accepted a teaching position at the Physiological Institute in Würzburg before ultimately becoming a professor of physiology at the Frederick William University in Berlin.

In April 1935, he was appointed director of the Berlin Research Institute for Aviation Medicine, operating under the auspices of the Ministry of Aviation. With the outbreak of the war, the institute was absorbed into the Luftwaffe Medical Corps, renamed the Air Force Institute of Aviation Medicine, and placed under the command of Generaloberstabsarzt Erich Hippke.

In October 1942, Strughold took part in a conference at which Dr Sigmund Rascher presented the results of experiments carried out on prisoners in the Dachau concentration camp. These included physiological tests in which inmates were submerged in icy water, placed in pressure chambers, and forced to endure exploratory surgeries without anaesthetic. As a result, many of them died.

It is not known whether Strughold personally took part in these experiments. What is certain, however, is that he must have been aware of them and possessed knowledge about them. The results would have been of great interest to him, since he himself studied such issues, and many of his assistants and collaborators were personally involved in the experiments. It is therefore hard to believe that such topics were not brought up during their daily conversations.

In 1944, a group led by Professor Strughold was relocated to a small palace in the village of Rząsiny in Lower Silesia. The transfer of the research team was a consequence of the bombing of the Berlin Institute for Aviation Medicine Research. Interestingly, the scientists, including, among others, Professor Hansjochem Autrum and Dr Hans Denzer, were accompanied by their entire families.

Professor Autrum had already been conducting medical experiments. At that time, however, instead of people, he used specially trained German shepherd dogs. He recalled his research as follows:

> At the end of 1942 or the beginning of 1943, I was assigned different tasks in Berlin in addition to working on the adaptation of the eye to darkness – namely, studying the effects of oxygen deficiency on mammals. The order came suddenly, and in Professor Strughold's eyes it was a matter of urgency. These studies were extremely important because aircraft crews suffered from low pressure and, as a result, oxygen deficiency, which within minutes could lead to loss of consciousness. We investigated how quickly a paratrooper would have to 'spread his wings' in order to remain sufficiently conscious to open his parachute. We examined how the time depended on altitude, at which sudden decompression and subsequent loss of consciousness occurred. During this, we monitored the ECG and heart rate. The pressure chamber was available thanks to Strughold's Institute. The test animals were shepherd dogs that had been properly trained.
>
> A few years later, we learned from Professor Strughold why there had been such urgency in carrying out the dog experiments. (…) In May 1942, Hitler and SS leader Himmler made the decision to annihilate the Jews. Shortly afterwards, a meeting was held at SS headquarters, to which Strughold was also invited. He was asked whether he would like to conduct his experiments on concentration camp prisoners. The professor rejected this proposal: in his opinion, experiments on animals were far more conclusive, since no psychological factors played a role here.

In Rząsiny, research was conducted on pressure and low oxygen levels. These studies later proved useful for NASA's work. But before that, the

German scientists experimented on themselves. Let us once again refer to the recollections of Professor Autrum:

> In 1944, the Institute conducted experiments in Rząsiny in Silesia, and the 'guinea pigs' were we and our fellow colleagues. My own experience looked like this: slow reduction of pressure, that is, reduced oxygen in the exhaled air, is unpleasant and of course reduces efficiency. At increasing altitudes there is no anxiety. (…) In the final phase, loss of consciousness occurs. As a result of the studies, it was shown that even a short oxygen deficiency has an irreversible effect on the brain and kidneys. Alongside these experiments, work on dark adaptation of the eye continued.
>
> Over time, the work in Rząsiny gathered pace. The only question that really interested us, concerning the measurement of the electrical potential in the human eye, was met with the greatest difficulties. Either the shielding was not correct, we had voltage in the amplifier, or we had to recharge the batteries. One day the oscilloscope, which we had received and partly rebuilt, also stopped working. It became tiresome to put a contact lens into one of our eyes, only to discover with disappointment that the two pieces of equipment did not work together. A substitute object instead of our eyes had to be moved further away in order to reach the apparatus. We never again received rabbits. They had been 'otherwise' utilised.

Strughold, too, likely out of curiosity, subjected himself to tests. He recalled it after the war: 'In the castle cellars I attempted a flight in a "rocket". I examined my own reactions. (…) I remember that everything shook, vibrated, to the point of danger. (…) After some time, it was impossible to steer; control over the rudder was lost.'

At the end of the war, as the Red Army advanced toward Rząsiny, the Germans began evacuating the facility.

As Autrum recalled:

> At the end of January 1945, Russian units (…) halted in Silesia before reaching Wrocław. In Rząsiny, we could hear the gunfire of retreating troops. We did not want to fall into the hands of

the Russian forces. Strughold had already settled in Göttingen in January. However, we did not want to leave behind our equipment, amplifiers, and oscillographs. We packed the most important apparatus into crates. (…) The landlord Schwertner transported the crates to the railway station in Gryfów. They were declared as goods belonging to the Wehrmacht. (…) We wanted to move these things as far west as possible. (…) When after several days the crates were still at the station in Gryfów, we resorted to 'criminal methods'. Together with Dr Hans Denzer, we frightened the station master in Gryfów by telling him that the crates contained important materials that could not fall into Russian hands. If they were not delivered to the West within two days, we had orders to blow up the baggage room.

We had neither orders nor explosives. The poor station master lived in an apartment above the baggage room. The next day, the crates were delivered to Suhl in Thuringia.[3]

At the same time, Professor Strughold was already at the University of Göttingen, preparing to begin his postwar life. After the war ended, in October 1945 he found employment at the University of Heidelberg as director of the Institute of Physiology. It is unclear whether he realised that his expertise was of immense value to the Americans, who already during the war had received information about the groundbreaking research being conducted. The number of victims these experiments had claimed mattered little at the time.

The key figures most interested in gaining a full perspective on German research were Major General Malcolm Grow, the Chief Medical Officer of the US Air Forces in Europe, and Lieutenant Colonel Harry Armstrong, then the Chief Medical Officer of the US 8th Air Force. These officers divided their tasks: Grow was to return to Washington to lobby for bringing over the 115 doctors and scientists he had selected, while Armstrong was to move to Berlin to locate them and persuade them to cooperate. Of course, the greatest hopes within the selected group were placed on acquiring Strughold, whom Armstrong had personally known since 1934. After the war, he recalled: 'We had a lot in common. He and I were almost the same age, both of us published books on aviation medicine in that year [1934], and he was carrying out in Germany the same role that I was fulfilling in the United States.'[4]

Strughold was located in Göttingen and persuaded to work for the Americans. In the United States Army Air Forces, he became the chief scientist of the Aero Medical Center, which was housed in the former Kaiser Wilhelm Institute for Medical Research. He personally selected fifty-eight of his collaborators, who over the course of two years were systematically transferred to the United States. In 1947, as part of Operation *Paperclip*, Strughold himself was also brought over and was assigned to the newly established US Air Force School of Aviation Medicine at Randolph Field in Texas, where he began work on the medical aspects of human presence in space.

In 1949, he was appointed the first and only professor of space medicine, focussing on research in 'astrobiology' and the so-called 'human factors' related to manned spaceflight. Between 1952 and 1954, he oversaw the construction of a space cabin simulator, a sealed chamber in which subjects were placed for extended periods to study the potential physical, astrobiological, and psychological effects of flight beyond the atmosphere.

In 1962 Strughold was appointed Chief Scientist of the Aerospace Medicine Division at the National Aeronautics and Space Administration (NASA). He played a key role in designing the pressure suit and onboard life-support systems used by astronauts during the *Gemini* and *Apollo* missions. He also oversaw the specialised training of flight surgeons and medical staff of the *Apollo* programme in preparation for the planned mission to the moon. He retired from his position at NASA in 1968.

Hubertus Strughold died on 25 September 1985, and it was only after his death that information about his activities during the Second World War began to surface. It was established that in 1943, six children with epilepsy, aged between 11 and 13, were taken from the Brandenburg Euthanasia Centre to Strughold's Berlin laboratory, where they were placed in vacuum chambers to induce epileptic seizures as a simulation of the effects of altitude-related conditions such as hypoxia.

However, these revelations did not prevent the Aerospace Medical Association from awarding a prize in his name between 1963 and 2012. Only in 2013 was the award discontinued. From then on, the shameful name of the 'scientist' began to be quietly erased from the chronicles of research institutions.

Chapter 28

The Mystery of the Last U-boats

On 25 March 1945, the German submarine U-234 set sail from Kiel. Its destination: Japan. Before that, however, the vessel headed to Norway to take on passengers and cargo. During its stop at the base in Bergen, it collided with U-1301, resulting in damage to the fuel tanks and the No. 1 diving tank. The crew, however, managed to carry out almost all the necessary repairs on their own. With that completed, loading operations could begin.

On board the submarine was placed cargo that had to reach Japan under the utmost secrecy. It included 500 kilograms of enriched uranium, a dismantled Messerschmitt Me-262 jet aircraft, and components of a V-2 rocket. One sailor remembered:

> In each of the six vertical mine shafts under the forward deck, a steel container resembling a giant cigar was to be placed. It was held in place by a mine-release mechanism. Loading was carried out in strict secrecy. In the keel, 25-kilogram steel flasks filled with mercury were stored. The holds contained optical glass, equipment schematics, cameras, sealed containers with secret documents, and even a Me-262 jet fighter in parts. Some of the forward mine shafts were loaded with Panzerfausts, other anti-tank weapons, and small rockets.[1]

In addition, eight members of the regular crew were replaced by eight mysterious passengers. Among them were: General Ulrich Kessler, a specialist in guided aerial weapons; Colonel Fritz von Sandrath, an expert in anti-aircraft defence; Colonel Erich Mentzel, a communications specialist; Lieutenant Commander Richard Bulla, responsible for air-naval cooperation; Commander Gerhard Falk, a naval construction expert; and August Bringewald, a civilian engineer from the Messerschmitt works. Two

Captain Johann-Heinrich Fehler surrendering U-234, 14 May 1945. The photograph was taken from aboard USS *Sutton*. (*Public domain*)

U-977 off Cape Cod, Massachusetts, shortly before being sunk during a US Navy torpedo test, 13 November 1946. (*Wikimedia Commons / US Navy photo 80-G-703417*)

Japanese officers also boarded: Colonel Genzo Shosi, an aviation engineer, and Commander Hideo Tomonaga, a submarine construction specialist.

U-234 was a 90-metre-long Type XB minelaying submarine, which was quite new for its time, having entered service on 2 March 1944. Its commander was the 34-year-old naval captain Johann-Heinrich Fehler, who was inexperienced in combat. Although this was to be his first combat voyage, he was immediately given the important and difficult mission of delivering materials and personnel to Japan. The fleet command had also prepared a contingency plan in case of difficulties in reaching the destination; the submarine could instead head to Argentina.

Wolfgang Hirschfeld, the radio operator serving on board, later recalled: 'In January 1945, we began the final preparations for departure to Tokyo.

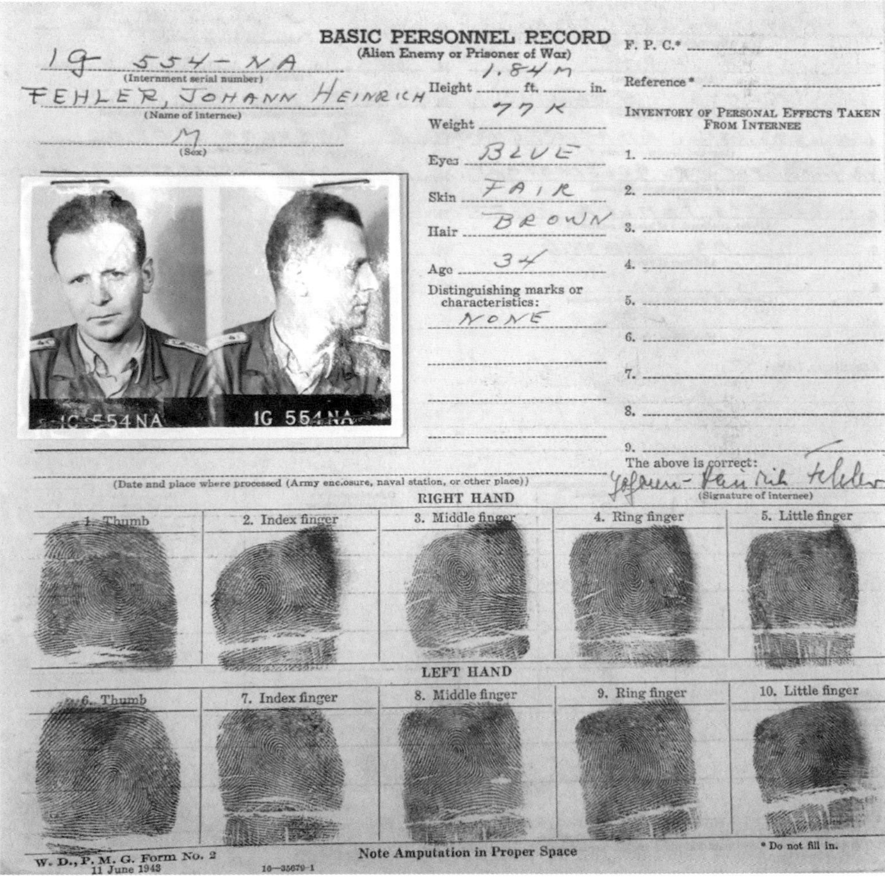

Registration card of Captain Johann-Heinrich Fehler. (*Mariusz Borowiak*)

A Hohentwiel radar, an invention of the Luftwaffe, was installed. (…) This radar allowed the U-Boat to detect approaching aircraft before they could pick up the submarine with their own radar, although it tended to overheat after extended use.'[2]

Life on a submarine meant that sailors rarely had the chance to breathe fresh air. For the next sixteen days, U-234 sailed entirely submerged. It was only on 1 May that Captain Fehler decided to surface. In the following days, surfacing took place only at night. During these times, the batteries were recharged, and the compartments were ventilated.

When the submarine was south of Newfoundland, it received word of the capitulation of the Third Reich. As naval historian Mariusz Borowiak calculates:

> As many as 174 submarines surrendered in bases in Germany, Norway, Denmark, France, Gibraltar, Great Britain, Canada, the USA, and the Far East. More than 200 commanders scuttled their vessels, carrying out the orders of Operation 'Regenbogen'. Two U-boats sailed to Argentina (U-530 and U-977) and surrendered there in the summer of 1945. Meanwhile, U-963 and U-1227 were scuttled by their own crews off the coast of Portugal, and U-979 ran aground southwest of the island of Amrum, near the German North Sea coast.[3]

The commander of U-234 decided to abort his mission. As he later testified before American investigators: 'Had the submarine not surrendered, [General Kessler] planned to make for Argentina. Using his contacts, he intended to approach the US Embassy and offer to hand over "U-234" to the US Navy in exchange for safe residence for himself and his men in Argentina. A list of addresses in Chile, handwritten by the general, was likely found. However, the list of addresses in Argentina disappeared.'[4]

Not everyone agreed with the decision to surrender the submarine. The two Japanese officers on board, upon learning that the vessel was to surrender to the Americans, committed suicide. After the war, Captain Fehler described the incident in one of his letters:

> When the radio brought to the deck of 'U-234' the information about Germany's surrender and the order instructing U-boats

to surrender and proceed to an Allied port, I informed the Japanese of the situation. I gave them my word that I would do everything in my power to prevent them from falling into Allied hands. I had planned to set them ashore somewhere on neutral territory Spain, Portugal, or the Canary Islands. Unfortunately, they either did not trust my word or thought the plan seemed unrealistic.

Be that as it may, during the night, while 'U-234' was running at full speed in very poor weather conditions and heavy seas, they ingested a large dose of Luminal. When they were found the following morning, nothing could be done. We kept their bodies on board for twenty hours until the next morning. They were wrapped in material from the hammocks they had been issued, and buried at sea in proper naval fashion, with a prayer and wrapped in the Japanese flag. This occurred [...] before the surrender of 'U-234' to the American destroyer *Sutton*.[5]

According to Allied directives, U-234 was supposed to enter the port of Halifax and surrender to the Canadians. However, the submarine's commander believed the Americans would treat the crew more leniently and decided instead to head toward the American sector; a decision he later came to regret.

On 17 May, the U-boat reached the base at Portsmouth, Maine, where several other German submarines had already surrendered to the Americans. The entire crew was sent to the Portsmouth prison for initial interrogation. Afterwards, the sailors were separated from the officers and the special passengers carried on board. Almost all of them were subjected to exhausting interrogations, and their personal belongings were unceremoniously looted.

Two years after the surrender, U-234 was sunk as a target ship during US Navy exercises.

Not all commanders, despite receiving orders to surrender, chose to comply. The longest-operating of them all was U-977, which, according to some claims, carried Adolf Hitler himself to Argentina.

This vessel was launched on 31 March 1943 at the Blohm & Voss shipyard in Hamburg. It spent practically the entire war in the Baltic Sea, training successive crews. On 1 April 1945, the submarine was stocked with supplies needed for a two-month voyage, as well as ammunition.

The second commander of the vessel, after Leutnant Hans Leilich, was 24-year-old Leutnant Heinz Schäffer, who had previously commanded the Type II D submarine U-148.

On 13 April 1945, U-977 left the port of Kiel and headed for the Norwegian port of Horten, arriving there after seven days. Then, on 30 April, it set out for the port of Kristiansand, which it reached later that same day. On 1 May, the radio broadcast the address of the new Führer, Karl Dönitz, declaring that Hitler had died a heroic death defending Berlin.

The following day, a ceremony was held during which the flag on the mast was lowered to half-mast in mourning for Hitler's death. Around 10:00 pm, the submarine set out on its final combat patrol. Its mission was to operate near the port of Southampton, with the possibility of penetrating the harbour itself. In practice, such an assignment meant certain death for the crew.

On the night of 4-5 May, a radio message was received ordering the cessation of hostilities. Many U-boat commanders, including Schäffer, believed the message to be false, assuming that the transmitting station had likely fallen into British hands. After a heated discussion with his senior officers, the captain decided not to inform the crew of the order that had been received. However, when it became clear that the Third Reich was indeed capitulating, a decision had to be made regarding further action.

The captain refused to surrender and instead announced his intention to head for Argentina, which sparked a lively debate among the crew. In a vote held among the forty-eight men, thirty chose to sail to South America, while only two expressed the desire to disembark in Spain, though they ultimately gave up on that idea. The rest of the sailors, mainly those with families in Germany, decided to disembark in Norway.

Those who remained on board undertook an extremely difficult voyage. Since the submarine travelled almost the entire time submerged, the quality of the air quickly deteriorated. Food and fresh water supplies also dwindled at an alarming rate. A decision was made to ration water to half a cup per day, used only for brushing teeth. Beyond that, water could be used solely for drinking or cooking. The use of fresh water for bathing or shaving was strictly forbidden. Washing underwear in seawater caused itching and boils, and clothing laundered in salt water refused to dry properly. The cooks also struggled with the growing mass of waste, which rapidly began to rot.

The lack of fresh air, food rationing, and constant tension pushed the entire crew into a state of apathy. At 6:00 am on 23 July, U-977 crossed the equator at around 30°W, where twenty-eight out of thirty-two officers and sailors underwent the traditional equatorial crossing ceremony. On 7 August 1945, after 108 days at sea and covering 7,600 nautical miles, U-977 entered the Argentine port of Mar del Plata, where the crew surrendered to the local navy. Before entering port, the idea of scuttling the submarine and secretly making their way ashore was considered, but for various reasons, this plan was ultimately abandoned.

After establishing contact with the Argentine vessels assigned to escort the German submarine into port, the captain called a crew assembly. He then delivered his farewell speech:

> Friends [...] we have reached the port of Argentina. I am certain that we did the right thing. None of us will ever regret this voyage. For most of us, it will forever remain the greatest experience of our lives, an achievement of which we can be proud. This is a hard farewell for us. Our lives have become so intertwined that we almost became one, but now each of you will be master of your own fate, free to go your own way. Yet we must never forget that we are German sailors, those who have survived the most terrible kind of war. That thought will bind us together in the years to come. Thank you for your trust and loyalty. I wish you the fulfilment of your hopes and the realisation of your dreams.[6]

The Argentinians immediately interned the entire crew, causing great surprise among the Germans, who had not expected to be treated like criminals. The reason behind the Argentine's behaviour lay in a certain misunderstanding that U-977 was accused of having sunk the Brazilian light cruiser *Bahia*.

Additionally, during the interrogations, the commander of the German U-boat had to defend himself against accusations of secretly transporting Adolf Hitler to Argentina. Although Schäffer's assurances seemed to convince the officers questioning him, the articles published in the local press, filled with claims that Hitler had indeed been on board, did nothing to improve the crew's situation.

On 5 September 1945, the submarine, together with its crew and ten numbered crates, was handed over under pressure to the US naval attaché, Captain W.W. Webb. After being transported to Fort Hunt, the Germans were subjected to interrogations once again. What interested the Americans most was, of course… Adolf Hitler.

The German submarine was included in the so-called Victory Parade and later, on 13 November 1946, was sunk during tests by a torpedo fired from the American submarine USS *Atule*.

The Americans released the crew at the end of 1946. Most of the sailors returned to Argentina. Freedom, however, was not granted to the commander. At the end of 1946, Schäffer was transported to Britain, where he once again had to undergo endless interrogations. For six months, the British kept him in a special camp for high-ranking German prisoners. They were unable, however, to prove any war crimes or the transport of gold and other valuables. Classified as a political prisoner, he was sent back to Germany and placed in a camp in Paderborn near Dortmund. Thanks to the help of friends, in the spring of 1947 he was finally able to leave its walls.

A year later, he rejoined his sailors in Argentina. There he married Ingeborg, an Argentine woman of German descent, with whom he had a son. He worked as a captain on various Argentine ships and towards the end of his life, seriously ill, he decided to return to Germany to die in his homeland. He passed away on 15 January 1970 in Berlin, aged 58.

Chapter 29

Nazi Hunters

Each of the victorious states of the Second World War sought German scientists, technicians, intelligence officers, and soldiers who could be used to strengthen their own military potential. Yet, despite this, there were also those who made it their personal mission to track down as many Nazis as possible and bring them to justice, with the main targets being those individuals connected with the Holocaust. The most famous of these Nazi hunters was Simon Wiesenthal, but he was not alone, and it is worth taking a closer look at several others.

The greatest success of the Nazi hunters was, of course, the tracking down and abduction of Adolf Eichmann in May 1960. One of the people who took part in this operation was Tadeusz Jasiński, born on 23 January 1922 in Radom, and better known today as Tuviah Friedman.

During the Second World War, Friedman was placed in the Jewish Labour Camp on Szkolna Street in Radom, where prisoners were forced to work in weapons production. In 1944, when the Germans evacuated the factory ahead of the advancing Soviets, he hid in a boiler room shelter, thus managing to avoid the almost certain death that befell many of the camp's forced labourers. After the war, he returned to Radom, but as he later recalled in an interview: 'The synagogue still stood, but there was no one there. Nowhere, where I had once known anyone, was there anybody. The houses still stood, but mine was gone.'

In 1945, Friedman joined the militia. As he later remembered, his unit's task was to put an end to the anarchist activities of the Home Army, as well as to track down and arrest Germans, Poles, and Ukrainians who, during the war, had acted against the best interests of Poland and the Polish nation. As he explained: 'I undertook this mission with tremendous enthusiasm. Together with several militiamen under my command, armed at my side, I arrested known war criminals one after another.'[1]

Friedman was sent to Gdańsk, where he was tasked with closely observing the Germans leaving the city. Some looked pitiful because they could barely walk, with bandages on their heads stained with blood. 'We were incapable of compassion, of pity. Not long before, they had been in a murderous frenzy. They were responsible for the consequences. My heart was filled with hatred. I hated them in defeat just as I had hated them as brutal victors.'

In Gdańsk, he carried out a selection of Germans. 'I decided arbitrarily: who had been in the police, in the SS, or simply who I didn't like. That was my whim, so what? (…) I beat Germans in the face. Just as I had once been beaten. Oh, it felt good to strike back. I was taking revenge for my father, for my mother, for my sister, for my little brother, for all my murdered loved ones.'

During a leave spent in his native Radom, he committed a robbery. The raid failed, and Friedman was unable to escape the scene. He was caught by

Above left: Beate Klarsfeld (Beate Auguste Künzel, 1939-), photographed in 2015, is a journalist who was known for her efforts to bring Nazi criminals to justice. (*Public domain*)

Above right: Serge Klarsfeld (1935-) is an historian, lawyer, author, and formerly a long-time Nazi hunter active in France. (*Public domain*)

a nearby militiaman. Ultimately, however, he managed to flee and soon left Poland, making his way to Israel. He later became the director of the Jewish Historical Documentation Center in Vienna, where he worked alongside the institute's founder, Simon Wiesenthal.

Bringing Nazi war criminals to justice was steadily pushed further down the list of priorities in postwar Europe. As a result, the flow of necessary funds for continued activity grew smaller and smaller. As Friedman recalled: 'My files were bursting with sworn testimonies. But no one wanted to use them to prosecute Nazis. The Germans didn't want them, the Austrians didn't want them. Neither did the Western Allies, nor the Russians.[2]

In 1952, Friedman closed his office and left for Israel, where after a period of work at the Yad Vashem Institute, in 1957 he founded the Institute of Documentation for the Investigation of Nazi War Crimes. Running it, he continued to track down Nazi criminals and exerted pressure on various governments, leading to their extradition.

He contributed to the capture and trial of 250 war criminals, including Adolf Eichmann. He tracked down Eichmann's trail in Argentina practically at the same time as Mossad. The documentation he gathered played a crucial role in sentencing Eichmann to death. Friedman died in 2011 in Haifa.

Great publicity worldwide was also gained by the married couple Serge and Beate Klarsfeld. Serge was born on 17 September 1935 in Bucharest, and his future wife on 13 February 1939 in Berlin. As can be seen, during the war both were mere children. After completing his studies in the humanities, Serge, while working as a lawyer, became interested in tracking down Nazis.

In 1979, in France, he founded the Association of Sons and Daughters of Jews Deported from France (FFDJF), which played an important role in the French authorities' recognition of their responsibility for the deportation of Jews. He is also the vice president of the Foundation for the Memory of the Shoah and a member of the Auschwitz-Birkenau Foundation Council, and since 2012, a member of the International Auschwitz Council.

Beate's career turned out to be far more turbulent. Her father had served in the Wehrmacht, and as she later recalled in an interview:

> My parents were not Nazis, but they voted for Hitler. They did not feel guilty for the crimes committed under his rule, even though they supported his rise to power. Before the war, my mother stayed at home while my father worked in an insurance

company. He served in the Wehrmacht on the French and Russian fronts but was discharged due to tuberculosis. After the war, my mother would meet with neighbours, and they would lament their fate. They recalled the prosperity of the past. They complained about injustice, forgetting that it was the result of their earlier choices – even if none of them had personally murdered anyone or stolen anything during the war.

Beate first gained knowledge about the Holocaust around 1960, after meeting her future husband, whom she married on 7 November 1963. As she herself remembered: 'We were preparing for a stable, organised life, like that of thousands of young married couples.' Two years later, the Klarsfelds' son was born, and they named him Arno.

Professionally, Beate worked as a secretary at the Franco-German Youth Cooperation Organisation. Her husband became deputy director of a radio and television agency. Nothing at the time suggested the direction their future would take. Beate could rather have been suspected of wanting to begin a political career, and it became increasingly clear that she was leaning toward the left and giving her support to the SPD. She also became more active in promoting feminism, turning into a passionate advocate of the movement. This displeased her superiors, who held conservative views and had previously been involved in the activities of the NSDAP.

When Kurt Georg Kiesinger became Chancellor of Germany, Beate saw it as a personal affront and at the same time, a challenge. Kiesinger had been a member of the NSDAP since 1933 and had

SS-Hauptsturmführer Nikolaus 'Klaus' Barbie (1913-1991) was the head of the Gestapo in Lyon. Owing to his crimes, he became known as the 'Butcher of Lyon'. (*Public domain*)

also served as deputy director of the Radio Division at the Ministry of Foreign Affairs.

At the time she wrote: 'As a German woman, I condemn Kiesinger's assumption of the office of Chancellor. Sociologist Hannah Arendt used the phrase "the banality of evil" when speaking of Eichmann. For me, Kiesinger represents the respectability of evil.'

Only a month after her article was published in the leftist magazine *Combat*, Beate was dismissed from her job. It was only then that her husband began to take a deeper interest in the story of his father, who had been deported and murdered in Auschwitz. When war broke out in 1967, he volunteered for the army and left for Israel. By the time he arrived, however, the conflict later known as the Six-Day War was virtually over. He therefore did not take part in combat, yet for him personally, the most important thing was that he had made the decision almost without hesitation. As he claimed, his courage came from the example of his father who, when struck by a camp *kapo*, simply struck back. He paid with his life, but showed extraordinary bravery.

'In 1943, I was 8 years old and we were hiding with the whole family in Nice. When the Gestapo appeared, he left the hiding place in order to save us. He convinced them that there was no one in the apartment, because the whole family had fallen ill and gone to the countryside. He was deported to Auschwitz,' Serge later recalled.

The radicalisation of both their public actions, however, led to a certain crisis in their marriage. Many friends advised them to let it go and live a normal life. Nevertheless, Serge, filled with postwar courage, told his wife: 'How can I accept your dismissal and not protest? You are the first woman in France since the war to have spoken the truth about a Nazi. That would be submission in the worst sense.'[3]

The decision was made, and the Klarsfelds began a long and exhausting legal battle against Beate's dismissal from her job. They also appealed to the French authorities, but were met with silence. Serge did not remain idle. During his vacation, he travelled to Berlin to examine the personnel file of the new chancellor in the archives of the Ministry of the Interior. He returned to Paris with copies of many documents, which he quickly used to write a book on Kiesinger's wartime propaganda activities. At that point, the Klarsfelds came under even stronger attack, with the main argument of their opponents being that both received support from Eastern Bloc states, mainly East Germany. Serge Klarsfeld did not deny this, but insisted that it was only a matter of access to documents, not financial backing.

Caricature of Klaus Barbie and his defence lawyer, Jacques Vergès, during the trial in Lyon in 1987. (*Wikimedia Commons / Calvi CC BY-SA 4.0*)

In 1970, Beate travelled to Warsaw, where she chained herself to a tree as part of a campaign to draw attention to Poland's ongoing 'anti-Zionist' campaign. However, the attempt failed and she was expelled. The same happened in Czechoslovakia, where she distributed leaflets in Prague. Yet she no longer needed such publicity. The book about the West German chancellor was selling well and had brought the couple enormous popularity.

They gained even greater fame through their pursuit of Klaus Barbie, the 'Butcher of Lyon', who was hiding under the pseudonym Klaus Altmann. 'In 1971, I learned that the prosecutor's office in Munich, at the request of a German organisation of Nazi victims, had opened an investigation into his case. Altmann, living in Bolivia, was said to be Klaus Barbie. I went to track him down and find proof that it was indeed him. Thus began the struggle for his extradition.'

Barbie was born on 25 October 1913, in Bad Godesberg. He studied at the Friedrich Wilhelm Institute, after which he joined the SS. He was accepted into the SD, where he underwent appropriate training in Bernau, and was then assigned to Düsseldorf. In 1937, he joined the NSDAP. He likely would have done so much earlier, but after Hitler's rise to power in Germany, new membership in the party was temporarily banned. Hitler wanted to guard against an influx of opportunists.

At the end of 1938, Barbie was required to serve in the Wehrmacht, where he was assigned to the 39th Infantry Regiment. Afterwards, he returned to the ranks of the Black Order and was sent to the SD officers' school in Charlottenburg. In 1940, following the Wehrmacht's occupation of the Netherlands, he was assigned to the SD office in The Hague, where he worked on developing SS plans for the anticipated invasion of the British Isles. Soon after, however, he was transferred to Office B4, which dealt with Jewish affairs within Section IV of the Gestapo.

When stationed in Amsterdam, he took part in public executions in the Jewish ghetto established there, often personally commanding the firing squad. In preparation for the attack on the Soviet Union under Operation *Barbarossa*, the SS reinstated the structures already tested in Poland: special units known as *Einsatzgruppen*. These formations, composed of members

Simon Wiesenthal (1908-2005) was an architect and engineer, as well as one of the most renowned Nazi hunters. (*Public domain*)

of the police, SD, and Gestapo, carried out mass executions. Klaus Barbie also served in one of these units.

In the spring of 1942, after enduring brutal service on the Eastern Front, the future 'Butcher of Lyon' was transferred to Gex, located about 10 kilometres (6 miles) from the border with neutral Switzerland. His strong command of the French language proved to be a major asset. His mission was to abduct Alexander Foote, a Soviet agent operating in Geneva. The plan, however, never materialised, as Foote had already left the city.

In June 1942, Barbie was reassigned to the *Kommando der Sipo-SD* in Dijon, from where he was deployed as an agent to Charbonnières-les-Bains in Vichy France. In 1944, when Hitler decided to put an end to the autonomy of this puppet state and ordered the occupation of southern France, Barbie was placed in charge of Section IV of the Gestapo within the Sipo-SD headquarters for the Rhône-Alpes region. He was responsible for combating the Resistance, counterintelligence, implementing the Holocaust, overseeing forgeries, and maintaining intelligence archives.

Devoted to his work, Barbie hardly ever rested and became notorious for his dynamism, ruthlessness, and cruelty. He was responsible, among other crimes, for the deportation of forty-four Jewish children and seven adults from Izieu to an extermination camp, the execution of twenty-two hostages including women and children in retaliation for an attack on two German policemen, as well as the killing of seventy Jews in Bron and others among the 120 Montluc prison inmates executed in Saint-Genis-Laval. In the first half of 1944, he took part in anti-partisan operations in the Jura and Ain regions, brutally pacifying local communities. He was also indirectly responsible for actions against the *maquis* (Resistance fighters) in other parts of the region, including in the Azergues valley and on the Vercors plateau.

Barbie's position within the Sipo-SD rose significantly after the capture and arrest of Jean Moulin, codenamed 'Rex', the chairman of the National Council of the Resistance and the delegate of Free France tasked with unifying the underground movement. Yet by now, German domination in France was nearing its end, after the Allied offensive launched on 6 June 1944, with the successful Operation *Overlord*, sealed the fate of the occupation.

In September 1944, after Lyon was liberated by the *Forces Françaises de l'Intérieur* (FFI), regular French troops, and the US Army, Barbie was transferred to the Vosges, where he organised operations against partisans.

Following the liberation of France, he continued his work in Baden-Baden, Halle, Düsseldorf, Essen, and Wuppertal. According to precise and documented calculations, he was co-responsible for the deportation of 7,500 Jews to extermination camps, the murder of 4,342 people, and the arrest and torture of 14,311 Resistance fighters. It was because of the scale of these crimes that he earned the notorious nickname the 'Butcher of Lyon'.

When the war came to an end, Barbie had to first avoid accountability for his crimes and then think about securing his future. This did not take long and he soon entered the service of the Americans and the British. He worked in intelligence, focusing on combating left-wing opposition to the Western Allies' occupation of Germany.

In 1951, Allied intelligence concluded that his services were no longer required. The knowledge he supposedly possessed proved of little practical use, and his value had been overstated. As a result, no obstacles were placed in his way when he fled to Argentina, taking his entire family with him. Soon after, however, he moved to Bolivia, where, under the alias Klaus Altmann, he engaged in drug trafficking. According to some sources, during the 1960s he also took part in crushing the guerrilla National Liberation Army and advised on the capture of the Argentine revolutionary Ernesto 'Che' Guevara.

In January 2011, it was revealed that between 1965 and 1966 Barbie had also cooperated with the German Federal Intelligence Service (*Bundesnachrichtendienst*, BND). According to its assessment, he 'held genuinely German convictions and was a determined enemy of communism'. Operating under the codename 'Eagle', he was considered a valuable source of information for West Germany, partly thanks to his connections with right-wing politicians in Bolivia.

In 1971, Barbie was tracked down by the Klarsfelds, who made their discovery public. At the beginning of 1972, French journalist Ladislas de Hoyos, accompanied by a cameraman, travelled to Bolivia. Officially, their purpose was to interview Klaus Altmann, but in reality, the subject of the conversation was Klaus Barbie. Barbie evidently felt secure enough in his assumed identity that he agreed to this unusual request, likely believing that such openness would help dispel any lingering suspicions.

The interview was conducted primarily in German and Spanish. Suddenly, the journalist asked in French: 'Have you ever been to Lyon?' Altmann immediately denied it without hesitation. To the Frenchman, this reaction seemed highly suspicious. He believed that Barbie should have at least paused, pretended to think, or shown some sign of surprise. This only strengthened de Hoyos's conviction that Altmann was in fact the wanted Klaus Barbie.

Until 1983, the Bolivian government refused all requests for his extradition. The hunt for Barbie nearly cost Beate Klarsfeld her life on more than one occasion. As she later recalled in an interview: 'In 1972 I received a package containing a bomb. In 1979, a time bomb was planted in my car. It exploded when no one was inside. I was repeatedly threatened by phone and mail. I won't even mention the pressure and the "good advice" whispered by various officials. They tried to manipulate me, appealing to my patriotism.'

Ultimately, Barbie's life in freedom came to an end on 18 January 1983. After being arrested, he was extradited to France. On 11 May 1987, his trial began before a French court in Lyon. The 'Butcher of Lyon's' defence attorney, Jacques Vergès, attempted to argue that Barbie's actions were no worse than those of French colonialists in the Americas. Faced with overwhelming evidence of his crimes, however, this line of defence failed, and on 4 July 1987, Barbie was sentenced to life imprisonment. He died of leukaemia in prison in 1991.

After Barbie's conviction, Beate Klarsfeld did not abandon her political activism. In the 2012 German presidential elections, she was nominated as a candidate by the Left Party. She was also chosen as an elector representing the Saxon Left, which gave her the right to cast a vote. In the election held on 18 March, she received 126 out of 1,232 electoral votes.

The most famous of the Nazi hunters, however, was Simon Wiesenthal, whose renown stemmed largely from the role he played in the capture of Adolf Eichmann.

Wiesenthal was born on 31 December 1908 in Buczacz, which at that time lay within the Austro-Hungarian Empire. During the First World War, he lost his father, after which he and his mother briefly moved to Vienna. When his mother found another suitor, she returned with her children to their hometown. It was there that the future Nazi hunter began his education, completing his secondary studies in 1928.

He then turned toward the Lwów Polytechnic, hoping to study in the Faculty of Architecture. However, he was not admitted due to the then unofficial policy of numerus clausus, which imposed limits on the number of university students. These restrictions were motivated by political or purely practical reasons, but in Central Europe they were often applied specifically against Jews.

Wiesenthal therefore went to study in Prague, where he graduated in 1932. He then settled in Lwów, where until the outbreak of the Second World War he ran his own architectural firm. The good life ended with the entry of the Red Army into Lwów, whereby the Soviets immediately set about imposing their own order, targeting primarily clergy, Polish soldiers, and the intelligentsia, which included Wiesenthal. Repression struck his entire family: his father-in-law was arrested, and his wife's brother was shot by the NKVD. The Soviets also nationalised all industry and confiscated private property. Wiesenthal lost his firm and, in order to survive, had to take whatever work he could find. He eventually secured a position in a state-owned factory, where he worked as a mechanic. But the Russians did not relent so easily, and Wiesenthal was placed on a list of those destined for deportation to the far east. He escaped this fate by bribing one of the NKVD men.

After the first wave of terror, there was a brief sense of relative safety. This lasted until June 1941, when the Third Reich launched Operation *Barbarossa*. As is well known, alongside the communists, Jews were its chief ideological enemy. The Jewish community of Lwów was forced to pay a levy of 20 million rubles. At the same time, the Germans did not restrain themselves from organising pogroms, often inciting the local Ukrainian population to take part. On 6 July, Simon Wiesenthal found himself among a group designated for execution. He was saved from death by a former acquaintance, who at the time was serving in the Ukrainian police.

When the Germans began constructing the ghetto, not a single day passed without someone from Lwów's Jewish community losing their life. Among the victims were Wiesenthal's mother and mother-in-law. In the autumn of 1942, while working on the railway, Wiesenthal established contact with the Polish underground. In exchange for intelligence on German trains, he secured false documents for his wife, allowing her to leave safely for Warsaw.

In April 1943, he narrowly escaped execution. On the occasion of Adolf Hitler's fifty-fourth birthday, the camp commander planned to kill fifty-four Jews. Wiesenthal was among those selected. He stood naked in a group of people awaiting a bullet when fate once again intervened. He was pulled out of the crowd and ordered back to the camp. He was spared. As he later recalled: 'I was staggering like a drunk, Koller slapped me twice and brought me back to reality. Naked, I headed back (…) Behind me, the sound of shots rang out again, but they fell silent long before I reached the camp.'

Shortly afterwards, Wiesenthal escaped from the camp. His previous rescuer, senior railway inspector Adolf Kohlrautz, a declared anti-Nazi, proved helpful. For the next three months, Wiesenthal hid in nearby villages before eventually being captured and taken back to the camp, where he was brutally interrogated. Pushed to the brink of endurance, he attempted suicide. According to his own account, before another Gestapo interrogation he cut his veins with a razor blade. However, since he never revealed how he had obtained the blade, many researchers doubt the veracity of this episode.

Wiesenthal was said to have been transferred to a nearby prison hospital, where he remained for about a month. He was then returned to the Janowska camp. With the front approaching, the Jews there were transported to Płaszów, on the outskirts of Kraków, where the commandant was Amon Goeth. By that time, efforts were already underway to erase evidence of crimes and prepare for evacuation, and Wiesenthal's work consisted of grinding corpses.

In November 1944, he was moved to the overcrowded Gross-Rosen camp, where at first he was assigned to peeling potatoes. In January 1945, all prisoners were forced to march on foot for 250 kilometres (155 miles) to the camp in Chemnitz, from where they were transported further to Buchenwald.

On 7 February 1945, Wiesenthal was transported to Mauthausen. Exhausted, emaciated, and ravaged by infection, he was sent to the 'death block', where, according to his memoirs, he lay for three months until liberation on 5 May 1945. At that time, he weighed barely 50 kilograms. Thanks to the care of American medics, however, he quickly regained his strength.

Once recovered, he turned to the question of accountability for war criminals. He submitted a request to the Americans, asking to participate in the investigation of German crimes. He also listed ninety-one individuals whom he believed should be tried and punished. However, his cooperation with the Americans fell short of expectations, and so he decided to act independently.

In 1947, he founded the Jewish Historical Documentation Centre, dedicated to collecting documents and eyewitness accounts of German crimes. A year earlier, he had come into the possession of files concerning Adolf Eichmann's crimes, which he had received from Israeli diplomat Asher Ben Nathan. The problem, however, was that no one had a photograph of Eichmann. After six months of effort, one was finally obtained.

Through Dieter Wisliceny, they managed to secure the address of Eichmann's wartime driver, who still maintained contact with his former boss's mistress.

Wiesenthal learned that Vera Eichmann had filed a petition in court to have her husband declared legally dead. If the court had granted her request, Eichmann would have been automatically removed from all registers of wanted war criminals. After all, why search for someone who was officially deceased? Wiesenthal, however, suspected that his target was still alive. His conviction grew stronger in 1951, when Vera left Europe for Argentina. He then tracked down her mother, from whom he learned that Eichmann's false identity was Ricardo Klement. This was another major breakthrough in the search, which ultimately led to Eichmann's abduction by Mossad in 1960, his transportation to Israel, and the administration of justice.

Wiesenthal's name secured a permanent place in history books, opening further opportunities for his work. In total, he contributed to the capture of more than 1,000 Nazi criminals, including Franz Stangl, the commandant of Treblinka, who had been hiding in Brazil.

In 1954, Wiesenthal closed his Documentation Centre, yet remained active for the rest of his life, striving to exclude former Nazis from public life and to hold additional Germans and Austrians accountable for their crimes. For this, he often faced harassment from certain Austrian politicians. 'The only value of almost five decades of my work is the warning to future murderers that they will never know peace,' he said in an interview with the Polish Section of Radio Free Europe.

Wiesenthal died in Vienna on 20 September 2005, aged 96.

Conclusion

The history of the Second World War and, more broadly, the twelve years of the Third Reich's existence left behind not only ruins and graves, but also a vast shadow zone: half-truths, missing documents, deliberate disinformation, and questions that refuse to disappear with time. Some riddles have been solved, but many still await their explanation. It is precisely these mysteries that continue to fire the imagination; the sense that somewhere, in a sealed file, a private diary, or a forgotten archive, the missing piece of the historical puzzle is still waiting.

This book has sought to show that a 'mystery' is not merely a label. The same hunger for sensation that drives conscientious researchers to seek facts also creates a market for shortcuts: forged documents, sensational 'discoveries', and stories constructed to impress rather than to withstand critical scrutiny. The episode of fabricated diaries or invented 'treasure' trails is not an amusing footnote to history; it is a warning that the past can be forged almost as easily as money, sometimes for profit, sometimes for influence, and sometimes simply for notoriety.

In the chapters contained within this book, the same pattern returns: the Third Reich was a system that fed on secrecy, myth-making, and the control of information, and it generated myths even as it was collapsing. In the final months of the war, rumours could move armies. The very idea of an 'Alpine Fortress', amplified by propaganda, influenced Allied decisions and sustained one last illusion of strategic depth at a moment when Germany no longer had the means to create it in any real, military sense. Even an illusion could become 'operational reality' in the minds of generals and politicians.

The same mechanism operated after the war. Stories of secret organisations, escape networks, hidden treasures, or wonder weapons endure because they offer emotional simplicity: one explanation, one culprit, one plan. Reality is usually less elegant. Escape routes did exist, but they were often improvised, opportunistic, and dependent on local contacts, silence, and corruption. The myth of a single, perfectly organised 'apparatus' can be a convenient veil. It sometimes helps conceal the uncomfortable truth that various institutions and individuals, for various reasons, assisted criminals in disappearing and starting new lives.

The most troubling continuity, however, was not institutional but human – continuity in compromise. After 1945, the world did not become morally simple. Victorious states courted German specialists and intelligence assets, while survivors, investigators, and activists fought to keep justice from slipping down the agenda. In that climate, prosecuting perpetrators was often postponed, not only because of exhaustion and bureaucracy, but also because the new geopolitical order encouraged selective blindness. The Cold War created a reality in which 'usefulness' could matter more than guilt, and morality was too often exchanged for strategic advantage.

That is why the final parts of this narrative, devoted to Nazi hunters, are so important. They remind us that justice rarely arrives on its own. It is chosen, fought for, funded or quietly abandoned. It requires documentation, persistence, and a willingness to endure years of struggle against indifference. The greatest successes in bringing war criminals to account were not inevitable; they were the result of long, painstaking work, often in defiance of the political mood of the time. The bitterest lesson is this: even when justice does come, it usually comes late, often after decades of comfortable anonymity for perpetrators and a lifetime of trauma for victims.

We must also accept an uncomfortable truth: time is the enemy of certainty. Witnesses die, traces vanish, and documents remain classified. Many looted records produced by German institutions still lie in archives with restricted access, and the political will to open them fully is far from guaranteed. As long as files remain sealed and collections scattered, speculation will fill the gaps. That does not mean the search is pointless; it means it must be disciplined, cautious, and honest about what can and cannot be proven.

Will the remaining mysteries ever be solved? Some will. Many will not. But reasonable hope is not naïveté. It is the awareness that history is not closed as long as archives can still be opened, graves can be identified, and documents can be reread with fresh eyes. Even if the final answer never comes, the pursuit still has value: it teaches us to distinguish evidence from legend, and truth from desire.

Endnotes

Chapter 1

1. D. Irving, *Wojna Rudolfa Hessa*, Pruszków 2002, p. 111.

Chapter 2

1. Bernadotte wrote letters to Himmler concerning the release of Jews from German concentration camps. See: G. Fleming, *Die herkunft des 'Bernadotte briefe' an Himmler vom 10 marz 1945*, [w:] Vierteljahrshefte für Zeitgeschichte, r. 26 (1978), Heft 4, pp. 578-600.
2. N. Masur, *En Jude talar med Himmler*, Sztokholm 1945, p. 29.
3. S. Persson, *Białe Autobusy. Pakt z Himmlerem i niezwykła akcja ratowania więźniów obozów koncentracyjnych*, Warszawa 2013, p. 15.
4. In his report on the conversation with Himmler, Masur noted that Himmler appeared distraught over the alleged lies being spread about the conditions in the concentration camps liberated by the Allies, particularly Bergen-Belsen and Buchenwald. At the same time, Masur feared that, in the event of Germany's defeat, Himmler might issue an order to exterminate all prisoners still held in the camps. See: TNA, FO/371/51194.
5. J. Mayo, E. Craigie, *Ostatni dzień Hitlera*, Warszawa 2016, p. 32.
6. F. Bernadotte, *Koniec Trzeciej Rzeszy*, Warszawa 1946, pp. 73-74.
7. Ibid, p. 81.
8. M.A. Musmanno, *Ostatni świadkowie Hitlera*, Warszawa 2005, p. 124.
9. W. Schellenberg, *Wspomnienia arcyszpiega Hitlera*, Warszawa 2009, p. 268.
10. After the war, efforts were made to downplay Count Folke Bernadotte's role in favour of Felix Kersten and even Walther Schellenberg. These actions were allegedly motivated by claims of antisemitism on the part of the count. On 17 September 1948, he was assassinated. The attack was carried out by the Jewish organisation LEHI and the Stern Group. It was not until May 1995 that Israeli Foreign Minister Shimon Peres apologised to the Bernadotte family for the count's murder. See: D. Basista, *Misja dyplomatyczna Folke Bernadotte w Niemczech w 1945 roku*, in: 'Historia i Polityka', no. 5, 8.10.2015, p. 29.

Chapter 3

1. Ch. Krüger, *Mój dziadek fałszerz*, Warszawa 2017, p. 51.
2. Ibid, p. 51.
3. Ibid, p. 54.
4. Ibid.
5. Bad Arolsen, Zugangsliste KZ Mauthausen, 1945, sygn. 1.1.26.1/1321818, ITS Digital Archive.
6. Ch. Krüger, op. cit., p. 72.
7. *Testimony of Georg Kohn given before the Berlin Criminal Police on 15 October 1955*, [in:] StAL EL 317 III Bue 329.
8. Ch. Krüger, op. cit., p. 92.
9. F. Altenhöner, *Człowiek, który rozpętał II wojnę światową. Alfred Naujocks – fałszerz, morderca, terrorysta*, Poznań 2019.

Chapter 4

1. The Amber Room was an extraordinary Baroque decorative interior essentially a 'chamber' or a set of wall panels – crafted from amber slabs, gilded ornamentation, and mirrors. It was created in the early eighteenth century in Prussia (at the initiative of the Prussian court) and was later presented to Tsar Peter I as a political gesture aimed at bringing Prussia and Russia closer together. Over time, the room was expanded and installed in the palace at Tsarskoye Selo near St. Petersburg, where it became one of the greatest attractions of the imperial residence often called the 'eighth wonder of the world' because of the way light reflected in the amber. During the Second World War, after the German occupation of the area around Leningrad, the Amber Room was dismantled and taken away by the Germans. It was transported to Königsberg (today's Kaliningrad) and displayed there. Toward the end of the war, its trail goes cold: there is no certainty whether it was destroyed in bombings and fires, looted, or hidden and still lies somewhere undiscovered. Between 1979 and 2003, a faithful reconstruction of the room was created, which can be seen today in the Catherine Palace in Tsarskoye Selo.
2. The search for the so-called 'gold train' near Wałbrzych is essentially an effort to verify a legend that, at the end of 1945, the Germans hid an armoured train loaded with valuables somewhere in a sealed tunnel in Lower Silesia. The story flared up again in August 2015, when it was announced that an object had been 'detected' with ground-penetrating radar, and Poland's then General Conservator of Monuments, Piotr Żuchowski, publicly spoke of a very high probability that such a train existed. However, independent geophysical surveys (including work involving scientists from AGH University of Science and Technology) indicated that there was no train

at the stated location. The efforts culminated in test excavations and drilling in the summer of 2016 near the 65th kilometre of the Wrocław–Wałbrzych railway line, which ended without finding either a tunnel or a train. Despite the lack of hard evidence, the topic resurfaces from time to time. For example, in 2025 another group claimed to have new indications and received a limited permit for search work, but no confirmed discovery has been made to date.

Chapter 6
1. D. Irving, *Norymberga. Ostatnia bitwa*, Warszawa 1999, p. 321.
2. Ibid, p. 324.
3. D. Irving, *Marszałek Rzeszy Hermann Göring 1893-1946*, Warszawa 2001, p. 570.

Chapter 7
1. *Okupacja i ruch oporu w dzienniku Hansa Franka 1939-1945*, t. 1: 1939-1942, oprac. S. Płoski, L. Dobroszycki, Warszawa 1972, p. 98.
2. G. Ueberschät, *Wojskowe elity III Rzeszy*, Warszawa 2004, p. 46.
3. Dokumentacja Międzynarodowego Trybunału w Norymberdze, 3706-PS, *Oświadczenie generała pułkownika Johannesa Blaskowitza, 10 listopada 1945 r.* (USA 537).
4. *14 niemieckich generałów – zbrodniarzy przed sądem. Samobójstwo Blaskowitza w dniu rozpoczęcia procesu w Norymberdze*, 'Dziennik Zachodni', nr 36, 6.02.1948 r.

Chapter 8
1. J. K. Latimer, *Śmiertelna choroba Hitlera i inne tajemnice nazistowskich przywódców*, Warszawa 2000, p. 228.
2. Ibid, p. 232.

Chapter 9
1. M. Gilbert, *Druga wojna światowa*, Warszawa 2000, p. 522.
2. I. Perkowska-Szczypiorska, *Kartki z Oświęcimia* [w:] Kominy, Oświęcim 1940-1945, Warszawa 1962, p. 102; P. Skutecki, *Trzecia Rzesza i koncerny farmaceutyczne*, Bydgoszcz 2022, p. 245.
3. K. Wer, *Eksperymenty 'anioła śmierci'* [w:] Pharmacopola, 2 (5), 30 października 2022, pp. 16-22.
4. P. Włoczyk, *Byłam ofiarą doktora Mengele* [w:] 'Historia do Rzeczy' nr 4/2014.
5. G. I. Posner, J. Ware, *Mengele. Polowanie na anioła śmierci*, Kraków 2008, p. 155.
6. Ibid, p. 191, 192.

Chapter 10

1. T. Sawicki, *Rozkaz zdławić powstanie. Niemcy i ich sojusznicy w walce z powstaniem warszawskim*, Warszawa 2010, p. 31.
2. Zbrodnie okupanta podczas powstania warszawskiego w 1944 roku (w dokumentach), red. Sz. Datner, K. Leszczyński, Warszawa 1962, p. 387.
3. Zeznanie Wandy Lurie o zbrodniach popełnionych przez Niemców w fabryce 'Ursus' przy ul. Wolskiej w Warszawie, źr. https://pl.wikisource.org/wiki/Zeznanie_Wandy_Lurie_o_zbrodniach_pope%C5%82nionych_przez_Niemc%C3%B3w_w_fabryce_%E2%80%9EUrsus%E2%80%9D_przy_ul._Wolskiej_w_Warszawie (14.09.2025)
4. S. Jankowski, *Z fałszywym ausweisem w prawdziwej Warszawie*, t. 2, Warszawa 1985, p. 242.

Chapter 11

1. A paramilitary formation composed of members of the German national minority living in the territory of the Second Polish Republic, established in September 1939 in the occupied Polish lands. In the first months of the German occupation, the Selbstschutz took part in extermination actions directed against the Polish intelligentsia. By the end of 1939, tens of thousands of Poles had been killed at the hands of Selbstschutz squads, the largest number on the territory of Pomerania.
2. AIPN, sign. IPN GK 164/68; APB, OKBZH w Bydgoszczy, sign. 93, s. 75; W. Trzeciakowski, *Selbstschutz w Bydgoszczy i powiecie bydgoskim 1939-1940*, Bydgoszcz 2017, p. 61.
3. AIPN, Interrogation of Teofil Czerwiński, sign. IPN BY 25/25, k. 27.
4. P. Longerich, *Himmler, buchalter śmierci*, Warszawa 2014, p. 530.
5. J. Camarasa, *El nazi que buscaba uranio* [w:] 'La Voz del Interior', 25.09.2011.
6. J. Camarasa, *El 1 de abril de 1970, un miercoles, Ludolf Hermann von Alvensleben murio en Santa Rosa de Calamuchita* [w:] 'La voz del Interior', 25.09.2011.
7. G. Negro, *Un tal Bubi en Calamuchita* [w:] 'La Voz del Interior', 25.05.2018.

Chapter 12

1. S. Lauryssens, *Dziennik nazisty. Wyznania Eichmanna*, Wrocław 2008, p. 126.
2. *Interrogation of Dieter Wisliceny by Colonel Smith Brookhart, Nuremberg, November 14, 1945* [w:] J. Mendelsohn, D. Detweiler, The Holocaust. Selected documents in eighteen volumes, T. 12, Nowy Jork 1983, pp. 6-24.
3. A. Eichmann, *Bożyszcza. Wspomnienia z celi śmierci,* Kraków 2001, p. 211.

Chapter 13

1. *Aktion Reinhardt* was the codename for a German extermination operation carried out in the General Government in 1942–1943, aimed at murdering Jews and plundering their property. Its 'core' consisted of the death camps of Bełżec, Sobibór, and

Treblinka (it was also linked to deportations and mass killings elsewhere, including at Majdanek). The operation was run by SS and police structures under the command of Odilo Globocnik from the Lublin District. As a result, approximately 1.5–2 million Jews were murdered, primarily from occupied Poland.

2. https://www.polskieradio.pl/39/156/Artykul/2872531,Franz-Stangl-Niemiecki-diabel-schwytany-przez-lowce-nazistow [3.01.2023 r.].

Chapter 14

1. I. Witkowski, *Kolonia Godność. Niemieckie imperium w Andach*, Warszawa 2021, p. 113.
2. *BODEUM Rome Group Willy FRIEDE*. 'Nazi War Crimes Disclosure Act', 1950-03-17.
3. CIA. *Background information on German military experts in Syria*. 'FOIA Collection', 1954-02-23. CIA.
4. O. Schröm, A. Röpke, *Cicha Pomoc dla nazistów. Tajna działalność byłych SS-manów i neonazistów,* Zakrzewo 2015, p. 58.

Chapter 15

1. O. Skorzeny, *Nieznana wojna. Moje operacje specjalne*, Gdańsk 1999, p. 260.
2. Ibid, p. 262.

Chapter 16

1. L. Degrelle, *Front wschodni 1941-1945*, Międzyzdroje 2002, p. 131.
2. Ibid, p. 202.

Chapter 17

1. A. Hitler, *Rozmowy przy stole 1941-1944*, Warszawa 1996, pp. 79-80.
2. D. Kurzman, *Misja specjalna*, Poznań 2008, p. 27.
3. U. Nersinger, *Szpiedzy Watykanu. Tajne służby w kościele*, Kraków 2022.
4. Ibid.

Chapter 18

1. R. Kaltenegger, *Operacja Twierdza Alpejska*, Warszawa 2002, p. 22.
2. V. Feurstein, *Irrwege der Pflicht 1938-1945*, München 1963, p. 298.
3. R. Kaltenegger, op. cit., p. 146.

Chapter 19

1. BA-MA, *Pismo Reichsführera SS do Kaltenbrunnera z 16.09.1944 r.*, sign. NS 19/1868.
2. BA-MA, *Reichsführer SS to Ernst Kaltenbrunner, 16.09.1944 r.*, sygn. NS 19/1868.

3. O. Skorzeny, op. cit., p. 207.
4. V. Koop, *Werwolf. Ostatni zaciąg Himmlera*, Warszawa 2016, pp. 182-185.
5. Ibid, pp. 203-204.

Chapter 20

1. R. Karlsch, *Atomowa bomba Hitlera. Historia tajnych niemieckich prób z bronią jądrową,* Wrocław 2005.
2. Ibid, p. 14.
3. R. Karlsch, op. cit., p. 173.
4. Ibid, p. 196.

Chapter 21

1. A. C. Hudal, *Römische Tagebücher. Lebensbeichte eines alten Bischofs*, Leopold Stocker, 1976, p. 21, cyt. za D J. Goldhagen, *Niedokończony rozrachunek*, Warszawa 2005, p. 185.
2. K. Grünberg, *SS-czarna gwardia Hitlera*, Warszawa 1985, p. 546.

Chapter 22

1. H. Thomas, *Sobowtór. Tajemnice berlińskiego bunkra,* Warszawa 1997, p. 95.
2. H. Trevor-Roper, *The Last Days of Hitler*, London 1950, p. 220.
3. J. O'Donnell, *The Berlin Bunker*, London 1979, p. 184.

Chapter 23

1. J. von Lang, *Martin Bormann. Człowiek, który zawładnął Hitlerem*, Warszawa 1995, pp. 443-470.

Chapter 25

1. D. Doyle, *Adolf Hitler's Medical Care*, [w:] 'Royal College of Physicians of Edinburgh', nr 35, pp. 75-82, Edinburgh 2005.
2. D. Irving, *Tajne dzienniki lekarza Hitlera*, Pruszków 1999, p. 17.
3. Ibid, p. 47.

Chapter 26

1. J. Pomezański, *Wielkopolskie tajemnice III Rzeszy*, Warszawa 2021, pp. 123-141.

Chapter 27

1. Operation *Paperclip* was the codename for an operation carried out by American intelligence services in the final phase of the Second World War and after its end, aimed at transferring leading German scientists to the United States. The operation was also known as Operation *Overcast,* which began before the war ended, and German scientists were to help in defeating Japan.

2. *Some of the Prisoners Hej dat Special Camp 11: Generalmajor Dr. Walther Dornberger, Island Farm Special Camp 11: The German Officers Held in Bridgend, 1946-1948,* http://www.specialcamp11.co.uk/Generalmajor_Dr_Walter_Dornberger.html [29.01.2023 r.].
3. Sz. Wrzesiński, *Tajemnicze eksperymenty w Rząsinach,* https://wydarzenia.interia.pl/prasa/odkrywca/news-tajemnicze-eksperymenty-w-rzasinach,-nId,909659 [23.01.2023 r.].
4. A. Jacobsen, *Operacja Paperclip,* Warszawa 2015, p. 129.

Chapter 28

1. W. Hirschfeld, *Ostatni U-boot,* Gdańsk 2008, pp. 260-261.
2. Ibid, p. 260.
3. M. Borowiak, *Kapitulacja U-bootów w Ameryce Północnej,* [w:] 'Morza, statki i okręty', nr 9-10 z 2019 r.
4. *Memorandum of Capt. John I. Riheldaffer, US-Subject. Report on Events at Portsmouth Navy Yard in Connections with the Surrender of German Submarines U 234, U 805, U 873 and U 1228, 22 May 1945*; NARA, sygn. NND 813024, cit. za M. Borowiak, op. cit., pp. 282-283.
5. M. Borowiak, op. cit., s. 286, p. 16.
6. H. Schäffer, *U-boat 977,* London 1953, p. 21.

Chapter 29

1. A. Nagorski, Łowcy nazistów, Poznań 2017, p. 47.
2. Ibid, p. 147.
3. B. Klarsfeld, *Wherever They May Be!,* p. 22.

Bibliography

Archival Sources

Archiwum Państwowe w Bydgoszczy
- OKBZH w Bydgoszczy, sygn. 93

Arolsen Archives
- Zugangsliste KZ Mauthausen, *1945*, sygn. 1.1.26.1/1321818, ITS Digital Archive.

Bundesarchiv Militararchiv
- *Pismo Reichsführera SS do Kaltenbrunnera z 16.09.1944 r.*, sygn. NS 19/1868.
- *Pismo Hildebrandta do Himmlera z 19.09.1944 r.*, sygn. NS 19/2884.

Centrall Inteligence Agency
- *BODEUM Rome Group Willy FRIEDE.* "Nazi War Crimes Disclosure Act", 1950-03-17.
- *Background information on German military experts in Syria.* "FOIA Collection", 1954-02-23.

Instytut Pamięci Narodowej
- sygn. IPN GK 164/68,
- *Protokół przesłuchania Teofila Czerwińskiego*, sygn. IPN By 25/25.

The National Archives
- FO/371/51194

Literature

Basista D., *Misja dyplomatyczna Folke Bernadotte w Niemczech w 1945 roku,* [w:] 'Historia i Polityka', 8.10.2015, nr 5.

Bernadotte F., *Koniec Trzeciej Rzeszy*, Warszawa 1946.

Borowiak M., *Kapitulacja U-bootów w Ameryce Północnej,* [w:] 'Morza, statki i okręty', nr 9-10/2019.

Borowiak M. Wytykowski P., *U-Booty Hitlera w Ameryce Południowej. Prawdziwa historia,* Chrzan 2021.

Camarasa J., *El nazi que buscaba uranio,* [w:] „La Voz Del Interior", 25.09.2011 r. [dostęp: 25.05.2018 r.].

Camarasa J., *El 1° de abril de 1970, un miércoles, Ludolf Hermann von Alvensleben murió en Santa Rosa de Calamuchita,* [w:] 'La voz del Interior', 25.09.2011 r. [dostęp: 25.05.2018 r.].

Degrelle L., *Front wschodni 1941-1945,* Międzyzdroje 2002.

Doyle D., *Adolf Hitler's Medical Care,* [w:] 'Royal College of Physicians of Edinburgh', nr 35/2005.

Eichmann A., *Bożyszcza. Wspomnienia z celi śmierci,* Kraków 2001.

Feurstein V., *Irrwege der Pflicht 1938-1945,* München 1963.

Fleming G., *Die herkunft des 'Bernadotte briefes' an Himmler vom 10 marz 1945,* [w:] 'Vierteljahrshefte für Zeitgeschichte', r. 26 (1978), Heft 4.

Gilbert M., *Druga Wojna Światowa,* Warszawa 2000.

Goldhagen D J., *Niedokończony rozrachunek,* 2005.

Grünberg K., *SS-czarna gwardia Hitlera,* Warszawa 1985.

Hirschfeld W., *Ostatni U-boot,* Gdańsk 2008.

Hudal A. C., *Römische Tagebücher. Lebensbeichte eines alten Bischofs,* Leopold Stocker, 1976.

Hitler A., *Rozmowy przy stole 1941-1944,* 1996.

Irving D., *Norymberga. Ostatnia bitwa,* Warszawa 1999.

Irving D., *Marszałek Rzeszy Hermann Göring 1893-1946,* Warszawa 2001.

Irving D., *Tajne dzienniki lekarza Hitlera,* Pruszków 1999.

Jacobsen A., *Operacja Paperclip,* Warszawa 2015.

Jankowski S., *Z fałszywym ausweisem w prawdziwej Warszawie, tom 2,* Warszawa 1985.

Kaltenegger R., *Operacja Twierdza Alpejska,* Warszawa 2002.

Karlsch R., *Atomowa bomba Hitlera. Historia tajnych niemieckich prób z bronią jądrową,* Wrocław 2005.

Koop V., *Werwolf. Ostatni zaciąg Himmlera,* Warszawa 2016.

Klarsfeld B., *Wherever They May Be!,* Ontario 1975.

Kuberski H., *Wschodnioeuropejska odyseja Leona Degrelle'a. Walońscy ochotnicy Waffen SS (1943-1945) na froncie wschodnim,* [w:] 'Studia z Dziejów Rosji i Europy Środkowo-Wschodniej'. XLIX (z. 2), 2014.

Kur T., *Trzy srebrne róże znaczą szlak zbrodni. Saga rodu Alvenslebenów,* Warszawa 1975.

Kurzman D., *Misja specjalna,* Poznań 2008.

Krakowski A., *Counterfeit Lives,* New York 1994.

Krüger Ch., *Mój dziadek fałszerz,* Warszawa 2017.

Krzyżanowski K., *Dziennik wojenny. Nowa odsłona,* [w:] 'Odkrywca', nr 6/2022.

Lang J. von, *Martin Bormann. Człowiek, który zawładnął Hitlerem,* Warszawa 1995.

Lattimer J. K., *Śmiertelna choroba Hitlera i inne tajemnice nazistowskich przywódców*, Warszawa 2000.

Lauryssens S., *Dziennik nazisty. Wyznania Eichmanna*, Wrocław 2008.

Longerich P., *Himmler, buchalter śmierci*, Warszawa 2014.

Masur N., *En Jude talar med Himmler*, Sztokholm 1945.

Marzec Z., *Umrzeć za Chile*, Warszawa 1980.

Mayo J., Craigie E., *Ostatni dzień Hitlera*, Warszawa 2016.

Mazanowska I., *Karolewo. Zbrodnie w obozie Selbstschutz Westpreussen*, Gdańsk-Warszawa 2017.

Musmanno M. A., *Ostatni świadkowie Hitlera*, Warszawa 2005.

Nagorski A., *Łowcy nazistów*, Poznań 2017.

Negro G., *Un tal Bubi en Calamuchita*, [w:] 'La Voz Del Interior' [dostęp: 25.05.2018 r.].

Nersinger U., *Szpiedzy Watykanu. Tajne służby w kościele*, Kraków 2022.

O'Donnell J., *The Berlin Bunker*, London 1979.

Perkowska-Szczypiorska I., *Kartki z Oświęcimia*, [w:] *Kominy, Oświęcim 1940-1945*, Warszawa 1962.

Persson, S., *Białe Autobusy. Pakt z Himmlerem i niezwykła akcja ratowania więźniów obozów koncentracyjnych*, Warszawa 2013.

Pomezański J., *Wielkopolskie tajemnice III Rzeszy*, Warszawa 2021.

Przesłuchanie Dietera Wislicenyprzez pułkownika Smitha Brookharta, Norymberga, 14 listopada 1945, [w:] Mendelsohn J. i Detweiler D., *The Holocaust. Selected documents in eighteen volumes*, tom. 12, Nowy Jork, 1983.

Sawicki T., *Rozkaz zdławić powstanie. Niemcy i ich sojusznicy w walce z powstaniem warszawskim*, Warszawa 2010.

Schäffer H., *U-boat 977*, London 1953.

Schellenberg W., *Wspomnienia arcyszpiega Hitlera*, Warszawa 2009.

Schröm O., Röpke A., *Cicha Pomoc dla nazistów. Tajna działalność byłych SS-manów i neonazistów*, Zakrzewo 2015.

Skorzeny O., *Nieznana wojna. Moje operacje specjalne*, Gdańsk 1999.

Skutecki P., *Trzecia Rzesza i koncerny farmaceutyczne*, Bydgoszcz 2022.

Świetlik J., *Alvenslebenowie*, Ostromecko 2005.

Thomas H., *Sobowtór. Tajemnice berlińskiego bunkra*, Warszawa 1997.

Trevor-Roper H., *The Last Days of Hitler*, London 1950.

Trzeciakowski W., *Selbstschutz w Bydgoszczy i powiecie bydgoskim 1939-1940*, Bydgoszcz 2017.

Ueberschär G., *Wojskowe elity III Rzeszy*. Warszawa 2004.

Wer K., *Eksperymenty „anioła śmierci"*, [w:] 'Pharmacopola', 2 (5), z 30 października 2022.

Zbrodnie okupanta w czasie powstania warszawskiego w 1944 roku (w dokumentach), red. Sz. Datnera i K. Leszczyńskiego, Warszawa 1962.

Internet

Franz Stangl. Niemiecki diabeł schwytany przez 'łowcę nazistów', PolskieRadio.pl, https://www.polskieradio.pl/39/156/Artykul/2872531,Franz-Stangl-Niemiecki-diabel-schwytany-przez-lowce-nazistow [dostęp: 3.01.2023 r.]

Some of the Prisoners Hej dat Special Camp 11: Generalmajor Dr Walther Dornberger, Island Farm Special Camp 11: The German Officers Held in Bridgend., 1946-1948, http://www.specialcamp11.co.uk/Generalmajor_Dr_Walter_Dornberger.htm [Dostęp: 29.01.2023 r.]

Wrzesiński Sz., *Tajemnicze eksperymenty w Rząsinach*, https://wydarzenia.interia.pl/prasa/odkrywca/news-tajemnicze-eksperymenty-w-rzasinach,nId,909659 [dostęp: 23.01.2023r.]

Zeznanie Wandy Lurie o zbrodniach popełnionych przez Niemców w fabryce 'Ursus' przy ul. Wolskiej w Warszawie, Wikiźródła, https://pl.wikisource.org/wiki/Zeznanie_Wandy_Lurie_o_zbrodniach_pope%C5%82nionych_przez_Niemc%C3%B3w_w_fabryce_%E2%80%9EUrsus%E2%80%9D_przy_ul._Wolskiej_w_Warszawie [dostęp: 30.12.2022 r.]

Index of Names

Dear Reader,

We hope you have enjoyed this book, but why not share your views on social media? You can also follow our pages to see more about our other products: facebook.com/penandswordbooks or follow us on X @penswordbooks

You can also view our products at www.pen-and-sword.co.uk (UK and ROW) or www.penandswordbooks.com (North America).

To keep up to date with our latest releases and online catalogues, please sign up to our newsletter at: www.pen-and-sword.co.uk/newsletter

If you would like a printed catalogue with our latest books, then please email: enquiries@pen-and-sword.co.uk or telephone: 01226 734555 (UK and ROW) or email: uspen-and-sword@casematepublishers.com or telephone: (610) 853-9131 (North America).

We respect your privacy and we will only use personal information to send you information about our products.

Thank you!

AN ENVIRONMENTAL HISTORY OF FRANCE